The Theory
of Absence

The Theory of Absence

Subjectivity, Signification, and Desire

PATRICK FUERY

Contributions in Philosophy, Number 55

GREENWOOD PRESS
Westport, Connecticut • London

Library of Congress Cataloging-in-Publication Data

Fuery, Patrick.
    The theory of absence : subjectivity, signification, and desire /
Patrick Fuery.
        p.   cm.—(Contributions in philosophy, ISSN 0084–926X ; no.
55)
    Includes bibliographical references (p.   ) and index.
    ISBN 0–313–29588–3 (alk. paper)
    1. Subjectivity.   2. Negativity (Philosophy).   3. Philosophy,
European—20th century.   I. Title. II. Series.
BD222.F84   1995
111—dc20   94–47437

British Library Cataloguing in Publication Data is available.

Library of Congress Catalog Card Number: 94–47437
ISBN: 0–313–29588–3
ISSN: 0084–926X

First published in 1995

Greenwood Press, 88 Post Road West, Westport, CT 06881
An imprint of Greenwood Publishing Group, Inc.

Printed in the United States of America

The paper used in this book complies with the
Permanent Paper Standard issued by the National
Information Standards Organization (Z39.48–1984).

10 9 8 7 6 5 4 3 2 1

For Horst, with thanks for his gifts of *großzügig*, *ésprit*, and *intellekt*.

Contents

Part Three: Towards a Semiotics of Absence

Acknowledgments

Books are never written alone, even if the hours spent at the computer make it feel so. I am grateful for the support of many people who contributed a great deal during the time of research, writing and final production of this manuscript. Their presence in this absence has been invaluable. At Greenwood Publishing Lynn Flint showed faith in the project, and Marcia Goldstein and Nita Romer were superb in their editorial and production skills. The professionalism of these three facilitated the book a great deal. I would also like to thank the staff of the Department of Literature, University of Essex. The friendship and intellectual support of Jonathan White in particular, as well as Francis Barker, Gordon Brotherston, Herbie Butterfield, Ana Gallegos, Peter Hulme is something dear to me. At Macquarie University Tom Burvill, Joan Kirkby and Nick Mansfield have contributed to the pleasures of completion, and will assist in the celebrations as only warm friends can. At Murdoch University David George is someone deeply significant through his generous support. Throughout the entire project Megan and Morgan have been there—showing patience, love and support. Without them not a single word could have been written. They are the birth of the word, and more. Finally, this book is dedicated to Horst Ruthrof for what he continues to show me—ideas and the vitality of thought.

I would like to thank the following for their permission to use copyright material: W.W. Norton and Company, INC. for Jacques Lacan *The Four Fundamental Concepts of Psychoanalysis*; The University of Chicago Press for Jacques Derrida *The Post Card: From Socrates to Freud and Beyond*; *Semiotica* for permission to reprint a version of 'Towards a Typology of the Absent Signifier'.

1

Negativity, Negation, Dialectics: Towards the Dialectics of Absence

What is Absence?

Presence is valued, held up, invested with power, and so can be said to have a pervasive quality. Presence, it appears, constructs, connects, holds together. Within this contrived order of things presence is the determining feature of being, subjectivity, ideology, textuality, systems of speech and writing, presentation and representation—the list is boundless. Presence is, non-presence is not. Such is the construction of presence, even absence, its taxonomic opposite, is seen as a formation and formulation of it. To have presence is also to have the capacity for absence. The force of this relational schema has led to the conceptual figuring of absence and absences only because there is presence, or a register of presence, to begin with. Absence is seen to be derived from a state of presence, as it is seen as the denial of presence.

One way of figuring absence(s) outside of this way of thinking is to specify two forms of absence: primary absences and secondary absences. These categories are necessarily broad and cannot be seen as ascribing a complete agenda to the issues. In this sense it is important to acknowledge the flexibility of the concepts—to recognise the chains of signification which determine not resolution and meaning, but the interplay of the discourses themselves. In their heterogeneity, polyglossia, and dynamic exchange they can be seen to offer not the classification of absence(s), but rather the methodological idea of absences distinct from a relational context of presence. Secondary absences are those which are always derived from a state of presence. They imply presence, acknowledge its relational context, gain their epistemological and ontological structures from it, and indicate sites of presence. They retain, and even reinforce, the binarism of presence and absence. Primary absences, on the other hand, exist outside of any relational context of presence. Primary absences exist in their own right, independent of any sense of presence.

Absence can be a status measured against other orders. Something is absent because it is not present, but the significant detail is that the absent something is figured as potentially present, that is, *held-in-readiness*. These absences are secondary because they establish forms of quasi-presences to fill the gaps, the holes and blanks, the simulacra, complex orders of signs which point and indicate until the absences themselves are denied. Bits of the missing presence are fleshed out, embellished, or signifiers are constructed to provide a presence. All the time these secondary absences are subforms of a presence because they have a referential system; in doing so they often suggest an originary position. This position is a constructed presence which takes on primacy, irrefutability, and, often, a sense of *truth*.

Part of the reason why absence is figured as a subform of presence is because the whole nature of perception, understanding, existence, and ways of dealing with the world is constructed in terms of mediation shadows on the cave wall. Every representation is a re[present]ation—the present is negotiated, arrives secondhand, is known only after a transformation. Presentness is only ever experienced in a secondary sense because it is mediated through signifying systems—language, discursive practices, ideology, models of representation. In this sense presence itself is an absence. Secondary absences suggest presence because the idea of presence is contained within them. An absent person enjoys the status of absence only because the sense of presence is held in readiness, in being. Primary absences operate external to any sense of presence, which is not to deny the possibility of measuring these absences against registers of presences. One of the major differences, however, is that primary absences are defined in terms of the centrality of absence rather than any referential action to a sense of presence and/or re[present]ation. The key areas of primary absence that will be considered here, in terms of operations and illustration, are absence as a determinant and constitutive element in the formation of subjectivity, desire as an operational system of absence, and the interpretative *value* of absence in terms of a semiotics. What is also part of the central contention is that absence forms a unifying principle in all three areas.

The claim here is that the relationship between primary and secondary absences can sometimes operate in terms of an ideal and its possible manifestations, of the abstract versus the concrete. This reading, however, has the potential to go against theorising absence as independent of presence because it suggests a relationship of rule and execution. It is critically more appropriate to see primary absences as an order unique within itself, even if this order is constantly shifting, and so operating as a dynamic, perhaps most often as an alterity. This is the reading of absence and presence favoured here, against the sense of zero-one and true-false sequences which are so often used to formulate models of expression and interpretation. Kristeva's poetic language and *le sémiotique* and Bakhtin's dialogism and the carnivalesque can be seen to operate in terms of the same derivation of non-binary relational contexts. Bataille, in dealing with being itself, evokes a sense of the non—zero-one sequence in terms of laughter: "Laughter intervenes in these value determinations of being as the expression of the circuit of movements of attraction across a human field. It manifests itself each time a change in level suddenly occurs: it characterizes all vacant life as ridiculous. A kind of incandescent joy—the explosive and sudden revelation of the presence of being—is liberated each time a striking appearance is contrasted with its absence . . ." (Bataille 1985: 176). Bataille's *laughter* shares a great deal with Kant's sense of presence and absence: "Something absurd (something in which, therefore, the understanding can of itself find no delight) must be present in whatever is to raise a hearty convulsive laugh. Laughter is an affection arising from a strained expectation being suddenly reduced to nothing" (Kant 1973: 201). The convulsive laugh is produced through an absence which can operate in both secondary and primary contexts, for it relates to the subject's self-conscious realisation of the *cogitatum/cogitationes* through absence. This complex relationship of being, absence, and presence can never be measured simply as being/non-being.

To divide the idea of absence into primary and secondary forms is not to establish distinct types—an important feature is that secondary absences provide a connection between the operations of the presence and all forms of absence. Although this does not provide a continuum between pure presence, that is a presentness, and primary absence, it does permit a reading of absence in terms of a relational context of presence, which, in turn, allows the continuation of a primary mode of absence, independent of any sense of presence.

The dynamics of primary and secondary absences mean that there are constant qualifying notions of the absent. No absence is ever fixed, and the connection of primary absences with any sense of presence through secondary absences indicates a sense of flux. Essentially, primary absences are determining principles and signifying practices in which absence is the defining feature and constant point of reference. In this sense it is a methodology of morphogenesis rather than a classification of types.

Negation—Negativity and Absence

In *Die Verneinung* Freud argues that expressions of the negative can be linked to the act of repression: "Thus the content of a repressed image or idea can make its way into consciousness, on condition that it is negated. Negation is a way of taking cognizance of what is repressed; indeed it is already a lifting of the repression, though not, of course, an acceptance of what is repressed" (Freud 1987: 437-438). Freud argues that the negative relates to the subject's sense of the external and internal, of subjectivity and objectivity. This can be seen as a function of absence and presence. Negation produces absence from presence—it is the denial of the existence of something (object, feeling, emotion, event)—in the attempt to safeguard the subject's sense of the world and his/her position in it. This can also be seen to be a model of ideological interpretation and signification because it necessarily involves the interplay of negation/negativity in signification.

Kristeva argues that the Freudian concept of the unconscious is a critically significant model in terms of understanding how negation operates both within a field of logic and in a trans-logical fashion, which strengthens the idea that negation is essential in, and to, the development of signifying practices: "true negativity is a dialectical notion specific to the signifying process, on the crossroads between the biological and social order on the one hand, and the thetic and signifying phase of the social order on the other" (Kristeva 1984c: 124). Part of the reason why negation can be seen as operating in this way is Freud's configuration of the unconscious and conscious.

It can be argued that meaning itself relies to a significant degree on the functions of negation/repression, which are fundamentally processes of absence and presence. However, in this model negation is not strictly a formulation of absence, rather it is a system of accounting for absences because it allows for the expression of something made absent through repression. Signification may well be tied to the interplay of repression and permitted expressions—of the syntagmatic and paradigmatic combinations—but the emphasis here is still on what is present (through direct expression or through disguise) rather than the absent. Do different models of negations construct different relational contexts of absence and presence? Sartre, examining various points of phenomenological ontology in *Being and Nothingness*, explores in some depth the relationship between negation and absence, although ultimately it will be necessary to distinguish between Sartre's conceptualisation of nothingness and absence.

Pierre is absent from the café—the café with "its patrons, its tables, its booths, its mirrors, its light, its smoky atmosphere, and the sounds of voices, rattling saucers and footsteps" (Sartre 1957: 9). In the context of multiple, almost excessive, presences Sartre finds an absence, a nothing. This absence is only found, however, because a presence was expected. The significance of these presences and the centrality of the nihilation is that rather than any presence, or presences, being emphasised, they instead become less significant. The focus of attention—Pierre and his absence in the café—determines all meaning, all signification. This is because the systems of meaning/signification are directed towards an absence, and this becomes the originary, determining, onto-epistemological signifying order. This absence is not found in a single space, or at a single moment, rather it is in all spaces and in all moments. Absence becomes the system which is utilised to construct meaning (the focus of attention and the dominating system of signification)—not the space filled with excessive presences, the person/object pursued, the action of perceptions or even the subject itself, but absence determines and orders meaning.

One of the central concerns throughout *Being and Nothingness* is to determine the relationship between what it is to be and the tensions of the loss or denial of that sense of being, that is, nothingness. Sartre, for example, measures this relationship by comparing a type of Hegelian dialectic of being and nothingness to Heidegger's (potentially) complementary model. This results in the postulation of a dynamic between subjectivity/being and nothingness, between what it is to be seen to have being and the fear of its loss. Nothingness becomes a categorising principle which must include systems of negation and negativity. Sartre coins the term *négatités* to link the various processes, judgements, and conditions of negation, and he lists examples of this: "absence, change, otherness, repulsion, regret, distraction" (Sartre 1957: 21). Absence as a *négatité* is important because it illustrates absence not as a nothing, or nothingness, which might in turn reduce things and subjects to nothingness, but as part of an active process. Sartre points out that when absence is experienced or constructed there must be a motivational force and a type of phenomenological intention. This intentionality, which both holds with and rereads Husserl's idea of empty (or emptied) intentions, is the qualifying principle of absence as an active, signifying force: "In short an empty intention is a consciousness of negation which transcends itself toward an object which it posits as absent or non-existent" (Sartre 1957: 27)—*négatités* are used to determine and produce meaning and not simply to specify an interpretation of status. For Sartre this is the bonding of human existence with nothingness, the intentionalities which produce the human condition made all the more complex through the self-consciousness of freedom. In terms of theorising absence it is further evidence of a primary absence because of the constitutive and deterministic qualities of the absences in signification.

Kristeva, engaging in the Hegelian tradition and some of Sartre's readings of it, links negativity closely to some specific issues of subjectivity—it becomes part of the definitional frame of a subject type constructed through absence as systems of formation: ". . . negativity can only produce a subject in process/on trial. In other words, the subject, constituted by the law of negativity and thus by the law of an objective reality, is necessarily suffused by negativity . . ." (Kristeva 1984c: 111). Kristeva's observation follows her reiteration of the need to distinguish between negativity, negation and nothingness—a distinction which Sartre sees as critically essential—which in turn allows the Hegelian assertion that nothingness must always be seen as part of being. Kristeva takes this issue further when she argues that ". . . Hegelian negativity prevents the immobilization of the thetic, unsettles doxy, and lets in all the semiotic motility that prepares and exceeds it" (Kristeva 1984c: 113). The disruptive, discursive nature of negativity, bound to the critical sense of being and subjectivity, here echoes Bataille's idea of the self-consciousness of laughter. For Kristeva, Hegelian negativity becomes a crossroad for the subject's relational context in the Symbolic, which eventually determines the very nature of subjectivity as process, on trial and is never able to unify. This split in the subject—the subject in process/on trial—is linked to desire and negativity, particularly in terms of the subject in a social and cultural (that is, largely Symbolic) context. Existing outside of this Symbolic interplay of negation and subjectivity is what Kristeva

terms poetic negativity as a third-degree rejection. This is in keeping with
negativity and negation being part of the repression process, and hence of
negotiating absence and presence. This positions negativity in terms of a (Lacanian configuration of) lack—substantially an issue of primary absence because
what is being determined is not simply a conditional frame, or even an
operational context, but an essential feature of the way in which subjectivity,
desire and signification are determined and operate. Absence is the common
determinate in and of all three.

Negation, Absence and *Aufhebung*

Measuring absence against *Aufhebung*—speculative negativity—provides a
possible escape from, or alternative to, the binarism of presence. The reason
for this is that the triple meaning of *Aufhebung* (cancellation, lifting onto a
higher plane, preservation) allows the positing on the one hand of a type of
binarism—the negation of something by something—and a non-binarism—the
lifting up and preserving of something through the dialectic. It is this double
level which leads Derrida to construct the concept of *la relève/la relevé* and
reveler which, like *Aufhebung*, can be seen to have within its critical frame a
qualifying sense of absence. The triple action of a preserving, heightening and
negation produces at least two forms of absence-once something is lifted up,
essentially transformed through the dialectic, it is made absent by that which
substitutes it (*la relève/la relevè*), whilst the act of negation can suggest an
absent opposite. For Hegel and the post-Hegelians, in particular Heidegger,
Aufhebung becomes one of the central models of space and time, uniting them,
utilising one to explain the operation of the other, and binding them to the issue
of being. Derrida demonstrates how this tradition allows the philosophical
configurations of space and time (and being, particularly in terms of Heidegger)
to form a relational context based on *Aufhebung*. One example of many is "the
relève (*Aufhebung*) of space is time. The latter is the truth of what it negates-
—that is space—in a movement of *relève*." (Derrida 1986: 89). Derrida's
central concern here is with the sign, and he goes on to argue that the sign itself
is a form of *Aufhebung*, and furthermore, and not surprisingly, that metaphor
too must be seen in terms of the *relève/relevé*.

If Derrida offers *relève/relevé* as a translation and commentary on
Aufhebung, he also offers *différance* as a concept which goes against this
Hegelian notion. He argues: "*Différance* . . . must sign the point at which one
breaks with the system of the *Aufhebung* and with speculative dialectics" and
that *différance* is "precisely the limit, the interruption, the destruction of the
Hegelian *relève/relevé* wherever it operates" (Derrida 1981: 44; 40-41). The
difference between *relève/relevé/Aufhebung* and *différance* is that the former
nexus always contains within its structure the interplay of binarism and nega-

tion, whereas this does not necessarily take place with *différance*. In this sense it is the crucial factor of absence in the "preserving elevation" that is shared by both *différance* and *relève/relevé*. This link is strengthened through the idea of sublation being the putting of something to one side, but still being in use—absence is not the end of effect, just as presence cannot guarantee influence, recognition, apprehendability. This influence of the absent, the force of absence, is of central concern in this theorising of absence.

We are brought to the situation of a register of absence which must attempt to differentiate levels of force, for surely not everything which is absent can be influential and powerful. There is also the issue of absence as a status and absence as an influence, absences which qualify and those which do not. How such a register might operate will be taken up at various points in the ensuing examination, but one of the guiding principles in such a study must be the combinational processes at work. Absence is at one level an alterant. Heidegger speaks of it as a modification of presence—of *praesens* into *absens*—particularly in the context of two orders. The first of these is the expectation of the missing which establishes a paradigm of possible presences: "to missing, as a specific enpresenting, there corresponds not no horizon at all, but a specially modified horizon of the present, of *praesens*. To the ecstasis of the unenpresenting that makes missing possible there belongs the horizonal schema of *absens*" (Heidegger 1982: 311). Which does not dismiss the possibility of being surprised, as Heidegger argues this is held within the same horizon—a dreamlike image is precisely this distortion of the expectation of the missing to create the unexpected, or even defamiliarization. Even the excessively familiar contains this relational context of absence; compare, for example, phenomenological intuition, which operates as secondary absences devising the presences.

The second order is when absence is seen to actually transform or modify the presences through the quality of negativity, and it is this sense of the negative that enables comparisons of absence and presence, at a number of levels, to the dialectic model. But if there is such a thing as a dialectic of absence, what form (or forms) would it take? Is it possible to articulate such a complex and variable structure, say, for example, in terms of Heidegger's model of horizonal expectations, variations of surprise, and the modification of *praesens* through *absens*? Any attempt to represent it must take into account both this complexity of form and variable modes of operation. It must be able to account for both major forms of absence—those that are connected to presences and those that are independent of any such reference. Such a dialectic might be formulated as follows. The initial binary structure of presence and absence, transformed into a dialectic proves too restrictive because it constantly demands a referential action back to the initial, (perhaps defined as originary) artificial binary relationship. Such a model cannot be dismissed outright however, and read against a dialectic of absence can prove insightful. The initial model then becomes: Absence—Presence, functioning in a dialectic, "produces" a paradigm which sustains Subjectivity—Desire—Signification.

Here Presence and Absence are read in a binary relationship, qualifying each other. The "Subjectivity-Desire-Signification" configuration represents part of the complex matrix which results from the interrelational context of presence and absence. It also reflects the various systemic and interpretative models which are overlayed on these relationships, including the ideological, hermeneutic, ontological, metaphysical, and political. Although this matrix is open-ended, these three issues, it will be argued, are central to the formulation of such an assemblage. Clearly this is not a true dialectic, and the rigidity of the model is apparent—presence and absence are seen as qualifying processes of the matrix and so the dynamic occurs within the matrix rather than within the organising binary system. To work towards a dialectic of absence the model can be constructed as: Absence—Non-Absence—Paradigm of *Aufhebung*.

For this to be seen as a dialectic two important interpretations must be made. Firstly, "non-absence" cannot be read simply as presence—at most it can be seen as a register with the potential to incorporate presence. Something can be non-absence without necessarily being an order of presence. Secondly, the Paradigm of *Aufhebung* must be recognised as a multiplicity of orders which are determined by the dialectic of Absence and Non-Absence. This means that the paradigm holds subjectivity, desire, and a semiotic (as systems of signifying chains, processes of signification, the composition of the sign and codes) as well as presence itself. Through these two qualifying interpretations it becomes clear that the only fixed point in the dialectic is the heterology of absence. Such is the nature of this dialectic and the determining factor of absence that no matter what order is drawn from the paradigm, it will always contain absence as an essential feature.

The emphasis of the *Aufhebung* here must be concentrated on the lifting up and transformation; however, this does not mean that (speculative) negation is to be dismissed. Absence transforms through its qualification of the non-absent (the non-binary dialectic) and its registering of absence as a particular status and force. Meaning—signification, or the essential issues of a semiotic, is, as Kristeva has pointed out in terms of Freud's theories, directly tied to negation. But meaning/signification is changed here so that any meaning or process of signification cannot be seen in terms of presence and absence (privilege and repression, valued and negated, thought and not-thought), but rather in terms of the unconscious which does not distinguish in this way and holds both at the same time. This does not mean that absence and presence are the same, or that they cannot be distinguished. Rather that they are not necessarily bound together so that we must think (or imply) one in order to understand and utilise the other. As Derrida points out: "In discourse (the unity of process and system), negativity is always the underside and accomplice of positivity. Negativity cannot be spoken of, nor has it ever been except in this fabric of meaning" (Derrida 1978b: 259). For as long as absence is thought of as a negativity of presence this will continue to hold true, but the restrictions set up by such a conjunction mean that the other side of absence—absence independent of presence—will be ignored. What is essential to this study is the recognition that absence can have a status outside of a mirroring negativity of presence.

This gives cause and legitimation for a third model which inverts the dialectic system and positions primary and secondary absences in a different way. This model can be represented as: Primary Absence——(*Aufhebung*)——Secondary Absence——(*Aufhebung*)——Non—Absence. Here the matrix of Subjectivity-Desire-Signification is located across the dialectic, modified by the action of *Aufhebung* to become secondary absences and non-absences. This does not negate its position within the system of primary absences, however, nor the idea that manifestations can be generated within the interplay of secondary absences and non-absences, for this is part of the construction of the registers. It is also important to recognise the heterogeneity within the orders of such a dialectical action.

Part One

The Subject of Desire and Absence

2

The True Aim of Desire: Subjectivity, Desire, and Absence

The true aim of desire is the Other.
Jacques Lacan

The central concern of this chapter is the ways in which desire and absence form fundamental structures in the determination and constitution of subjectivity and the subject position. The initial point of departure will be Lacan's description of the subject. This description, it will be argued, presents the definitional and operational sense of subjectivity as one of the desiring subject determined by absences. By arguing that desire and absence form fundamental structures in both the determination and constitution of subjectivity and the subject position(s), or sites of subjectivity, we shift the emphasis from the political centrality of presences to the more essential aspects of secondary absences as modality and of primary absences as constitutive processes. The intersection of modality and genealogy produces—as teleology, diathesis, process—one of the most *essential* sites of subjectivity, that of the desiring subject determined by absences. This site operates as a repository for different types of absences (including desire) as well as the scene of production and consumption of desire as an absence. The forms that these absences take are considerably diverse, but rather than directly engaging in issues of typology, what is of primary concern here is the dynamics of this system of subjectivity, desire, and absence/lack and the definitional qualities of each component as it is qualified by the other two. This site is the manacle of subjectivity devised by such an interplay when it operates as both adhesive and disjunctive. The subject does not simply engage in a complex order of absences, but is defined by, motivated by, and determines/is determined by absence.

The Lacanian Subject and the Configuration of Desire

To deal with the idea of a specifically Lacanian interpretation of subjectivity and the subject position requires a certain amount of contextualisation of Lacan's ideas on this issue. A comprehensive, perhaps historical, survey of this sort is beyond the direct concerns here; however, note should be made, no matter how brief, of Lacan's commentaries on the relationship between Descartes and Freud in terms of the defining of the subject. It is largely through these commentaries that Lacan establishes fundamental points on the definition of the subject and subjectivity. Such a note is largely prefatorial here, simply establishing some of the groundwork for the ensuing examination of Lacan's own ideas which, because of this lineage, demonstrates both philosophical and psychoanalytic concerns.

Lacan's "return" to Freud produces a number of critical positions in terms of the subject. This is so in part because Lacan both reworks Freud's ideas and at the same time determines his own perspective on the nature of subjectivity. For Freud, the subject is ultimately a divided and fragmented being, defined by its processes of conflict and subsequent struggles to be a united being. If the Cartesian subject can be summarily defined by the primacy of the *cogito*, its methods and processes, and the Freudian model as one of conflict and division, then the Lacanian subject's intrinsicality is its relationship to a particular type of desire and language. By locating the idea of systemic absences in terms of determining subjectivity, we are provided with a critical point of analysis and a definitional frame.

Lacan points out that the Cartesian *cogito* functions as a historically significant model for Freud's development of the theory of the subject. However, the Freudian/Lacanian interpretation of the constitutive elements of a theory of subjectivity radically splits from the Cartesian concepts in a number of crucial areas. These splits lead to the development, firstly by Freud and then by Lacan, of a subject position that is in many ways directly oppositional to the Cartesian model. For Freud, the idea of the subject and subjectivity is measured against the Cartesian *cogito*—the Freudian subject is the "subject of Cartesian origin" (Lacan 1986: 47) through the action of calling. One of the most striking aspects about this development is that the (Cartesian) originary critical position and the basis of the split (particularly in terms of the psychoanalytic methodology) from this position stem from the same set of fundamental issues of definition and critical inquiry.

The originary and defining position of the Cartesian *cogito* is concentrated in doubt. Descartes's Method of Doubt is not simply the negation of everything, rather it is devised as a tactic for certainty. This can be read within the same terms that were previously used to investigate a dialectic positioning of absence.

In this sense it is a system of doubt, read here as absence, and certainty, that is presence. Here we witness one of the major philosophical configurations of absence and presence, and of the (consequential) privileging of the present over the absent. The Method of Doubt utilises absence in an attempt to construct an indubitable, apodictic presence—it is a constructing absence that works on excluding everything that cannot be declared as certain. In this way Descartes in effect employs a double sense of absence in the Method of Doubt. By nominating everything (except the determining *cogito*) as suspect, Descartes is looking for presences in what is ultimately figured as a universe of absences—tricks, illusions, and hallucinations. He then employs a philosophical methodology to indicate these absences as absences—as gaps and tricks. This declarative action is supposedly the production of presences through certainty. Reading doubt and certainty in terms of absence and presence provides an important connection between the Cartesian (philosophical) subject and the Freudian (psychoanalytic) method and assists in bridging the distance between the aims of defining the subject and subjectivity on the one hand and determining how it operates on the other. This becomes an essential issue in Lacan's ideas, both as psychoanalytic methodology and the wider philosophical, textual, ideological issues that have developed from them.

Lacan argues that the connection between Freud and Descartes is based on this central issue of certainty and doubt, of the apodictic and its questioning: "The major term, in fact, is not truth. It is *Gewissheit*, certainty. Freud's method is Cartesian—in the sense that he sets out from the basis of the subject as certainty. . . . Now—and it is here that Freud lays all his stress—doubt is the support of certainty" (Lacan 1986: 35). This revelation through absence—the certainty through the presence of doubt—is part of the speaking of the subject in the unconscious. In this sense absence becomes the definitional order of being/subjectivity—it "proves" the certainty of the subject more than any assertion through presence. The dialectic of absence/doubt and presence/certainty that is to be found in the Cartesian *cogito* becomes unsustainable within such an order—for Freud doubt is "a sign of resistance" (Lacan 1986: 35). Doubt becomes one of the central indicators of a something other to the point where absolute certainty can also become a reason for doubt. The Freudian method must recognise both emphatic certainty and uncertainty as signifiers of something which is being left out, made absent, and it is this transcategorality of absence that becomes the defining feature of the subject and the basis of critical method. Consider Freud's analysis of the three caskets—what he concentrates on is not the fullness of the speech, the presences of the arguments, for choosing the casket made from lead, rather he argues that the greater the complexity of argument for the choice the more the analyst must suspect disguise, repression, and resistance. The certainty of the discourse becomes something to doubt. It is how this signifying order of resistance/doubt as certainty is read that leads to the methodological and definitional split from Descartes's formulation of the *cogito* position. Freud, and even more substantially for Lacan, alters the semiotic of this relational signification of doubt/certainty, and in doing so shifts the investigatory and analytic emphasis away from the need for certainty and onto the nature of the doubting, uncertain, divided subject. This is the point Lacan is making in the seminar "Of the Subject of Certainty" where he defends Freud's idea of the unconscious as distinct from its manifestations: "*The unconscious*, he [Freud] tells us, *is not the dream*. What he means is that the unconscious may operate in the direction of deception, and that this does not in any way count as an objection for him" (Lacan 1986: 37-38). This may sound like an inversion of Descartes's method, which attempts to produce a sense of the subject as a consequence of, among other things, the Method of Doubt, and so, consequentially, in the Freudian and Lacanian schema it appears to be a commencing with the subject and then arriving at a dialectical system of doubt and certainty. However the inversion is not that simple. The difference in Freud's interpretation of certainty, as opposed to Descartes—as positioned within a Cartesian world order—is that whereas the Method of Doubt starts from absences/doubt in order to abolish absence in favour of presence/certainty, Freud, it can be argued, reinterprets the doubt/absence and certainty/presence configuration within the context of the unconscious. Doubt/absence becomes a manifestation of the unconscious, acting as "proof" of its existence, and the double articulation of the dialectic of absence in this case becomes a triple articulation. This is precisely the same order of things that leads Kristeva to read Freud's concept of negation as essentially about meaning and signification. In a different, although connected, way this is the same debate that Derrida and Foucault take up in relation to the archaeology of silence.

This is not to argue that the sense of the apodictic is abolished from the Freudian and Lacanian systems and interpretations, but rather that it is repositioned in quite an extreme fashion. Lacan argues:

> *Le cogito cartésien, de cette expérience, est l'exploit majeur, peut-être terminal, en ce qu'il atteint une certitude de savoir. Mais il ne dénonce que mieux ce qu'a de privilégié le moment où il s'appuie, et combien frauduleux est d'en étendre le privilège, pour leur en faire un statut, aux phénomènes pourvus de conscience.*

> (Lacan 1971: 196).

Doubt as resistance is apodictic to the sense of the existence and operation of the unconscious, and as a functional process in and of the unconscious. Lacan, as indicated earlier, argues that dreams, parapraxis, etc., demonstrates the presence of the unconscious, and that the unconscious reveals itself as absent. Some of the most profound and essential processes of this revelation in absence are to be found in repression and censorship, and, importantly, such disguises (*Verkleidung*) share the same relationships and methods of operation with the subject position, absence, and the unconscious.

Lacan argues that Descartes did not fully engage in the self-consciousness of the *cogito*, and so missed the possibility of self-presence formulated through a reflexive discursive practice, and this is precisely what Lacan, and Freud, see as the central issue at hand. This idea of self-consciousness, and the attendant issue of self-reflexivity, as determinants of subjectivity is highly significant in understanding how absence features in defining subjectivity. It is this difference in the two formulations that provides the schism between the Freudian project and the Cartesian *cogito*, which operates on the assumption that the I is certain, without fully challenging it as an actual entity or describing its dynamics. For both Freud and Lacan it is precisely the constitutive factors of the I that determine and organise the investigation.

It would be an oversimplification, and dangerously close to error, to say that the formula "*cogito ergo sum*" does not contain evidence of this self-reflexivity of the I. Descartes's *Meditations and Discourse on Method* commences with a sense of self-reflection, and as Gasché points out: "the philosophy of reflection is generally considered to have begun with Descartes's *prima philosophia*. . . . With Cartesian thought, the self-certainty of the thinking subject—a certainty apodictically found in the *cogito me cogitare*—becomes the unshakeable ground of philosophy itself" (Gasché 1986: 17). However what is at issue is the orientation that such an inflection is given by Freud and Lacan, as distinct from the apodictic and central nature of it in Descartes. Descartes acknowledges the self-reflexive in order to move towards certainty. Lacan indicates that this philosophical tradition has bolstered and strengthened such a reading over time: "the philosophical *cogito* is at the centre of the mirage that renders modern man so sure of being himself even in his uncertainties about himself" (Lacan 1985: 165). For Lacan the presence of the *cogito* cannot simply become the apodictic proof of subjectivity, even if he accepts the complexities of loss and absence in the structure of the mind. The interplay between *cogitans* and *cogitatum* becomes a recurring issue, presented in many forms, in Lacan's works. A particularly striking example of this is Lacan's reading of this interplay and the configuration of the body, in which, at one point, he clearly announces his feelings with the description "that idiot Descartes" (Lacan 1988b: 73). Lacan may overcome some of his objections through the qualification of some aspects of the *cogito ergo sum*, but the need to develop further the *cogito* as central to the defining of subjectivity remains crucial. It is because the Cartesian method moves towards the closure of gaps, the dismissal of divisions, and the parenthesising of absence as qualifying status, that it is necessary to challenge its essential features in any consideration of subjectivity and absence.

One of the challenges to this philosophical tradition in the Lacanian formulation of subjectivity is that it operates as a site. This site is ideologically created in as much as it exists prior to the subject and comes to determine the subject. The subject attempts to occupy, and is compelled to attempt to occupy, this site through the philosophical, psychoanalytical, sociocultural, and ideological urgency of subjectivity as presence. This is true of both analytic

methodology and praxis. It is this site that is primary to the operation of the
subject, and this is why that subject is based on absence and desire—in the first
instance it is the desire for a site which is always positioned as absence, and
after that complex and multiple convolutions based on lack, holes, gaps, and
splits as they operate in the determination of the qualifying status of subjectivity. In order to understand more clearly what this site can be, how it is defined,
and its relational structure to subjectivity, it is necessary to understand the
nature of desire as a determining feature of the subject. From this configuration
of the subject defined through absence of the site of subjectivity and the desire
to fill this absence, we arrive at the desiring subject defined through absences.

The *Ichspaltung* and the Mirror Stage

The mirror stage represents a significant process in the development of the
subject position (towards the site of subjectivity) as it is determined by the
social order of the Symbolic and the subject's perspective via the Imaginary and
Real. There is, however, an ontological and hermeneutic disjunction between
the "subject position", the site of subjectivity, and the emerging subject who
identifies, or at the very least recognises, this positional site. It is this disjunction, and the subsequent (ideological as well as subjective) negotiations of it by
the individual, that contains the performative functions of absence in determining the subject.

The mirror stage, despite its configurations and gestures towards presence,
is fundamentally about absence. It is concerned with how subjectivity is derived
from absences and is motivated by a desire for something which is always
figured as a lack. The mirror stage positions the emerging subject in terms of
the Symbolic order, which represents and operates almost entirely as presence
(even if it is of the same order as the Cartesian hallucinations and illusions).
The subject becomes aware of his/her qualifying nature of lack (of speech, of
mobility, of power, of access to discursive practices) and so develops into the
desiring subject. From this point on the subject is defined by paradigmatic
system of absences and desires in all their most complex manifestations and
simplest requirements for satisfaction. What becomes even more striking about
such a reading of subjectivity in these terms is that desire itself is a lack in both
the transitional mirror stage and any sense of the subject emerging from this
stage. The emerging subject is born into the convolutions of absence/lack and
desire through the self-reflexive and sociocultural demarcation systems of the
mirror stage. The mirror stage is a consequence of the revelation of the absence
of the Symbolic order from the subject. Desire is constructed as a lack, and
through this the subject is fragmented and split within itself, and from
discourse, social institutions, the measure of histories and the objects of desire.
How this split takes place and the consequences of it can be seen in terms of the
status of *Ichspaltung* and the *imago*.

The passage through the mirror stage is demarcated by the imposition, in terms of the unconscious, of the Oedipal complex and the subject's desire to be able to control and manipulate language, which in effect becomes any, and all, discursive systems. Here the subject moves from the ego-centric world of the *moi* (the subject in the pre-Symbolic) to the socially defined realm of the Symbolic. Expressed in this fashion it is also possible to see how the Pleasure Principle and the Reality Principle play such a decisive role in this development. The mirror stage takes the subject from the ego-centric position so that he/she can no longer contemplate the world from the sanctity of the pre-Copernican universe and forces he/she to enter the maze of social praxis. In doing so the subject takes on the complex negotiations of desire and the Other. A further resultant of this process is that the subject comes to be defined, and defines himself/herself, as split and fragmented. Both the splitting of the subject and his/her fragmented being are manifestations of an order of absence: the split produces the absenting of part of the self from the self; there is the desire for different fragments and for unification; there is the absence produced within the split/fragmentation itself. This interstice becomes the frame of reference for itself. It is both the slip of light and the chasm which defines any sense of the presence of being.

In moving through the mirror stage the subject becomes the split/fragmented subject—the *Ichspaltung*—captured by desire and the desire for discourse. Lacan calls this fractured subject of the mirror stage the *imago*—a term which suggests a relational context insisted by the mirror stage for the subject in the formation of self-consciousness and the social order of discourse. The metaphoric sense of both mirror and *imago* operates on the reflection of the self for the self, as well as the reflection of the self in terms of the Symbolic order. The mirror stage articulates subjectivity (as site and as position) for the subject in external, absent terms. This is its horror as the subject wakes from the plea for the self (as social agent as well as for the self) to recognise the flames. The "reflection" of the self to the self means that subjectivity exists outside of—that is, in effect, is absent from—the subject itself. It is for this reason that the transition from the pre-Oedipal, pre-Symbolic, to the Symbolic order through the mirror stage can be seen as a significant contribution to the idea of a site of subjectivity defined as absent from the emerging subject, and desired by that subject. The *imago*/split subject is also linked to absence in terms of what it is split from, and to desire because of the desire to rejoin and regain the sense of wholeness. This motivational desire to be "whole" is a central feature of the *Ichspaltung*.

Lacan represents the *Ichspaltung* as the movement from S to the barred $\cancel{S}$—from a perceived sense of the subject as whole to the split/fractured subject. What is also significant about this transformation and realisation is the relationship between the S/$\cancel{S}$ and the signifier. Entry into the Symbolic order, and the connected sense of urgency to gain the signifier, is central to the splitting of the subject. The split subject, based on absences and desire, constantly attempts to move towards and so possess the signifier, and in doing so occupy the site of subjectivity. This is the subject of lack, splits and absence attempting to gain signifiers of presence and wholeness.

The tension of the *Ichspaltung* is originary, and as such has a very primary sense to it. Lacan (1985) argues that a significant aspect of the mirror stage is the disjunction between the emerging sense of subjectivity and the coming-into--being *(devenir)*. This is the tension of the I according to, and measured against the status of, the self. This is the dialectical process of attempted resolution between *devenir* and I in terms of reality (and distinct from pleasure rather than the Real). Any sense of synthesis occurs in the engagement with the signifier—although because of the centrality of absence to both subjectivity and the Symbolic this will always be a sense rather than any actual and complete synthesis—the *Aufhebung* carries with it (conserves) even what it seems to leave behind or negate. This is confirmed to some degree by the fact that the signifier cannot be possessed.

The Other as Absence and the Structure of the Unconscious

In Lacan the site of subjectivity—how and where a subject is constituted and determined—is based and ordered on the interconnected systems of absence and desire, and within the combinational systems derived from these two factors the notion of the Other figures prominently. In a great deal of Lacan's work on the Other there is evidence of the strong philosophical tradition, particularly the Hegelian model, which is concerned with the idea of the Other. Rather than any sense of coherent historical development, the idea of the Other has emerged in various guises and for different reasons. Lacan adapted and developed the philosophical concept of the Other specifically for psychoanalytic theory and practice. There is something to be said for retaining the idea of the Other as a multidisciplinary concept which shares certain features, particularly within the context of a group of contemporary works and projects.

Levinas, in "*La Trace de L'Autre*", argues that the notion of the Other has been in circulation for a long time, perhaps always embedded somewhere (in Western thought at least) in the form of fear: "Western philosophy coincides with the disclosure of the other where the other, in manifesting itself as a being, loses its alterity. From its infancy philosophy has been struck with a horror of the other that remains other—with an insurmountable allergy" (Levinas 1986: 346). Derrida takes up Levinas's reading of the Other and measures it against the larger tradition of what he calls the "ontology of presence" (Derrida 1986). In this sense Otherness has been denied the real central issue of absence—both as an order and as a mode of production, even if this sense of the horror is inflected in terms of absence. Levinas sees the horror of the Other as partly based on the compulsion for needing something which is always denied (desire for the Other) and as something which acts as a determining process for the subject's being. In this sense Levinas can be seen as providing support for the reading of the Other as part of the Symbolic: "This desire for another, which is our very sociality, is not a simple relationship with a being where, according to our formulas at the beginning, the other is converted into the same. . . . The manifestation of the other is, to be sure, first produced in conformity with the way every signification is produced. The other is present in a cultural whole and is illuminated by this whole, like a text by its context" (Levinas 1986: 350, 351). This idea of the Other as social function and the denial of access for the individual shares a great deal with Lacan's definition, particularly in terms of drives and the split subject, as well as the operation of the Symbolic. The Symbolic in this sense becomes defined by its relationship to signification and the determination of meaning. The Other is signification both for the individual and his/her sense of subjectivity, and the interrelational processes of meaning between subjects.

For Sartre the Other is essential to the self's encounter with self-consciousness. This is the Other as a necessary determinant of the self measured against the sense of the self. For a concept which carries so much force and influence, which determines fundamental aspects of being, sociality, and relational contexts, the Other is surprisingly intangible. Even though contextually it is part of the ontology of presence, the Other must always be absent—and it is this absence that defines the Other and gives it so much force. Sartre constantly speaks of the Other as not-here, as unfixed: "We can never apprehend the relation of that Other to me and he is never given, but gradually we constitute him as a concrete object. . . . To the extent that the Other is an absence he escapes nature. . . . The Other is the one who is not me and the one who I am not. This *not* indicates a nothingness as a given element of separation between the Other and myself" (Sartre 1957: 228, 230). Levinas, working towards specifying one possible permutation of this relationship between absence and the Other, states: "What then can be this relationship with an absence radically withdrawn from disclosure and from dissimulation? And what is this absence that renders visitation possible, an absence not reducible to hiddenness, since it involves a signifyingness—a signifyingness in which the other is not converted to the same?" (Levinas 1986: 354). This is the double bind of the Other—it qualifies, and therefore determines, desire through its alterity and absence, and yet there is the desire to keep Otherness absent, to not be exposed to the *eidos* of something absent. The horror of the Other is like Freud's *das Unheimlich*, for it uncovers the normally hidden uncanny. However this is not the only reading available to us in terms of the Other.

Otherness determines the relational context of the subject to the systems of absence and desire because the subject positions itself in terms of absence and/or desire through the Other. The effect this has is the production of relational permutations between the subject, the site of subjectivity, the Other, and desire, each linked by the concept of absence. These permutations include desire as Other, the desired Other, absence as Other, and subjectivity as Other.

Underlying each of these (and the various combinations of them) is the idea that Otherness itself operates entirely on absence. This is not simply the idea that to be Other is to be absent—Sartre's configuration alone dismisses that—although this can certainly be a central issue, but rather that alterity functions, can be made sense of and is defined, entirely through the concept of absence. It is important to note on this point that the sense of desire, subject, and absence as Other is distinct from Other as absence. The first of these is a form of typological ruling, whilst the second is a conceptual declaration on the nature of Otherness.

The idea of the *Ichspaltung*—its nature and operation—becomes clearer if we note that the relationship between the subject and the Other is an ontological imperative to the action of *devenir*. The subject is tied to the Other by "the signifying dependence in the locus of the Other" (Lacan 1986: 206). This relates to both the sense of meaning and signification and the centrality of language systems in the Symbolic order. The Other is the Symbolic (becomes the Symbolic) in terms of the definition of the site of subjectivity, so that all that is contained in the Symbolic is read as Otherness by the subject. The Other as locus of the signifier emphasises the idea that the signifier itself is a process of, and subject to, absence. What becomes increasingly evident is that the Other actually determines the site of subjectivity for the subject and, consequently, the nature of the subject—this is Sartre's idea of the absent Other acting as the point of differentia between the self and the perception/conception of the self. This in turn means that the particular type of relationship developed between the subject, the Other and the site of subjectivity will substantially determine the essence of that subject type. The interplay involved here is not lost on Lacan who seeks to negate any sense of binary order between presence and absence through the sign and the Other: "We should speak of it rather as of the combination of life with the atom O of the sign, first and foremost of the sign in so far as it connotes presence or absence, by introducing essentially the "and" that links them, since in connoting presence or absence, it establishes presence against a background of absence, just as it constitutes absence in presence" (Lacan 1985: 234). Of course to accommodate Lacan's "and" into the schema of primary and secondary absences it is necessary to enforce the operation of backgrounds not as closure, or even definitional points, but as one part of absence (that is, secondary absences). This is entirely in keeping with Lacan's two crucial defining features of the Other—that it functions as absence and is the site of the signifier for the subject.

The Other as the site of the signifier means that the Lacanian subject is determined through the interplay of at least three sets of absences: the Other as fundamental lack; the Symbolic as an order of absence, as well as being positioned as originary presence for establishing subjectivity; the denied signifier as lack. In each of these cases the propulsion of desire binds the subject to the absences. It is not simply a matter of choice, rather each absence, and the multiple combinations possible, are *insisted* through the complex network of demands and desires. The Other, the signifier, and these absences are desired for the sense of subjectivity (power, control, presence, existence) invested in them. This operates as a form of dependency: "Two lacks overlap here. The first emerges from the central defect around which the dialectic of the advent of the subject to his own being in relation to the Other turns—by the fact that the subject depends on the signifier and that the signifier is first of all in the field of the Other. This lack takes up the other lack, which is the real, earlier lack, to be situated at the advent of the living being" (Lacan 1986: 204-205). The defect of the dialectic of subjectivity can be seen as a systemic notion of the determination of being through an external (to the self) process established prior to any engagement by the subject. Such a defect is distinct from the order of absence which defines the Other. Defect here is taken to mean an absence which motivates the subject toward the site of subjectivity, in these terms the Other and the locus of the signifier. This is the dependency of the subject through desire and the drives for the signifier and the Other.

Central to this issue is the idea of the speaking/enunciating subject—the subject who is determined/constituted by and defined through his/her relationship to language and speech. Within the context of the present concerns it is significant that the Other is not just the locus of the signifier, but also of speech. The causal relationship is the subject's use of the signifier to establish subjectivity as presence both at the individual, performative level as well as the cosmogonical, the onto-theological, the metaphysical. The exact positioning of the subject by the signifier, and the signifier by the subject, plays an essential role in fashioning the nature of the site of subjectivity, for this site is not a fixed, stable space but rather a shifting dynamic, made up of dominant and subordinated paradigms. It is these paradigms of constitutive subjectivity that give a sense of the determinants of the subject/subjectivity at any one point in time. This positioning is true of the subject itself as well as the typology of absences (including lacks, gaps, splits) and the ideological functions. Primary to this is the idea that subjectivity develops precisely from this encounter with the Other, the realisation of the signifier figured as a lack, and the development of desire as a qualifying force.

Lacan argues that in the *Real-Ich*—the realm of the Real and the ego—it is possible for everything to remain constant without a sense of the subject. Subjectivity, for Lacan, comes into being—is realised as an essential feature—only with the positioning of the signifier in the Other. This means that the Other, along with the emerging subject in the Symbolic—the field of the signifier in the formation of the subject—does not simply demand an engagement with the signifier in order to make the transition, but that such a process actually creates, determines and sustains the nature and function of subjectivity. Lacan is most emphatic regarding this: "If the subject is what I say it is, namely the subject determined by language and speech, it follows that the subject, *in initio*, begins in the locus of the Other, in so far as it is there that the first signifier emerges" (Lacan 1986: 198). This means that the subject is created by the signifier in the Other and sustained (the identificatory process) through this relationship. It is a relationship based on lack/absence and desire, and the intensity of these two operational systems is made even more clear once there is a recognition of the ontological, epistemological, and ideological investments.

Part of this process is made clearer by considering the Other as a type of code system. The subject, in effect, finds itself in the Other, or at least finds a desire to find itself in the Other. *Où se trouve*? To find itself means that the self is looking for something that, paradoxically, it needs to have in order to find. The subject cannot be if it is looking for subjectivity. This is the double play of "*où se trouve*"—it is a question of where something is (absence), but is also asking where it finds itself (presence). The English "I found myself sitting by the river" is a similar construction because it sets up the split of the subject who is looking and the subject who is found. The split of the subject who finds him/herself by the river and the double play of "*où se trouve*" indicate the desire for the signifier and the Other. The search is on, and it is a search that cannot be satisfied because the rupture of the subject must already have taken place. The *Ichspaltung* is precisely this subject. This is why subjectivity has all the appearances of presence, but all the mechanisms, and definitional qualities, of absence. The presences of subjectivity are play and only become operational against the backdrop of secondary absences, and capable of signification through primary absences.

Part of the understanding of the Other in terms of subjectivity and desire is to read it as a code system. There is the initial obvious connection here with the idea of the Other as site of the signifier, with the Other acting as a repository for the range of signifiers possible. In these terms the combinatory qualities of the code system make sense of the signifiers and their combinations. The paradigmatics of the Other as a code system does not necessarily mean that signifiers of subjectivity, desire, and absence are interchangeable, although such a register is, within certain limits, possible. What would be more common, however, is the exchanging of signifiers within the syntagmatic orders. This is a substantial part of the reason why the subject can find itself sitting by the river—the displacement between the oppositions of looking and finding are negotiated by the code structure of desire and absence. What remains missing is the subject itself, because the subject is invested in the signifier and not the code. The Other as code is what is essentially desired—what is offered by way of appeasement is the *objet petit a*.

The complex nature of the Other as code, and *objet petit a* as one part—an especially important part it should be added—of the manifestation of this code means that the paradigmatics rely heavily on an external ordering process. What becomes evident with even the most cursory of glances at such an ordering is the artificial nature of the process. This is because even though the Other is a code, it is distinct from most other codes because of its dynamic nature emphasising the rules of combination rather than exclusion. Theoretically, as Sartre points out, nothing can be excluded from the realm of the Other because of the open-ended sense of its operation. Otherness is categorical, encyclopedic even, but as a code it does not operate with the same sense of exclusion that is common to other code systems. In effect what is being argued here is that there are three semiotic code systems (absence, subjectivity, and desire) read against a second order semiotic code which allows interconnection between these (and others). This is the reason why Otherness applies to desire, subjectivity, and absence in both differing and similar ways. This reading of the Other as code suggests a further link, to the idea of the Other as a discourse. This is the interconnection of the discourse of the Other as the unconscious and the unconscious structured as a language.

Two of the central features for this theorising of absence regarding the nature and function of the unconscious are the operation of the unconscious as language and the systems of gaps/absences inherent in such an operation. In both cases desire and subjectivity figure prominently in the interconnection between the unconscious and the Other. The sense of the Other as a code system operates to position the Other as an organising principle of meaning, as well as offering an explanation for the processes of gaps and absences in the subject's encounter with Otherness, the structure of desire, the signification of lack.

When Lacan speaks of the unconscious as structured like a language he has the Freudian model firmly in mind. This Freudian model is the unconscious figured in terms of repression and censorship, of the elaborate mechanisms for expressing the repressed, of the centrality of the drives in the connection between the ego, id, and super-ego. The structure of the conscious, preconscious, and unconscious is made sense of through the mechanisms of censorship, repression, wishfulfilment, parapraxis—in short the measuring of the present against what is absent, of what is manifested and what is intended. The essence of Freudian theory, it can be argued, is based on absence—*The Interpretation of Dreams*, for example, is a systematic examination of the ways in which absence operates to shape and control thoughts, desires, and wishes as they pass back and forth from the unconscious to the conscious. The passage, and even the creation and destruction, of these thoughts is continually shaped by the processes of repression, the return of the repressed, the need to express desires and drives, and the social function of censorship. It is in processes such as these that resistance is instigated and maintained, which in turn leads to a modification of thoughts. Censorship commands and determines the form of all conscious thoughts, feelings, etc.—that is, essentially, all structures that come to mean or have meaning determined for them—as they are translated from the unconscious to the conscious mind. In turn it also determines the presence and absence of all thoughts and their manifestations. This determining, constitutive action, which is based on the system of translation, is tied to the construction of subjectivity. Freud qualifies this when he states: "The mechanism of dream-formation would in general be greatly clarified if instead of the opposition between *conscious* and *unconscious* we were to speak of that between the *ego* and the *repressed"* (Freud 1986a: 710). The avoidance of binary opposites here does more than simply shift the issue from designating signifiers into conscious and unconscious types. It fundamentally shifts the emphasis of the interpretation of the signifiers and how they are seen to be organised. Furthermore, it is important to note that Freud is not aligning the ego with the conscious and the repressed with the unconscious. The ego does become contiguous with consciousness because of the urgency of presence in subjectivity, just as the unconscious becomes contiguous with the repressed because of the ordering prompted by notions of presence and absence. However, this should be seen as an ordering based on analytic concerns—dreams, as with most other manifestations of the mind, are elements of both subjectivity and repression, and are issues of both presence and absence.

All forms of repression and censorship of the unconscious can be read in terms of absence, which in turn allows consequences of these processes to be seen as indicators of absence, as resultants of absence, or as meaningful in terms of absence. An example of this is Freud's idea that the actions of repression and/or censorship produce *Entstellung*, or distortion which is produced in the attempt to avoid anxiety from the repression or censoring of a desire or drive. This is not to misread Freud's shifting stance on this issue—in early writings Freud argues that repression is a device employed to avoid anxiety, but later he qualifies this and sees repression as something which can also be caused by anxiety, hence any sense of causality:[repression/censorship] as causal—resulting in [anxiety]—and consequently [*Entstellung*] and is contextualised by the action of anxiety being seen as causal in itself:[Anxiety (of something)] as causal—resulting in [repression/censorship]—and consequently [*Entstellung*]. *Entstellung* is created by the repression and censoring of thoughts, and the greater the censorship and repression the greater the distortion of the signifiers and the number of symbols used (although it is necessary to avoid any sense of the quantitative being the sole indicator here). This whole process can be made sense of by reading such distortions as processes of absences. *Entstellung* is a form of absence because what is apparent, in a sense the denotative, to the interpreter (analyst or reader) is only part of the original message. A central contributing factor to the distortion is the exclusion of certain signifying elements, the multiple levels of the connotative. It could be argued that the motivation behind this action is what distinguishes this mental process from the lacunae which are a necessary part of the structure of the text.

This offers one demonstration of *Entstellung* as part of the code of the Other as language/discourse. *Entstellung* as absence (indicator of absence, absence in a representational sense, incomplete and uncompleted presences, and others) and the absences actually produced by these distortions are initially derived from the censorship and repression connected with the ego and id, which can be seen as being strongly connected to the Freudian formula *Wo es war, soll Ich weden*. Such a model holds significant potential in terms of interpreting the structure of the text and noting how absences operate in the act of reading. In these cases it is the balance of textual representations (conventions, lacunae, discursive practices, historical and social methods) and the desire and/or need to distort, disguise, and repress.

Part of the reason why Freud insists on distinguishing between conscious/unconscious and ego/repression is because repression and censorship do not take place in either the conscious or the unconscious, but rather between the two: "repression is a process which occurs between the systems Ucs. and Pcs. (or Cs.), and results in keeping something at a distance from consciousness" (Freud 1987: 208-209). This sense of no-place is comparable to the description Sartre gives the Other—it is neither regulative nor constitutive of the subject's sense of knowledge. This is important to the idea of the Other as code of the unconscious because it is an indicator that, like distortion, repression, and censorship, the Other is a vital part of the operation of the unconscious, but it does not constitute the unconscious. Another parallel that operates here is that by positioning repression in this manner, Freud is setting up the idea of the return of the repressed. Clearly returns and repetition are significant features in the function of absence.

A further example of the relationship between repression, censorship, and the Other is parapraxis and the act of forgetting. The forgetting of names and places serves as an example of presence and absence operating through repression. Here the failure to recall, or the demonstration of parapraxis, becomes a signifier of repression and so can be read as an absence. What is made present (parapraxis) is a substitute for the repressed absent, and what is forgotten represents an absence through denial. Freud's example of the forgetting of names and the subsequent substituting of them (Boltraffio, Botticelli) because of the unconscious links with death and sexuality demonstrates the connection between repression and substitution. What is substituted and what forms it takes—that is, the acting present—becomes a further issue of analysis. This is why one signifier, chosen over others, can be used to define the absence, distortion, repression, and censorship processes involved in the production of the text. There can be no final text, however, even a final deconstructed one, because it is retold, reread—elements previously "unseen" because they seemed insignificant are suddenly filled with importance because of the different perspectives adopted. The idea that all repression and subsequent absences must somehow produce a presence (or series of presences) is a crucial issue. If this is correct, and all absences produced from repression and censorship must produce a substitute presence (even if this is the act of forgetting itself), then the code of the Other becomes part of the production process. Central to Freudian theory is the idea that absences cannot be left, that the repressed returns, and that a distorted presence stands in its place. The need to establish such presences (no matter how distorted) stems from desire, and the actual production of these presences is derived from the Other as code. This is ascribing a central, active, and creative role to the Other which is distinct from the more passive configuration of the Other as site of desire via the *objet petit a*. This creative function is attributed to the Other as code, rather than being based in any encoding sense already there.

This creative function of the Other as code is distinct from, but not unrelated to, sublimation. In terms of absence sublimation operates in a similar manner to the paradigmatics of metaphor and metonymy—that is, it sets up a presence which is an "acceptable" alternative, in terms of the register of presences and the context of the conscious, to that which is made absent through repression and/or censorship. Strictly speaking, Freud uses the term to explain how intellectual and artistic activities replace/sublimate sexual drives and activities. However, as with resistance, the general notion of sublimation/replacement (why it occurs, what happens to the originary signifying order when it has been sublimated) can be read within the context of absence. The processes of sublimation are also processes of absence in a wider context. Sublimation and resistance in these terms are mechanisms of analysis that help to explain how absence as process affects the form and structure of the signifier as it appears in the final reading act.

The failure to remember and parapraxis are both systems of absence demonstrating particular forms of repression. How this repression and subsequent replacement or manifestation occur and why they do so are connected to the subject's relationship to desire. This necessarily includes repressed desires as well as the repression of elements that run counter to the subject's desires. It is not simply a case of desires being repressed, for there is also the action of hegemonically managing structures and systems that oppose such desires and their operation. In this way the systematic process of subjectivity as presence becomes linked to the repressive/sublimation action. The operation of absences of this type develop a code system independent of the Other as code, but often deal with the constitutive signifiers and their combinations in a similar fashion. Part of the reason why such a distinction needs to be made is because of the definitional qualities of these codes in terms of subjectivity and desire. Repression and the concomitant action of sublimation forms part of the code system of lacunae.

Freud argues that there are two levels of repression—*Entstellung* and the suppression of affect. Both are consequences of censorship. This is significant in relation to the somatic and ideational aspects of dreaming and the operation of suppression. Linked to the suppression of affect is the idea that every train of thought in the unconscious "is yoked with its contradictory opposite" (Freud 1986a: 604-605). This bond allows the imposition of opposites at the level of the signifiers produced through distortion and repression without creating a need for further censoring—that is, the suppression of affect—and at the level of the signified in condensation and displacement. A further aspect of this idea of the contiguity of linking opposites or seemingly disparate images/themes, etc., is that censorship, through repression and sublimation, compels a displacement of signifiers. In Freudian theory this form of displacement is particularly important in the hysteric. The second dream in the case study of Dora is based almost entirely on reading such a relationship. An example which demonstrates this is the reading of "box" (*Schachtel*) for female genitals in a derogatory manner: "Where is the key? seems to be the masculine counterpart to the question Where is the box? They are questions therefore referring to the genitals" (Freud 1985: 137). This reading of *Schachtel* recurs throughout Freud's work—it is found, for example, in the analysis of both of Dora's dreams, in *Jokes and Their Relation to the Unconscious*, and in *The Interpretation of Dreams*—each time operating within this context of the contiguity of ideas through the action of censorship.

The processes of censorship, distortion, and repression are linked to the idea of the Other as code through the shared interests of the subject's construction of desire through absence. This connection is strengthened even further through the reading of the unconscious as a site of the Other and the fundamental issue of language to this site. These intersections of codes are also evident in the issue of why processes of censorship and repression take place at all. Freud indicates that the key to understanding repression rests in the idea that the very action is inextricably tied to the avoidance of unpleasure. This is formulated in the link between repression as a function of absence and desire/wish fulfilment. It is also connected to Freud's idea that whereas dreams are always processes of wish fulfilments—and so the avoidance of unpleasure—activities such as jokes are processes of realising pleasure. The nexus of repression, pleasure/unpleasure (which should be read not as a binarism but in terms of an analogic system), language, censorship, desire can be read as a signification order based on absence. Where within one system (e.g., certain language constructions, jokes, parapraxis) absences are based on pleasure and negotiating the actions of censorship, and in the other system (e.g., dreams) the nature of the absences and their origins are based on the avoidance of unpleasure. Clearly it would be incorrect to see these as exclusive divisions, hence the reason why absence becomes a unifying concept in these terms.

It is possible to link this ordering of absences with the distinction of primary and secondary processes. If absence is to be seen as part of the way in which meaning is constructed, of how language operates, and perhaps, ultimately, of the basis of textuality and the motivation for reading, then these two fundamental processes must be taken into account. This is true in part because they can be seen as explanatory indices for such models and actions, and in part because primary and secondary processes are revisionary and there-fore, it can be argued, attached to making things absent. This is also true of Freud's concept of mobile and quiescent psychical energy which shapes both the eventual form of representation and the paradigmatics of constructed meaning. In terms of repression Freud points out that because the permitted thoughts of one system are categorically distinct from another—the secondary process being more severely censoring—the manifestations, which are the presences devised through the action of *Entstellung* as well as other processes such as consider-ations of representabilty, are significant in their formal features. So the form that is adopted indicates something about the absent. Distortion must also accommodate the concept of disguise, which is usually motivated in the same way as the censorship itself. Disguising the repressed signifiers (the signifiers of repression as well as the actual signifiers which are repressed) is a further indicator of absence operating within the signifying process. Lacan introduces a stronger sense of the textual when he argues that distortion can be read as an interplay of the signifier, the signified, and the sliding action of the bar. The sense of autonomy attributed to the signifier must be a contextual one, related to the operation of the signified in terms of meaning and not a more universal sense of directly attributable signifiers to signifieds, for this would go directly against Lacan's own sense of the sign and its operations.

When the butcher's wife desires caviar but asks her husband to withhold it, she enters into a signifying order of the repression and disguising of desire itself. Her desire operates on at least two levels—the desire for caviar and the desire for her much-loved husband to demonstrate similar feelings for her by keeping it from her. She wishes to strike a balance between desire and denial. But within this seemingly organised system of the exchange of signifiers between husband and wife there is the further complication of the friend and her smoked salmon. The woman dreams of a dinner party that cannot be held because she cannot obtain any smoked salmon—the favourite food of her friend. Freud reads this as a wish fulfilment because the woman's friend cannot become stout, and so her husband, potential inamorato of Rubensian women, will not be seduced by the friend. The caviar and the smoked salmon become metaphors of desire and its denial and absence. Lacan reads this as the desire for the Other: "Since this desire is totally inadequate (how can one receive all these people with only one slice of smoked salmon?), I really must when all (or the dream) is said and done give up my desire to give a dinner (that is, my search for the desire of the Other, which is the secret of my desire)" (Lacan: 1985: 262). The butcher's wife, because she enters into a hysterical identification with her friend, becomes the metonym for the desire and its absence. The dream itself abounds with absences—the dinner party, the smoked salmon, the caviar, the husband and his demonstrations of fidelity through denial can all be read in terms of absence. In such a catalogue of absences rests the disguise of the signifier of desire and its motivational force. Through this sense of desire in its disguised and repressed form it becomes evident that the site where caviar and smoked salmon operate as desire and as meaningful is the Other, and as such it is possible to read them, and all the absences featured in this example, as signifiers organised through the code of the Other.

When Freud attempts to map out the connection between the process of repression, and its consequences, and the order of the conscious, he ends up driving a theoretical wedge between the orders of the mind. In effect Freud is arguing that repression is allowed to operate freely in the unconscious and preconscious, but is actually only an effect in the conscious. This means that repression and its derivatives are processes that make things absent in one system, but in doing so produce and/or sustain presences in another—which in turn suggests that we must speak of absences crossing the boundaries of primary and secondary types depending on the context of their production and operation. This supports the idea of a Freudian sense of absence which has as its central edict not absence as negativity, but absence as "non-apparent". Such an idea finds further evidence in the other key readings of the action of repression: that it is often derived from an earlier action of expulsion of something from the conscious by the conscious; that the two types of repression—primal and proper—are connected to *trieb* as an active and motivational force, and in this sense continue to operate as a presence figured as an absence; and that the key idea of derivatives and substitutes can be read within this context.

To argue that repression is only an effect in the conscious and a process in the unconscious and preconscious would seem to go against the understood "logic" of the action. The idea of repression is usually seen in terms of whatever is repressed is done so from the conscious to the unconscious and/or preconscious. This is a reading in keeping with Freud's own desire to position it within the context of economic, topographical, and dynamic processes, and hence the "quota of effect" for repression. Simply put, this seems to argue that repression takes place in the conscious after which there is a subsequent transference of the repressed to the unconscious/preconscious. However, to make sense of the absence such a schema must be read via the non-apparentness of the absence because of the insistence on the presence through *Entstellung*, derivatives, and substitutions. This sense of the insistence on the presence shares a number of common features with the critical and hermeneutic issues that Derrida specifies in the deconstruction of the metaphysics of presence as determinant of subjectivity, meaning/signification, and history in Western philosophy.

Repression does not create an absence in the sense of negation—in fact repression is a highly productive activity which results in a dynamic paradigmatic of polyonymous signifiers. The reason for such a dynamic is the antithetical forces which come into play against what is eventually repressed. In these terms of the operation of absence, it would be incorrect to see repression as an action of the conscious or, for that matter, the unconscious or preconscious. Repression is part of the non-apparentness of absence because of the two functions it contributes—derivatives and substitutes in the conscious, and their coextensive production in the unconscious and preconscious. This does not go against Freud's notion that the instinctual representative can be split to produce an idealisation of fetishism and repression, rather it means that fetishism can be read as part of the non-apparentness, polyonymous signifying order of absence.

Repression in these terms operates in the unconscious because it prevents the manifestation of the repressed signifiers from entering the conscious. Repression, then, does not remove signifiers from the conscious and reposition them in the unconscious, for the signifiers were never in the conscious to begin with. The absences produced through repression stem from the non-apparentness of the "originary" signifiers and the substitution of them through the language and code structures of the Other. This is entirely in keeping with the idea that repression itself is only ever known by its effects and that the actual process of repression is never witnessed. This would suggest that there are two types of non-apparent absences in this field—the system of repression itself, and the manifestations of repression in the permitted signifiers.

The non-apparentness of this type of signifier extends to other aspects of Freud's work, of particular note is the act of forgetting. However, in the case of forgetting the signifier, as opposed to the sign which might require a more complete sense of the act of reading, or at least registering, the action draws attention to itself and there is the potential situation of the non-apparent absence being discovered for what it is—an absence disguised as a presence. To avoid the realisation of this the action of forgetting sets up various defence mechanisms. The process of forgetting is not homogeneous in terms of the rationale behind its function, which makes the task of designating discriminatory features a difficult one. The forgetting of names in *The Psychopathology of Everyday Life* is a repression through avoidance. However, in the case study of Dora repression operates, through forgetting, as a defence against interpretation, specifically Freud's own interpretative actions, and it does have other possible meanings. At various points in the text Freud argues for the act of forgetting: as something actually forgotten (in essence a mechanical process); a disguise for the willing and intentional withholding of information (". . . patients consciously and intentionally keep back part of what they ought to tell—things that are perfectly well known to them" [Freud 1985: 46]); as a system contrasted to the "wholeness" of remembering ("Nothing that could help to confirm this view had escaped her perception, which in this connection was pitilessly sharp; *here there were no gaps to be found in her memory*" [Freud 1985: 63]; and as the replacement of forgetting by other signifiers to fill up the gaps in remembering. In a footnote in *Jokes and Their Relation to the Unconscious*, Freud attempts to knit together these and other models of forgetting. In three primary texts of dreams, jokes, and the normal, everyday forgetting shares the sense of repression in forgetting, but the more insidious sense given to it by Freud in Dora's case study (and others) adds a further, political dimension to this form of absence.

It is noteworthy that Freud reads Dora as a woman very much motivated by revenge. This quality of vengeance ascribed to her is seen by Freud as directed not just towards the others in her everyday life, but also towards Freud, the analyst, the interpreter of her words and actions. In the case study we find such examples as: ". . . you gave free rein to your feelings of revenge" (p. 148); ". . . she might just as well have been merely provoked into satisfying her craving for revenge . . ." (p. 151); ". . . this was an unmistakable act of vengeance on her part" (p. 150); "Now I know your motive for the slap in the face with which you answered Herr K.'s proposal. It was not that you were offended at his suggestions; you were actuated by jealousy and revenge" (p.

147). For Freud Dora's motivations through revenge determine all of her actions, including forgetting and remembering. This clearly sets up a type of politicised forgetting that is beyond repression. And it is political on two fronts: Freud's reading of it as a political act against psychoanalysis and himself, with the politics of patriarchy and phallocentric readings being a different discursive practice. The non-apparent absence is shifted from an emphasis on the substitution of the repressed signifier to fill in the gap created by the act of repression to the deliberate manipulation of this non-apparent absence as a defence/attack mechanism. This introduces a wider category of absence which is crucial to the understanding of absence as a theoretical model, for this is the politicised absence, bound to the orders of discourse and their powerful systems of signification. Control of such absences and their interpretation constitutes a fundamental part of the determination of meaning, of discourse, of the figuring of subjectivity—it is an essential part of the operation of signification as it comes to be. At a meta-critical level this also reveals the absences produced within specific paradigms. In as much as Freud is also a product of his own time and culture he is unable to notice many of the absences within his own critical frame. He does not make the connections between power and discourse that have become part of the post-structuralist critical paradigm.

Distortion (*Entstellung*) and the suppression of affect imply a transformation of the original into a particular configuration. The greater the repression the more convoluted and extensive the transformation becomes, and the greater are the number of substituting signifiers. To understand this more fully it is necessary to return to the issue of the unconscious and its systemic function as a language. This model of the unconscious ties in with Lacan's assertion that the unconscious is structured like a language. There is a duality in this reading: the unconscious *as* a language; and the language *of* the unconscious. Such a duality need not be seen as mutually exclusive, that is we need not choose an answer for the question "is the equation saying that the unconscious is like positive language, or is it saying that the unconscious can be read like a language system?" For even in the above passage there is not the dismissal of the double play that occurs in the equation. In fact it is important that the equation retains its duality as its sense hinges on the retention, particularly in terms of the Other as code, as well as mapping the subject's relationship to the Other. Furthermore, the equation must retain this dual function in order to operate within the Freudian context of the unconscious and processes like repression and *Entstellung*. This idea that the unconscious is structured like a language is concomitant to the unconscious being the discourse of the Other.

One of the central concerns here is to consider the ways in which the subject position—which includes the relational context of the site of subjectivity—is connected to the Other as absence. Because of the centrality of the unconscious to the discourse of the Other what becomes evident in such an examination is the investment of subjectivity in its discourse and its articulation. Lacan ascribes to the language of the unconscious the determination of the subject: "The unconscious is constituted by the effects of speech on the subject, it is the dimension in which the subject is determined in the development of the effects of speech, consequently the unconscious is structured like a language. Such a direction seems well fitted to snatch any apprehension of the unconscious from an orientation to reality, other than that of the constitution of the subject" (Lacan 1986: 149). The key to understanding this is the idea that the determination of the subject in the unconscious is done through the signifier and its relation to signification. It is this matrix which produces what Lacan calls dialectized significations—a dialectic, it can be argued, sustained by the operations of absences and desire. In these terms subjectivity is based on the code structure of the Other as it operates in the language structure of the unconscious. The investment of subjectivity in the discourse of the Other, and even more specifically in the signifier(s) of this discourse, can be seen as further evidence of the centrality of absence to the subject's relationship to the site of subjectivity, as well as the organising principles of this site in itself.

Lacan speaks constantly of the unconscious in terms that can be read as part of the order of absence. He refers to Freud's seeking of the unconscious in the "sense of impediment" (Lacan 1986: 25). This impediment, which Lacan describes at various points as a failure, a split, and, perhaps most significantly here, as a gap, is both a system and a manifestation of absence. Impediment suggests Freud's idea of repression—the impeding of thoughts from entering the conscious; failure is linked to Lacanian *méconnaissance*; split to the *Ichspaltung* (especially in terms of subjectivity, although there are many other connections). Most clearly, however, it is when Lacan speaks of gaps in terms of the unconscious that absence is evoked, and it is to this that we must now turn our attention.

Lacan argues that the revelation of a thought in the unconscious occurs through an absence. This relates to what has been described here as the non-apparentness of the signifier caused by absence—which necessarily includes the unconscious as absence, lack, and gap, as well as the actual absences, lacks, and gaps that are in the unconscious. What must also be included is otherness. The centrality of the Other in terms of the unconscious is primary to this because it acts both as an independent system of absences and as a referential point of absences in, and as, the unconscious. The distinction between the unconscious as absence and the absences which constitute the unconscious can be measured in terms of Lacan's reference to the gap of the unconscious, whilst this paradigmatic of non-apparent absences can be seen, at least in part, as a consequence of this gap and its manifestations. It is not simply products from the unconscious that can be seen in this light, rather it is the whole realm of the unconscious and the discursive practices: "the unconscious is not an ambiguity of acts . . . but lacuna, cut, rupture inscribed in a certain lack" (Lacan 1986: 153). One of the strongest links made by Lacan is between the unconscious and gaps. At many points in his writings Lacan actually infers that it is the gap which most clearly defines the essential feature of the unconscious—which

includes the unconscious as a gap as well as absences in the unconscious—as a
"hole", as a "split", and as the order of the "nonrealised". Tied in with this is
the concept of the refusal and its link with repression. The lacunae of the
unconscious define its quality as Other and provide a central link to the notion
of absence and desire in constituting subjectivity.

The gap of the unconscious is an issue of ontology, but not simply because
of this sense of subjectivity and the process of desire. Desire develops the
ontological sense of the unconscious as gap, but Lacan positions the "gapness"
as pre-ontological because of the discrepancies between the unconscious and
ontological orders. It is the *epoche* which operates in the critical interpretation
of the unconscious and ontology that further positions the Other and the Real
as the absenting realm of the unconscious. This elusive nature is the disjunction
between the unconscious and the ontologically defined aspects, events, and
processes. The elusive unconscious is demonstrated in Freud's division of latent
and manifest and Lacan's division of Imaginary, Symbolic, and Real. The
ontological difference demands critical systems of this type. The definition and
management of the unconscious in the ontic is part of the previously mentioned
concepts of impediment (and deception should be added here as part of the
order of impediment) and gap—how the ontic is "defined" and "managed" in
the unconscious is yet another issue. In these terms it is significant that Lacan
argues that the problematisation of cause in the philosophical tradition—his
central model being Kant's use of the gap in the *Prolegomena*—is in some ways
answered by the Freudian conceptualisation of the unconscious, and his own
subsequent readings of it as a gap. This is the "domain of cause" of the
unconscious. So when Kant claims that cause "must either be grounded
completely a priori in the understanding, or must be entirely given up as a mere
phantom of the brain, (Kant 1973: 125), the unconscious can be seen as part of
this phantom of the brain in a manner quite oppositional to the ways in which
The Critique of Pure Reason positions it.

The unconscious has a pulsative function, that is, the need to "close up
again upon itself . . . to vanish, to disappear" (Lacan 1986: 43). The pulsative
function of the slit (the Freudian metaphor for the unconscious) is part of the
manifestation of the unconscious through absence. It is this elusive aspect of
disappearing that makes the desire of the Other so complex in terms of the site
of subjectivity—the subject becomes tied to the signifier in the Other. The
subject becomes the gap and various aspects of it (e.g., the body, the operation
of the mind, the relationship to others, social discourse) can be read in terms
of the gap—that is, essentially, absence. Just as there are absences in the gap
and absences of the gap, so we also find similar types in these absences. This
is the interplay between primary and secondary absences in the dialectical
structure and the dialectization of signification.

The connections of subjectivity to the Other and the unconscious operate
in a series of folds, each convoluted and bound to the other systems. The
subject is continually embroiled in the process of determining its own sense of

subjectivity, insisted in the Other as the discourse of the unconscious. The dual catalysts of desire and absence provide the impetus of this insistence traced along the drive. The subject is motivated towards this site of subjectivity by a complex interplay of absences, one of the most significant and powerful being desire and its manifestations. Before turning to a closer examination of the nature of desire and subjectivity within this context it is necessary to take note of the relationship between the subject and the object in these terms.

Lacan coins the term "*co-naissance*" to describe the connection that the subject constructs towards the object. As with the division of Sartre's "*pour-soi*" and "*en-soi*", *co-naissance* suggests a political urgency in the action of differentiation by the subject towards the object. The subject wants to exclude through distinction the object from the realm of the self because such an action emphasises and (seemingly) strengthens the subject's own claim to being/existence. This sense of differentiation has its roots in Heidegger's *Das Nichts* and Sartre's *le Neánt*—hence the almost simultaneous desire for the subject position (occupation of the site of subjectivity) and the anxiety of potential objectness. The nature of the object is born out of a desire for the object and/or fear for the loss of the self as object. *Co-naissance* carries with it both the desire for the object (its possession and the control of it) and the urgency of the subject position partly stimulated by the anxiety of real or possible loss. This is strongly reminiscent of the operations of the *objet petit a* in the discourse of desire.

The development of the object by the subject through these two structures suggests a further link to object-relations and the political agenda for the subject. The fear of objectification by the subject is based on the complexities of the nature of absence in subjectivity, in these terms the absence is the self reduced to the object, the denial of subjectivity. The object is read by the subject as being without a relational context to the Other (and the unconscious)—which is to say that the object may be ontically Otherness or have its Otherness deleted through objectification, which can occur in the subject's desire for the order of the Other itself. This does not refute the sense of the object as Other for the subject. The subject attempts to align itself with the order of the Other through the pulsative action of the desire for the Other. Similarly, the desire for the object can be based on the very absence of the object. This is the bipartite system of the chisel (^ and v) in the subject's relationship to the *objet petit a*. These are the *vels* of alienation and separation of the subject from the object, which can include the subject itself. This is the evoking of presence in absence and can be seen to be strongly connected to the model of *fort/da*. It is possible for the fear of objectness and the desire by the subject for the object (in its capacity of metonymic Otherness) to be combined. The notion of the subject distinguished from the object is central to the psychoanalytic process: "It [psychoanalysis] stresses that man isn't an object, but a being in the process of becoming, something metaphysical" (Lacan 1988b: 105). It is significant that Lacan emphasises the incompleteness—the gap—of the process of subjectivity in this definition, which aligns it with the critical order of the subject-in-process.

A primary motivating force of the subject's relationship to the Other is in desire and absence. Lacan constantly stresses this connection. One example, from "The Function and Field of Speech and Language in Psychoanalysis", will serve to illustrate this point: "desire finds its meaning in the desire of the Other, not so much because the Other holds the key to the object desired, as because the first object of desire is to be recognised by the Other" (Lacan 1985: 58). This desire to be recognised by the Other, in something that is always absent, that allows the construction of the central idea of desire as a system of absence, and absence as a system of desire in the subject. Much less than a negation of desire, this convolution of the subject into the desire of/for the Other, liberates desire. What it does to the subject, on the other hand, requires a different critical agenda.

3

Desire, Pleasure, and the Subject of Absence

Desire and Pleasure—Some Connections

Pleasure is a manifestation of desire, a type within a larger order of (potentially) categorised types. This implies that there might be other manifestations of different categories and types, and some of these will be taken up in the ensuing sections on abjection and the enunciating subject, as well as in the consideration of a semiotics of absence. This is not, however, a categorisation of types of desire and its manifestations. Rather, what is at issue here is the operation of desire/pleasure in terms of the subject and absence, and part of the legitimation in considering a concept such as pleasure lies in the implicating corpus which already exists. This corpus suggests that pleasure exists a priori to desire, and so we are dealing with issues of production as well as pulsation.

What such a division of types suggests is that if desire operates as an absence, then pleasure can be read as one of its manifested presences. These manifestations can be seen as "positive" (for example pleasure) or "negative" (for example unrequited love) or even neutral (for example repetition), but none are the total satisfaction of the act of desire itself. What also needs to be avoided is the idea that there is a straightforward correlation between desire/pleasure and absence/presence—pleasure cannot be seen as simply an attempt to create presence within the context of the absences of desire. The presences of pleasure are attempts to alleviate the tensions, which are carried with the absences of desire, in the subject, or text—any signifying order in fact. In this sense it can be seen as a primary force in the act of reading. However, pleasure, no matter in which way it is developed, is ephemeral whilst desire is atemporal and resides in the Other and its discourse. This is why the cultural diachronics of pleasure are so dynamic. Some of the fundamental aspects which need to be investigated under such a rubric include: i) the relationship between desire as absence and pleasure as presence; ii) how pleasure operates to escape repression and censorship connected to the processes of desire and the unconscious; iii) how pleasure is managed in this presentational and representational sense; iv) the connection between the *objet petit a* and pleasure and, as a consequence, the connection between the subject—object and desire—pleasure. What such issues initially suggest is that different pleasures are made present (and represent) differently. These representational aspects or, to contextualise this in Freudian terms, the considerations of representability, become central to the analysis of processes of presence and absence and their political/ideological manifestations and management.

The Concept of Pleasure: *Fort/da*

The opening definition of pleasure in "Beyond the Pleasure Principle" is striking in its semiotic construction. Here pleasure is defined by its opposite, that of unpleasure and so mirrors the structure of the sign and so of *différance*, difference, and *Aufhebung*. The introduction of the particular reading of the economic at this point in Freud's theoretical development supports the reading that pleasure is initially defined in negative terms. What is pleasurable is defined by the qualitative and quantitative avoidance of unpleasure. The economics of this is that the amount of unpleasure that is avoided is measured against the resulting pleasure. This operates as a dynamic—that is, that the psychic response is constantly attempting to move away from unpleasure and towards that which is pleasurable. We rediscover this feature of the dynamic in the notion of desire, the insatiable urgency of striving for the Other which can never be attained. Desire and pleasure are dynamic economies rather than nodal points of resolution. This qualifies the idea that pleasure is simply a manifestation of absenting desire (essentially read as a satisfaction of desire) and attributes a semblance of absence to pleasure itself. This absence within pleasure is distinct from the force of absence known as desire.

The economic function involved with pleasure/unpleasure, Freud argues, relates to "quantity of excitation" (Freud 1987: 276). These quantities are supposed to be kept low, or at the very least constant, so in this sense Freud is attempting to read the action as one of management. The reason why this managing is necessary is that there is a tension of forces between those directed towards pleasure and those oppositional to it. The tension rests in what Freud describes as the reality principle. According to Freud, the pleasure principle is a dangerous force because it has such little regard for the survival of the self. The reality principle is not oppositional to pleasure, but seeks its deferment. This deferential quality involves the insistence of presence of the reality principle and its consequences, and making pleasure absent, which is an absence of quite a different order than the absences connected to desire. The reality principle allows the manifestation of particular signifiers and seeks to defer or absent other signifiers connected to the pleasure principle, which often, argues

Freud, involves the sex drives.

It is in terms of the pleasure principle and the reality principle that Freud introduces the idea of *fort/da*. Clearly *fort/da* is a very significant concept in terms of theorising absence and represents a point of intersection for a great number of concerns. Lacan, for example, attributes it with a fundamental role in the development and function of language for the self when he describes it: "through the word—already a presence constructed out of absence—absence itself comes to giving itself a name in that moment of origin whose perpetual recreation Freud's genius detected in the play of a child" (Lacan 1968: 39). Derrida points out that all that Freud builds into the child's play with the wooden spool is not certain, and that Freud himself never claims closure and resolution with the theory of *fort/da*.

There are four central ideas within the context of how *fort/da* relates to the pleasure principle and the reality principle. These four can be designated as: i) the play as cultural achievement; ii) the pleasure involved with repetition; iii) the transformation of passivity to activity; 4) the act of revenge. In drawing up such a schema it is also possible to integrate those critical concerns of *Aufhebung* and the eternal return as issues of pleasure as a political process.

The first of these four, the configuration of pleasure as play, is one of the primary ways in which cultures allow manifestations of pleasure. This can be read in terms of a shift in the encoding of the signifiers of pleasure and play. Gregory Bateson's example of the playful nip of the animal operates in a similar fashion—the falsification of the signal allows the manifestation of pleasure through play. The reading competence of both the sender and receiver of the message is crucial to its success. Both parties must acknowledge—to themselves and/or each other—the sense of play, the falsification of the signifiers via specific code systems, in order that the sense of pleasure can operate. In a similar way the inversion of the social order, and the concurrent pleasure of this, in the carnivalesque is permitted because of the cultural definition of play as semiotic system. Kristeva's postulation of the carnivalesque as the residual of a cosmogony aligns it at once with the subversive and marginal. A cosmogony necessarily, through both design and intent, orders and explains. The residual offers no methodology, whilst its epistemological structure operates under a different modality. This modality initially appears to be indecipherable but remains so only under the stricture of the cosmogony. The carnivalesque, then, is a separate discourse which has abandoned Foucault's playful dictum that desire and institution must combine to give sense to utterances. The institution forsaken allows forbidden speech—madness and desire—to promulgate the text's signification.

The pleasure of the carnivalesque lies in its antithetical (and, as Kristeva points out, antitheological) nature because it prescribes to the fortunes of the illogical, or rather the "antilogical", for it does have its own internal and systemic logic. It is this internal, systemic logic which is established as a code system, even if it only ever operates at the level of recognition. Such fortunes carry with them the possibilities of silence or misunderstanding, but have the subversive advantage of being defined as external to the ruling value system. Divorced from the established sense of *vraisemblance*, the carnivalesque is free to establish its own dynamics and rule-governing codes. The specific play of *fort/da* can be seen as a more universal property of pleasure in play. All play is based on configurations of presence and absence, and the pleasure of play is to be found in the double semiotics of this interplay of presence/absence with the insertion of the subject, and the disturbing of the cultural order, that is, the momentary arresting of the reality principle.

The pleasure of repetition operates in a similar manner. This pleasure is oppositional to the dialectical reading given to it by Artaud and then Derrida, and yet it is unarguably part of the same conceptual frame: "Dialectics is the movement through which expenditure is reappropriated into presence—it is the economy of repetition. The economy of truth. Repetition *summarizes* negativity, gathers and maintains the past present as truth, as ideality" (Derrida 1978a: 246).The negativity attributed to repetition by Derrida is part of the same process which enables it to be pleasurable, just as a different dimension of negativity enables the carnivalesque to be defined as such. This pleasure in repetition is not simply the satisfaction of prediction because it is more directly connected in *fort/da* to the play of subjectivity, with subjectivity. Repetition of absence and presence permits the subject position to be located and lost, located and lost in an endless cycle. The individual may be no closer to achieving the desired site of subjectivity, but pleasure is derived from the regaining of the absent, and the sense of controlling the present. The dialectic of negativity in repetition is translated into pleasure in *fort/da* largely because of this sense of control—of planned and reversible absences. Freud asserts that the greatest pleasure of *fort/da* rests in the repetition rather than in the initial act. Derrida takes up this point in terms of the completion of the "game": "What the speculating (grand)father calls the complete game would be the game in the duality of its two phases: disappearing and coming back, absence and re-presentation. What links the game to itself is the *re-* of the return, the extra turn of repetition and reappearing. He insists that the greater quantity of pleasure is attached to the second phase, to the *re*-turn that determines everything, and without which nothing would come about" (Derrida 1978a: 131). It is in this pleasure of repetition that the principle is both founded and gone beyond.

Another reason why the pleasure of repetition is not just about predictability and control is because it is connected to the return of the repressed. Although not specified by Freud, it is possible to read the continual repeating of presence and absence in *fort/da* as an enactment of the repetition of "the return of the repressed". This requires us to read the repressed as potentially pleasurable and its continuing attempts to return (or the return to it) as altering the economic by adjusting the quantity of excitation. This can only be applied to a certain type of repression, especially if we are to remain true to the Freudian idea that what is repressed is unpleasurable. It seems likely, moreover, that repression is also applied to things pleasurable, particularly if we are to read the reality principle as a type of repression of the pleasure principle itself. In some ways such a reading complements Lacan's notion of the inversions of pleasure and pain in the reality principle and pleasure principle. Freud does argue that repetition is connected to repression through the compulsion to repeat (*Wiederholungszwang*)and it is precisely this compulsion to repeat that is the "beyond" of Freud's essay, and it is this compulsion which has the ability to "override the pleasure principle" (Freud 1987: 293-294). Lacan takes up this compulsion to repeat and stresses it even further by employing one of his key signifiers, that of insistence. The insistence of this compulsion results in it being unavoidable.

The third aspect of the transformation of the passive into the active can be more directly tied to the centrality of subjectivity. As Derrida points out: "Not that Freud says so, but he will say, in one of the two notes I've mentioned, that what in the child's "game" appears and disappears does indeed include the child himself or his image. He is part of his *Spielzeug*" and "But none of this (spontaneity, self-production, the primeval quality of the first time) contributes any descriptive content that does not go back to the self-engendering of self-repetition: the heterotautology (the definition of the speculative in Hegel) of repeated repetition, of self-repetition, in its pure form, which will constitute the game" (Derrida 1978a: 125-126 and 117). By repeating the *fort/da* the subject asserts a sense of having/owning subjectivity, and of control over systems of presence and absence, which includes those transcategorical orders such as signification, discourse, subjectivity, and desire. The pleasure of repeating what is potentially an act filled with anxiety (absence as loss and lack) lies in the predictability of the outcome—the reel (signifier of the mother) always returns to the status of presence, as well as this sense that it is essentially about the repetition of the self, of self-repetition. The subject becomes active by the repetition of the reconstructed return, and in this activity exists the claim for the site of subjectivity, of a control over absence and presence. *Fort/da* then becomes an action based on the subject's attempts to gain the Other, which is ultimately the satisfaction of desire and its absences. However, as with all such attempts, it is a simulacrum. The *fort/da* simulacrum is unique in a number of ways, particularly in terms of absence.

This aspect of subjectivity and the centrality of absence to desire is used by Barthes to investigate the very nature of desire in the form of love. For Barthes it is not a question of whether absence is an issue, but rather just how extensive is the effect: "But isn't desire always the same, whether the object is present or absent? Isn't the object *always* absent?" (Barthes 1990: 15). This is unification through the bonding of presence and absence: "Desire for the absent being and desire for the present being: languor superimposes the two desires, putting absence within presence" (Barthes 1990: 156). Barthes takes up the model of *fort/da* to explain the centrality of absence to desire in the lover's discourse: "Absence persists—I must endure it. Hence I will *manipulate* it: transform the distortion of time into oscillation, produce rhythm, make an entrance onto the stage of language (language is born of absence: the child has made himself a doll out of a spool, throws it away and picks it up again, miming the mother's departure and return: a paradigm is created). Absence becomes an active practice, a *business*" (Barthes 1990: 16). Desire in the practice of love concentrates on this business of absence and how best to utilise it. It is not simply the absence of the Other, creating a lack and emptiness. The persistence of absence means that it becomes part of the entire operation of desire and of subjectivity. It is not an issue of choice—I will or will not engage in absence—but an issue of how absence will be dealt with in language, in desire, in the sense of the self. This is the issue of how the lover creates meaning out of nothing.

The fourth aspect of the *fort/da* game is closely connected to this sense of subjectivity and control. Revenge is a manifestation of the active self, operating as evidence of the presence of the subject itself and the power of the subject over his/her environment. It is in this second sense that revenge operates as a post-mirror stage construction. This is similar to the way revenge is analysed by Freud in the "Dora" case study and in various dreams analysed in *The Interpretation of Dreams*. Revenge is also a reaction, demonstrating a second order of action (a variation on the dialectics of negativity) which aligns it further in *fort/da* with presence, which is also seen as a reaction to the initial absence.

Lacan seeks to blur the oppositional sense that has developed in the critical analysis of the reality principle and the pleasure principle. Lacan argues that they are not antagonistic forces, as may first seem to be the case, but operate towards the same end: "The reality principle consists in making the game last, that is to say, in ensuring that pleasure is renewed, so that the fight doesn't end for lack of combatants. The reality principle consists in husbanding our pleasures, these pleasures whose aim is precisely to end in cessation" (Lacan 1988b: 84). To understand the seeming inversion that operates here it is necessary to take into account the idea of "homeostasis". Lacan is defining the action of the reality principle in terms of the pleasure principle's aim to end pleasure. The pleasure principle is not the production of pleasure, rather it is the attempts to satisfy pleasure. This provides an even more direct link to the idea of desire as a system of subjectivity. The pleasure principle is the mechanism which allows the attempted satisfaction of never-ending desire. In turn, the reality principle is not the censoring of these attempts, but the economic management, the deferral, of them. Lacan's answer to the complexity of the operations of the reality principle and pleasure principle is to critically realign them. In this way the reality principle, through the processes of deferral, sustains the pleasure rather than destroying it and in doing so refuses the homeostasis that would result from the pleasure principle.

Any analysis involving concepts such as pleasure and unpleasure must include, directly or indirectly, the subject, and it has already been noted that the subject, and the determining site of subjectivity, is central to *fort/da* and its sense of repetition and pleasure/unpleasure. As Derrida puts it: "For the speculative heterotautology of the thing is that "beyond" is lodged in the repetition of the PP [pleasure principle]" (Derrida 1978a: 118). This is the determination of the subject through the control of pleasure as it is constituted by absence and presence. This sense of the subject is a tenet fundamental to the Lacanian system. To deal with one particular aspect of the relationship of the subject to the pleasure principle and the reality principle Lacan proposes the model derived from a heteroglossic and interrelational basis. This diagram (Lacan 1986) of the "proof" of the subject via the *objet petit a* represents three interconnected circles constructing relationships between the status of the *Ich* and Lust and Unlust. It is important to recall at this point that within the Freudian view the pleasure principle and the reality principle are fundamentally located with the subject's positionality to the Symbolic. Determined through the rent of the ego-ideal and the ideal ego, they illustrate the entwining of the subject to desire and social processes. This model represents the relationship of the subject to the two principles within the context of homeostasis and pleasure. Lacan is using the terms *Lustprinzip* and *Unlustprinzip* and *Lust* and *Unlust* in the sense of pleasure and unpleasure. To understand the operational sense of the model it is also important to recall Lacan's ideas regarding the locating of the subject in terms of the object (as referent and as a frame of reference), and the consequential fears that such a collocation produces.

The schema is made up of three interconnecting circles, which in turn produce subsystems through their collision. The *Ich* is not placed in a central position, as might be expected in such a schema of subjectivity, because this is a model of consequences—notably the consequences of *Lustprinzip* and *Unlustprinzip* in blurring and meeting. They only make sense in terms of the subject, just as the subject can only be made sense of in terms of them. The orders of the schema are not uniform, most significantly *Lust* is of a different order and is more appropriately designated as part of the *objet petit a*: "As for *Lust*, this is not a field strictly speaking, it is always an object, an object of pleasure, which, as such, is mirrored in the ego" (Lacan 1986: 241). The underlying sense of the subject as opposed to the object, and the hegemonic implications, should not be missed here.

The circle within circles, internal and external divisions of the schema, are part of the presence and absence structure of the subject, object and pleasure. Pleasure/Lust becomes embedded in the realm of the *Ich* to form *Lust-Ich*. That which is defined as unpleasure is always external to this realm because of its particular relationship to the subject. Hence a categorisation of signifiers cannot occur in such a schema because of this relationship. What may be figured as *Unlust*/unpleasure for one subject may well be firmly located within the realm of *Lust*/pleasure for another. In terms of a textuality of *Lust/Unlust* it can be argued that there are dominant and subversive models, determined to a large extent by the sociocultural climate, diachronic and synchronic variations. This schema is Lacan's model of the *Lust-Ich*, which is the specific conflation of the subject position and the objects of pleasure according to that (social and cultural) subject. This is not to suggest that there is a deliberate and calculated construction of the orders of *Lust* and *Unlust* by the subject. Rather, the subject and the site(s) of subjectivity are constructed by the presences and absences of *Lust* and *Unlust* in relation to the *Ich*.

The relationship of the site of subjectivity to the presences and absences of *Lust* and *Unlust* also takes into account the positioning of the object. This object can be an actual object, a process by the subject (for example, the gaze, language), another person, or even the subject itself. In short, the object of the *objet petit a* is not fixed to a paradigmatics of signifiers, but instead slides according to a set of external factors. In doing so the forbidden object is created. The relationship of the subject to the forbidden object requires a further clarification of pleasure/unpleasure in terms of desire.

Pleasure, Desire, and *Jouissance*

Desire and pleasure are distinct but interrelated. Here the relationship has been argued in terms of system and manifestation, absence and presence. Desire is a further "beyond" of the pleasure principle, denying the limits of homeostasis which are so central to this principle. Desire does operate beyond the pleasure principle because it articulates its own boundaries, and then seeks to extend beyond the limits set, which is part of the reason why the ordering of system and manifestation is significant here. Desire as system is operationally distinct from the homeostasis imperative. The nature of this transgression is formulated in *jouissance*.

Part of the transgression of *jouissance* is "the dialectic of desire" (Lacan 1985: 319). This is the dialectic which contributes significantly to the formation of the *Ichspaltung*—the split subject who is barred from the Other, that is, the discourses of desire. All desire is orientated towards the Other, deployed in the *objet petit a* and the subject's own sense of the self. The dialectical *jouissance* is a "*jouissance* beyond the pleasure principle" (Lacan 1986: 184) because of its relationship to the Other. There are at least three primary levels of interplay in such an equation: *jouissance* and the Other; *jouissance* and the pleasure principle; *jouissance* beyond the pleasure principle. These levels indicate the dialectical nature of desire as it functions in terms of subjectivity and the Other, and suggest a dynamic based on the operation of lack as a central determinant.

The first two of these interplays, the relational context of *jouissance* to the Other and the position of *jouissance* and the pleasure principle in terms of one another, have, to a certain degree, already been indicated. At this level *jouissance* is to be read in the same typographical manner as pleasure—that is, orientated towards the Other by the motivations of desire and absence, absent

desire, and absence and subjectivity. It is the illusionary projection of presence
in the *objet petit a* (the assertion of the subject against the status of the object)
to counter the overwhelming domination of absences. The impossible register
of a *jouissance* of the Other is contrived but never realised—this is the point of
excess which transforms pleasure by reading it within a sense of the Other.
Bernini's rendering of the ecstatic face of St. Teresa can be read as just such
an attempt to depict the point of pleasure turning to excess through *jouissance*
in the sense of the Other. Lacan writes: "you only have to go and look at
Bernini's statue in Rome to understand immediately that she's coming, there is
no doubt about it. And what is her *jouissance*, her coming from? It is clear that
the essential testimony of the mystics is that they are experiencing it but know
nothing about it" (Lacan 1982: 147). Her ecstasy is based on absence more than
presence, just as the reader's gaze must be located at a point beyond and outside
the image. Bernini's St. Teresa is the *imago*, caught between discourse and
desire in the field of absence.

Jouissance beyond the pleasure principle, connected as it is to *fort/da*, must
include a sense of repetition and the compulsion to repeat. There appears to be
two ways of interpreting repetition and compulsion in this sense: the compulsion
to repeat the experience of *jouissance*, and/or to read *jouissance* as part of the
reality principle. The difficulty is that this suggests two contradictory positions.
One interpretation argues for *jouissance* to be seen as part of desire, the other
argues that *jouissance* is part of the restrictions placed on pleasure. The
property (including its quality) of transgression that Lacan ascribes to
jouissance—that it goes beyond the pleasure principle—would seem to support
the first of these two interpretations, although the deferential—and so absenting—potential of *jouissance* cannot be ignored. The Derridean idea of *différance*
may offer a possible mediating position, allowing for the differences in
jouissance found in desire or in the reality principle, and also in keeping with
the Other as deferred *jouissance* and the deferral of *jouissance* by the reality
principle. This is also linked to the systems of absence and presence that
operate as part of the carnivalesque, the borderliner, the thetic ruptures, the
uncanny—in short that whole paradigm of subversive agencies of absence
against the order of the known presences. A further, complementing, aspect is
that the reality principle is not antithetical to pleasure and so can accommodate
jouissance. Such an interpretation supports Lacan's idea of a supplementary
jouissance, although with a distinctly different political sense. The supplementary here is a beyond because of the operation of the phallic law. In one sense
this is what Lacan attempts to examine and critique in *Seminar XX: Encore*,
when he speaks of a *jouissance* of the body beyond the phallus.

Note has already been made of the connection between desire and
Lust/Unlust, and of the connection between the *Ich* (here used in the sense of
the self, as well as the sense of the self for the self) and the narcissistic drive

to the object—the *Lust-Ich*. *Ich* is supplemented by this relational context of a narcissistic drive in the sense of subjectivity based on *fort/da*, or the *fort/da(sein)*. Sartre's "existence before essence" view of subjectivity would permit such readings of the *Ich*, but this is not to argue for an existential basis of any definition, but serves as a further illustration of the subject determining itself through the absence/presence of the action and status of *fort/da(sein)*. *Lust* contains the object that the subject desires (the *objet petit a*), which ascribes to it certain elements of a field as well as the pulsatory drive. *Jouissance* must figure in such a definitional concern as it is part of *Lust* through the subject's experience/creation of it. The subject/*Ich* of *jouissance* exists before the essence and, more significantly here, this essence is part of the absent Other. This is why it can operate as a methodological structure—*epoche* in a sense—and as something definitionally absent. It is for this reason that Sartre's Cartesian disruption is comparable to the way Lacan deals with Freud's relationship with Descartes.

An important feature in terms of this sense of pleasure and the subject is how *Unlust* is regarded as negation, as split from the ego, or the formation (to establish distinguishing types) of the non-ego, as Lacan calls it (Lacan 1986: 241). In these terms *Unlust* becomes aligned to the Other because it is positioned as external to the ego/self. The non-ego of *Unlust* operates in terms of the Other here, but is not the Other, because of the fundamental aspect of narcissistic operations, which are the primary processes of the *Lust-Ich*.

Jouissance is a fundamental part of the *Ichspaltung* and its relationship to the Other. This is because *jouissance* itself can be read as a system of absence. It, like lack, is a signifier of a gap rather than any specific set of discursive practices. This is in keeping with Lacan's construction of the *objet petit a*, the subject who is split and within the larger order of a dialectics of desire. The subject must be split because it is from just such a schism that the attempts to gain *jouissance* (experience it, manage or control it, produce it) are devised. *Jouissance* in these terms becomes pleasure for the self and the pleasure of the self. The unrelenting force of desire produces the narcissistic demand of this very action. Which is not to argue for a complete grounding of *jouissance* in the narcissistic action, but for the acknowledgment of this action in a primary form of *jouissance*, particularly in terms of the formation and operation of subjectivity as a site.

The narcissistic drive of the subject towards *jouissance* is in fact directly tied to the sense of the Other as a determining absence. It is this nexus which makes the Other necessary to the pleasure/*jouissance* of the self, for the self and for others. Barthes defines this as a relationship of subjectivity and desire, but always in a manner complicated by the distinction of the self measured against the Other:

The other is my good and my knowledge: only I know him, only I make

him exist in his truth. Whoever is not me is ignorant of the other. . . .
Conversely, the other establishes me in truth: it is only with the other that
I feel I am "myself." I know more about myself than all those who simply
do not know this about me: that I am in love. Or again, instead of trying
to define the other ("What is he?"), I turn to myself: "What do I want,
wanting to know you?" What would happen if I decided to define you as
a force and not as a person? And if I were to situate myself as another
force confronting yours? This would happen: my other would be defined
solely by the suffering or the pleasure he affords me.

(Barthes 1990: 229; 135).

In the lover's discourse the Other (person, force, object, institution) is reflected
in the sense of the self (the narcissistic) and passion. *Jouissance* is part of this
defining, and qualification, of the subject by his/her sufferings and passions. It
is not simply the desire/need to internalise the external Other, but the Other
acting as signifying practice—the Other becomes the referential point of
disclosure. Even in this convolution of presences, *jouissance*, and any object of
jouissance (its textuality), is always incomplete, always has a lack. This is why
there exists a multiplicity of absences and gaps—of subject, of ego, of object,
of represented drive—and why absence forms the fundamental quality of the
subject and *jouissance*. Even the incomplete *Lust* combined with the subject of
jouissance (*Lust-Ich*) forms a set of absences.

To illustrate this in the first instance we can return to that text produced in
the intersection of subtexts by Freud, Lacan, and Dora. This intersection of
sub-texts operates in the sense of Barthes's notion of the self, determined in
truth by the Other—Dora's truth (her subjectivity) is determined in truth by the
texts of Freudian and Lacanian analytic otherness. What is of primary interest
here is the construction of Dora through the (Lacanian) sense of pleasure,
jouissance and desire, and how all of these are based on absence. The idea of
"constructing" Dora is appropriate because this is what first Freud, then Lacan,
and then those who followed, have done. Dora passes out of the individual
ontology of the historical person and becomes a metonymic (political,
ideological, psychoanalytical, cultural, fictional, filmic) subject figure. Dora
does exist before her essence, but she is denied the *jouissance* (or otherwise)
of creating that essence because, especially in this textual sense, this is the
jouissance of those who come after. The political (re)presentations of Dora have
formed an ontology within their own right, independent of the originary
subject—if such a subject can ever have existed.

Lacan's central text in terms of the Dora case study is "Intervention of
Transference," but to understand what is taking place in this essay it is
necessary to consider the Freudian origins of the case study itself. In terms of
the issues at hand this means a reading of the texts based on the concepts of
absence as an interpretative system. There are a number of further critical
issues in such an examination which include: the idea of masculine and feminine

jouissance; interconnections between the idea of the subject determined through absence and desire; and, particularly in terms of Lacan's essay, the aspect of transference.

In the case study of Dora Freud connects doubt and the processes of censorship. This is something that is to be found in other parts of his work; however, it reaches a particular level of critical force in this reading. Freud uses the Dora case to argue that anamnestic knowledge of forgetting, of producing absences in the recounting of its history by the subject, is connected to repression and surrounded by doubts. The forgetting of dreams, names, and events is linked to the repression of the signifier, which can be seen as operating in a sense of syntagmatic signifiers selected and organised from the larger order of (repressed) signifiers from the paradigmatic base. Doubt, in these terms, is not simply the act of being unsure, but a set of absences that directly determines the status of the subject—that is, the determination of the truth of the subject by the Other through the initial sense of doubt (lack, absence, gap). For this reason it is possible to see doubt operating as part of the censoring process which constructs absences in the construction of a text, or of texts, as well as part of the absences of the analysis and language of the text, on the discourses of the text (its history, the construction and deconstruction of the texts).

The primary function of doubt for Freud is to ensure that whatever signifiers have been censored, but not made totally absent (and so allowed a semblance of presence), will be read/interpreted as insignificant—in effect made critically and hermeneutically absent. A related, although seemingly opposition-al, type of absence is those in the *condition seconde*—that is, the hallucinatory absences of Anna O's clouds (Freud/Breuer 1980). This establishes the idea that signifiers may be absent through censorship and repression, or that presented signifiers will be distorted so that their "true"—the determination of "truth" through the Other—signification (which necessarily includes the denotative) will be made absent through doubt. Doubt restructures the meaning of the signifiers, often yielding a double meaning based on the interpretation of the signifier within the textual world order, and an opposite one by the reader of the text.

Displacement, along with doubt, forms a fundamental issue in the interpretation of absence in the Dora case study. The reading of displacement as a system of absence can be illustrated through the case study. At one point in the case study Freud discusses the displacement of sensations from the lower to the upper part of the body. The scene is where Herr K. kisses Dora, which she speaks about with a sense of disgust. There are three crucial configurations of absence in the recounting and subsequent analysis. The first absence is articulated by Freud: "I have formed in my own mind the following reconstruc-tion of the scene" (Freud 1985: 60). Here Freud acts as the archetypal reader, reconstructing the text from its lacunae. This lacunal quality permits the political re-reading of the text, which has, historically, become an extremely contentious issue. This is related to the second configuration of absence.

Freud's reading/reconstruction of the scene denies Dora her own *jouissance*, or any capacity for pleasure—it is made absent in order for the signifiers to fit within the reading of the reconstruction. The analysis performed by Freud centres on why Dora is repulsed by Herr K.'s actions, why she does not find it pleasurable to be kissed by someone "young and of prepossessing appearance," in short, why she has an absence of pleasure. The idea that Dora may well have a sense of *jouissance*, but that it is being denied, or is quite different from anything he can imagine, does not occur to Freud in part because he reads her actions as hysterical, in part because of the current attitudes towards feminine sexuality/pleasure, and in part because such a reading would go against the one being constructed. There is, of course, a further corollary - that Dora has the right to find another's advances unattractive, repulsive, invasive; of how Freud and Herr K., as phallic law, operate as a threat to Dora's autonomy, and to the autonomy of her sense of pleasure.

The third configuration of absence in this scene and the subsequent analysis/reading relates more directly to displacement. This is the displacement of sensations from the lower part of the body to the upper. Freud's reconstruction is: "I believe that during the man's passionate embrace she felt not merely his kiss upon her lips but also the pressure of his erect member against her body. This perception was revolting to her; it was dismissed from her memory, repressed, and replaced by the innocent sensation of pressure in her thorax" (Freud 1985: 60-61). This is the production of absences through displacement, which is in effect the production of absences through the re-reading of present signifiers. Freud interprets this as the significant encounter with demonstrative masculine sexuality, which is repressed and displaced to another part of the body. But what he does not note, in fact cannot note, is that his re-readings and analysis form part of the same manifestation of the phallic law, so that the absences through displacement he allocates to Dora's physical sensations operate in the same way as the interpretative acts of power and control. It is this junction of absences, and their political signification, which brings into question the act of analysis—it becomes a meta-analytic reflection based on the manipulation of absence.

At a later point in the case study Freud reads Dora's supposed knowledge of fellatio as a repressed desire. It is this desire, he argues, that accounts for the displacement of this repressed sensation specifically to the throat. Lacan, in turn, corrects Freud and argues that what Dora is referring to is not fellatio but cunnilingus—an interpretation which has become central to a number of subsequent readings of the text. Even in this sense the idea of Dora's *jouissance* is not fully taken into consideration, although Lacan does set up other possible interpretations based on the idea of feminine *jouissance*.

The other correlation is speech and denial—the link with sexuality and orality is extended to the processes of power and discourse. This extension is part of the particular quality of the displacement—it is reinforced or supervalent (*uberwertig*), stemming directly from the unconscious, and so can be seen as part of the discourse of the Other. This supervalent displacement operates in an overdetermined sense, which partly explains the multiple connections and levels of meaning produced in the history of this text, particularly the repositioning of Freud by others. The transformation of the signifier through disguise (e.g., displacement, condensation, censorship, repression) results in an interpretative battle. This relates to the critical imperative—its political agenda—of doubt as absence and the need to recognise when it is occurring.

The significance of Lacan's essay "Intervention on Transference" to the concerns here rests largely in the ways in which Lacan deals with the idea of the subject and its relationship to desire and *jouissance*. The opening sentence of the essay declares that the objective is to "accustom people's ears to the term subject" (Lacan 1982: 62). Subject and pleasure in this sense are positioned in terms of transference, which, for Lacan in particular, constitutes one the four key concepts in psychoanalytic theory—the other three being the unconscious, repetition, and the drive. It is noteworthy that Lacan requires a distinction to be made between repetition and transference at the analytic level. Transference may well serve as part of the process of repetition, but this does not mean that the two are synonymous or even necessarily connected. Lacan argues that transference explains the process of repetition, how it is structured, and some of the reasons why it is required. What is also important about this sense of transference and repetition is the interplay of connections between the two in terms of the unconscious. From this set of connections it is possible to argue that transference is not only hermeneutically orientated towards repetition (it explains why repetition takes place, demonstrates and critically isolates repetition, defines the repetitive act) but also, largely as a consequence of this, reveals absences and their connections. An illustration of these connections is contained in Lacan's account of the pulsative function of the unconscious. In this Lacan allows for the relational context of repetition and transference, but distinguishes them in terms of what is missing.

The issue of the missing is relevant to the concept of transference as it is seen as part of the censoring act. It functions within the primary and secondary processes in the overall construction of the manifest signifier which has been distorted and/or disguised through absences. In this sense it is comparable to the system of absence producing a distorted presence. In the case of transference and repetition it is the production and utilisation of certain signifiers to bridge the gaps created by the repression of the primary presences of thoughts, desires, feelings, etc. Freud attempts to establish a direct link between transference and repression as products of hysteria when an abnormal psychical treatment of an unconscious wish occurs. With Dora, Freud uses this correlation to analyse the cough that she develops as part of the repression of sexuality. This is the sexuality that Freud defines as "normal", but clearly must be located within a particular historical and cultural setting. It is the insertion of the phallocentric, patriarchal, and heterosexual configuration of pleasure and sexuality, and does not allow for legitimate variations of any of these types. This is the normative as producer of presences and differences as absences.

Transference is derived from two distinct subject positions, both related to the operation of the presence and absence of "knowledge", which must be distinguished here because of the discursive aspects. As Lacan states: "As soon as the subject who is supposed to know exists somewhere . . . there is transference" (Lacan 1986: 232). The subject who is supposed to know—the *sujet supposé savoir* (S.s.S.)—is the analyst as seen by the analysand, and the transference occurs through the subject who desires the status of *sujet supposé savoir*. In these terms the model can be extended so that the initial model of transference becomes a model of desire and Otherness. Such a reading allows the *sujet supposé savoir* to be seen in a much wider context—notably desire and absence, as well as the issue of subjectivity itself. This can also be extended to include the interaction of transference and repetition as an order of reading and textuality.

Transference is "bound up with desire as the nodal phenomenon of the human being" (Lacan 1986: 231). This clearly indicates that for Lacan transference is as much about subjectivity and desire as it is about psychoanalytic techniques. Transference can be interpreted as a semiotic model of textuality—something which is of central concern to a semiotics of absence and its reading model. This also relates to the *savoir* aspect of the *sujet supposé savoir*. This knowledge of the subject who is supposed to know is about signification and desire—not simply the knowledge of something, but the knowledge of knowledge and the desirable status of this knowing. Of course the subject does not know—the *supposé* operates within a register of the actual because of the connection between desire, subjectivity, and the Other. *Supposé* indicates the centrality of absence in the subject, because *savoir* is a false presence. It does not exist, and cannot exist, as a presence in the subject (any subject) because it is part of the Other—it defines the otherness of subjectivity. This in turn means that the *sujet supposé savoir* is never an actual subject, but a configuration of subjectivity by the "reader" in transference. In this sense it can be seen to be related to Lacan's concept of the *Je-ideal*, which is a significant aspect of the reading of the ego as object. This is why transference mirrors the act of reading; the reader measures his/her own readings against other readers—actual and imagined as well as the order of readerness—who are supposed to know (about the text, reading, interpretation), in historical, critical, and cultural/ideological senses. There is also the measuring of the reading of the text against all texts that are supposed to know. The act of transference in the reading of the text is not the projection of the self into the text (character identification) but the transference of the *act* of reading and interpreting itself, as well as a sense of the text to all texts.

The *sujet supposé savoir*—the absent subject position of desire through knowledge—operates as a *fort/da*, compelling repetition. Transference and the compulsion to repeat contribute to the splitting of the subject of desire. Repetition in transference is grounded in the split subject. The speculative discourse of repetition in transference (for transference is a discursive practice) makes present and emphasises the status of the split in the subject. Transference through the *sujet supposé savoir* deepens this split. The speculative quality produced through the transference-repetition action is significant to the concerns here because it makes present to the subject the split which constitutes (in a sense defines for the subject) subjectivity. Speculative discourse is crucial to subjectivity and its various manifestations, such as the speaking subject and the specular subject.

Lacan reads Freud's formula *Wo Es war, soll Ich werden* as part of this transference process. The *Es* is connected to the *sujet supposé savoir* through the action of transference, that is, absence and desire in the figuring of subjectivity. This is the juxtapositioning of speculative subjectivity and the speaking subject at a point defined as absent:

> This *Es*, take it as the letter S. It is there, it is always there. It is the subject. He knows himself or he doesn't know himself. That isn't even the most important thing—he speaks or he doesn't speak. At the end of the analysis, it is him who must be called on to speak, and to enter into relation with the real Others. Where the S was, there the *Ich* should be. That is where the subject authentically re-integrates his disjointed limbs, and recognises, reaggregates his experience.
>
> (Lacan 1988b: 246-247)

It is necessary to read this final point not as one of (psycho)analytic closure (perhaps success), but as the moment of self-reflexivity within the subject. How such a realisation might take place varies, but within a textual sense (i.e. the reader's relationship to the text, to other readers, to textuality) of transference is the point of realising the self as reader and the splits and desires both resulting from this and attendant to this development.

Denied wholeness, *Es*/S is the split subject in search of an operational system of subjectivity and the satisfaction of desire. This search is more clearly demonstrated if we apply the *Es*/S and *sujet supposé savoir* of absence to a dynamic model developed by Lacan (1988b: 243). This is a typical structure which recurs in Lacanian theory—covering, as it does, this feature of the subject and the Other and, as will be considered shortly, the nature of desire. Lacan constructs this model to discuss the operation of the ego, however it can be interpreted as part of the convergence of *Es* and S (of the S.s.S.) through absence.

The model is not perfectly symmetrical—it would collapse if such an idea were to be forced upon it. Otherness does not define the right-hand side, and aspects of subjectivity the left. However, the *objet petit a* must be read as construction from the subject (*Es*/S) and the ego. Furthermore, the nature of absence is operationally distinct at different points in the model—in terms of *Es*/S, in the Other (the line of the unconscious) and the *objet petit a* (the permutation from the intersection between the *Es*/S—A and the ego—*objet petit a*). This intersection in effect produces two triangles which merge in the intersection of the unconscious and the imaginary. The merging is produced through desire and the force of absence.

The connection between ego and *objet petit a* is derived almost entirely from the *Es*/S as a function of desire. This is the point of signification, that is, the semiotic locale of the subject in the signifier as that set of signifiers come to represent the subject to itself. The insertion of the specular subject in the filmic discourse, for example, occurs at that point in part because the text invites it through the establishment of absences within the text, and in part by engaging in the scopic drives—this is a fundamental process in the gaze and the related site of subjectivity. The same sort of relationship can be argued for the speaking subject (the subject position determined by the relationship to discourse and discursive practices) through what Lacan calls the wall of language. Language—and here it is used in the most extensive sense of heteroglossia—is particularly significant to transference because of the basis of power (whether seen as inherent or constructed) and the relationships devised by or for subjects based on power in the language of the act of transference. Lacan argues that transference cannot be seen as a sensible analytic process without an acknowledgment of the centrality of speech. However, the subject of *Es*/S is split from itself so it cannot hope to be united with other subjects—"I always aim at true subjects, and I have to be content with shadows" (Lacan 1988b: 244). These shadows are products of absent subjectivity and the phenomenon of the splitting of the subject. These shadows can also be produced through transference.

One interpretative sense of the self that is operating in the absenting shadows is the transference of the self to another. This is manifested, to a large extent, because of the desire invested in the *sujet supposé savoir*—only here the *supposé* is denied by the subject who reads the configuration. The motivation for such a reading must stem from an accentuation of the *je me deux*. In the case of Dora this is external to the self through the sexual politics of Herr and Frau K., Dora's father, and, eventually, Freud. Dora attempts to define desire but has conflicting messages from her own sense of desire and the shadowy others, including seeing herself as an object of desire by being forced into the object position of "woman [as] the object of a divine desire, or else, a transcendent object of desire, which amount to the same thing" (Lacan 1982: 99). The beyondness of subjectivity (even as an object of desire) echoes the beyondness of the unconscious as demonstrated in transference. Transference, in analytic terms (which is to distinguish between the process and its analysis), is essential to the understanding of the language of the unconscious and the operation of the Other. This is also an aspect of countertransference with its relational context of power and the politicisation of the subject.

The interplay of transference and countertransference is, ultimately, about the subject's manipulation of manifestations of desire within the sense of the self, as well as desire's manipulation of the subject. In the *Es*/S model this is the division of otherness (the axis of *objet petit a* and Other) as the field of desire which qualifies the relationship and operation between the *Es*/S and the ego—that is, desire as determinant of subjectivity. In the inversion of this, the lines of "Imaginary relations" and the "Unconscious" become the processes of aligning the subject's sense of desire as it is found in the Other. Transference is part of the construction of the subject through presence and absence of desire. This can occur within the subject or can be determined by another subject, an institutional model, or an order of discourse. In these terms *jouissance* is a political process embodying the construction of the subject through its desires (*Es*/S—Other; ego/a—*objet petit a*) as determined by lack and *manque-á-être*. Read in this way, desire is like a language of absence operating in terms of the production and representation of the subject through assertion or negation.

Jouissance and the Text: Some Notes on Fantasy

Freud can be seen as arguing that the subject can become his/her own text—at least two of the vicissitudes of an instinct (reversal to an opposite and the turning around to the self) can be read in this way. The narcissistic process, the scopophilic imperative of masochism, and the projection through active scopophilia in exhibitionism (to list a few) are all transformations of the self into a text for the self and for others. For Barthes this textualisation of the self operates in the discourse of love. It is the transformation of all facets of the self as perceived by the self (the body, the voice, the mark of violence which disappears, the look, the transcribing of love into a discourse) into a text, and to be read as a text by the self and by others. Freud's qualification that certain actions of textualisation are transgressed does not negate the textualisation of the self by the self (as, for example, described by Barthes) because this transgression is only a management rather than resolution. So even if an important phase in the realisation of the subject (the site of subjectivity as well as the positioning of the subject) is the acknowledgement of a separation between the subject and the object, this realisation can be a source of conflict rather than resolution. This line between conflict and resolution is of the same order as the distinction of the object from the self as determined by the self (Kant), or the object as paradigm object (Hegel). Textualisation of the self operates in at least two fundamental forms: the self seen by the self as text (the non-distinction of subject from object, or the conscious and deliberate transformation of the self into a different ontological [textual] order); and the reading of the process whereby the self distinguishes between the subject (both of the self and others) and object. Both these readings are entirely in keeping with the idea of the mirror phase as a determining factor of the subject's attempted entry into the Symbolic.

Other than this sense of the subject becoming the site of textuality in terms of *jouissance*, either via the self and/or through others—and hence the absenting of subjectivity through textualisation—there is also the more literal *jouissance* of what is defined as a text (literature, film, painting, music). One of the central concerns here is to examine how this pleasure/*jouissance* of the text relates to the issue of absence. This necessarily includes the transformation of the self into a text (e.g., the body as text, the history of the self as text—such as the autobiography—as well as features of subjectivity as a text) by the self or others, in addition to the transformation of the text into the self. The second of these can be traced to the relationship of the subject to the Other, which is, at least in part, constituted by the confluence of Imaginary Relations and the unconscious.

It can be argued that what Barthes does in his semiotic readings of pleasure and textuality, particularly in defining *jouissance* as a textual issue, is comparable to the ways in which desire and subjectivity have been positioned thus far. Essentially this is the idea that *jouissance* is inextricably tied to subjectivity, and both operate, and can be made sense of, in terms of a dynamic of absence and presence. This is connected to the dialectic of subjectivity, absence, and desire, and that this desiring subject is defined by the systems of absence. This is why *jouissance* is examined here in terms of transference, the subject, and the Other.

Jouissance can only be made sense of if the issue of subjectivity is accorded a pivotal role. This incorporates the further consideration of subjectivity being defined through the experience of *jouissance*. Barthes describes this moment in terms of the anti-hero, but of greater significance in the antithetical sense of this position is the temporal dimension that he designates to it—that is, it is in the moment of pleasure that the reader/subject exists. This coming-into-being is the site of *jouissance* and the "possibility of a dialectic of desire" (Barthes 1988: 5) because it is the negotiation of absences (both primary and secondary) as they determine the subject's relationship to subjectivity.

Barthes's "dialectic" is a product of the operations between the reader, the text, and the cultural frame, or institution. It operates largely within a phenomenological context in that it has a strong sense of the type of reception theory developed by Roman Ingarden (via Husserl), and later by Wolfgang Iser, as well as certain elements of Umberto Eco's semiotic theory. In this sense a number of Barthes's concepts, such as the active and passive reader and the distinction between texts of pleasure and texts of *jouissance,* carry with them a phenomenological underpinning. In terms of theorising subjectivity what is most striking about Barthes's examination is the definition of the active reader and text—that is, the text of *jouissance*. This definition, and the referential sense of difference, is based on absence, and it is on this basis that it is directed towards the issue of subjectivity. The text of *jouissance* is one of subjectivity and textualisation because it involves the destabilisation of the reader. This is not necessarily pleasurable, just as *jouissance* is not simply a site of pleasure. Compare Kristeva's concept of poetic language, which "through the particularity of its signifying operations, is an unsettling process—when not an outright destruction—of the identity of meaning and the speaking subject. . . . [This is the] questionable subject in process . . ." (Kristeva 1984b: 125). Kristeva's poetic language and the subject in process operate in much the same way as Barthes's text of *jouissance* and the coming into being of the reader. The unsettling through signifying processes creates a reflexive point which contains or, at the very least, suggests the reader's relationship to the text (the self as reader and the self-consciousness of the relationship between text and reader). However, this reflexive point of coming into being (as reader) also incorporates more essential features of subjectivity and the sense of the self. The constitutive function of the subject in process in the formation and operation of poetic language is a point of *jouissance*, a temporal frame and the revolutionary feature of the anti-hero. Temporality includes the Heideggerian correlation of beingness and time and a further process of the disruptive.

In terms of absence this temporality has a number of important features. The Heideggerian temporality links the past and future as being carried away—this is their *ecstatic* nature (after the Greek *ekstatikon*—stepping outside itself). Being itself becomes ordered in terms of the ecstatic nature of temporality, which is fundamentally a self-reflexive position, and the intentionality of this being. Although Heidegger specifies that this ecstatic quality is this stepping outside itself, it is still possible to locate it, in terms of absence, as part of the self-reflexive *jouissance* of the subject in process, be it the phenomenological subject or the reader.

A number of comparisons can be made between the way Barthes deals with the relationship of the reader and the pleasure of the text, and Lacan's discussion of the connection between fantasy and the subject in terms of desire. Of particular significance is the connection between the semiotic sense of the text (via Barthes's and even Kristeva's category of the poetic) and the psychoanalytic sense of fantasy. Such a comparison requires a positioning of "fantasy" in terms of desire and the textualisation of the subject (the self as text, others defined as texts by the self, the interplay of the self and the Other as textual issue). This, of course, also operates in the opposite sense so that the text becomes subject.

The psychoanalytic interpretation is important to this discussion because of this relationship between text, subject, object, and desire. There is further support for this comparison if we bear in mind Barthes's distinction between "work" and "text". Textuality is determined because it necessarily involves *jouissance*—the distinction can only operate if *jouissance* is positioned as part of the text, which is not always a transformational process (that is, transformed from the status of "work" to "text") but is certainly a possibility. Similarly, it is not necessarily a divisional system ("work" as opposed to "text"), but such an evaluative operation is also possible. This critical praxis is comparable to certain aspects of Lacan's theory of the subject and desire—one defines and constructs the other within a context of absence and presence.

For Freud fantasy is an operation related purely to the pleasure principle, being antithetical to a number of the operations of the reality principle. The distinction between fantasy and reality does not occur in the mental processes, and such indiscrimination is important to the sense of the formation of reality and fantasy, and ties them inextricably to absence and presence. For example, what effect does it have that reality is absent as a critical concept to the construction of fantasy? What is the relationship between a non-distinction of reality and the text? How is the absence of reality accounted for and accommodated in the construction of the text by the reader, as well as in the subject's *jouissance* of the text and desire? What is the relational context of ecstatic temporality to the formation of fantasy in terms of absence and presence? These sorts of questions become crucial to the operation of textuality and the subject's determination of the object as absence and presence. Lacan reminds us that "phantasy is the stuff of the I" (Lacan 1985: 314), and that *jouissance* is bound up to the eroticism of the self: "*mais bien que leur outrepassement signifie ce qui ramène toute jouissance convoitée à la brièveté de l'auto-érotisme*" (Lacan 1971: 185). This development of *outrepassement* occurs at that point when the desire for *jouissance* becomes reflected, or more correctly centred, in the self. This is the insertion of the self into the desiring action. Furthermore, the I of the auto-eroticism, the fantasising I, is embedded in the ego: "the notion of unconscious fantasy, of the activity of fantasy, is supported only by taking a detour via the ego" (Lacan 1988b: 214). This detour is the *outrepassement* of *jouissance* in terms of the determination of the subject.

The situating of mental functioning in fantasy is important here because it locates the centrality of the subject within the context of the system of analysis. This is the objectification of the subject as it appears in both the assertion of the subject, that is the presenting, and the loss (actual or potential) of the subject (e.g., aphanisis), as absence. The distinction made by Laplanche and Pontalis (1986), based on this analytic system, is between an external and an internal reality. This is a crucial point in the definition of fantasy and mental operations. Such a definition illustrates the ontological slippage and heterology of the text as fantasy—it possesses elements of both realms, altering its materiality in terms of the subject and *jouissance*. This possession is based on the blurring of divisions (pleasure/reality, real/non-real, truth/lies, actual/contrived) that are an essential feature to fantasy. Freud's analysis of Hoffmann's "The Sand-Man" in "The Uncanny" is based precisely on this slippage and the inability to distinguish the real from the non-real. The uncanny is a slippage of what is considered to be the familiar and the known into the realm of the unknown. And as Freud himself points out, the uncanny—*das Unheimlich*—contains the sense of the unfamiliar and the no-longer hidden. It is the making present of the uncomfortable absences.

Another feature of the Freudian interpretation of fantasy is the primary role given to the seduction scene. Two important aspects occur in the seduction scene as related to fantasy: i) Freud wanted to establish the "intrinsic relationship between repression and sexuality" (Laplanche and Pontalis 1986: 10); and

ii) in the seduction scene there is the injection of desire and "the language of passion" (Laplanche and Pontalis 1986: 11) into the child's discourse from the adult eroticism. The sense of passivity that Laplanche and Pontalis ascribe to the subject outside of the seduction is misleading, however. Freud clearly positions this subject as active within its own sensibilities of seduction. In his essay "The Paths to the Formation of Symptoms" Freud indicates that exposure to the seduction scene produces a creative response, in much the same way as the subject of *fort/da* is experimenting with creative, active responses to subjectivity and absence/presence. This response is translated into fantasy, which in turn is a form of textualisation. The subject who observes the seduction, and so experiences the discourse of desire, does not simply absorb the scene, but attempts interpretation. This is the action of constructing fantasy through the negotiation of repression in terms of the reality principle.

Trieb, Desire, and Absence

The concept of *trieb* is of central significance to the Freudian and Lacanian models of desire and subjectivity. It is because of this critical significance that the isolating of the terms is a difficult undertaking as more often than not they operate within a network or sequence of ideas. It is partly for this reason that this section ties *trieb* and desire together. The term *trieb* carries with it the difficulties of translation. Lacan argues that the fundamental errors committed in the translation of Freud's use of *trieb* actually shifted the original and intended meaning of the term. *Trieb*, Lacan emphatically states, is not instinct. A more appropriate translation is drive or *pulsion*. Lacan argues the issue further by suggesting *dérive* if *pulsion* is not strong enough: "*et ce pour quoi le mot dérive serait en français notre recours de désespoir, au cas où nous n'arriverions pas à donner à la bâtardise du mot pulsion son point de frappe*" (Lacan 1971: 162). The significant point here is the connection made between *trieb/dérive* and desire. This same issue is also raised in Lacan's specification of *besoin* as different to *trieb*/drive. We must not lose sight of the theoretical sense that surrounds *trieb*/drive. As Lacan points out: "The theory of the drives is not at the base of the construction, but right up at the top. It is eminently abstract, and Freud later was to call it our mythology" (Lacan 1988a: 120). The compulsion to act, to think, etc. is tied to the strength of *trieb*/drive and the unresolvable desire. *Trieb*/drive, in these terms, can be seen as the manifestation for the absenting desire.

For Freud the most powerful form of *trieb*/drive is connected to sexuality. At various points in his writings he links sexuality and *trieb*/drive, a notable example being the role of this link in the formation of hysteria. In a similar way, Freud connects wit/jokes to the sexual *trieb*/drive through the mediating structure of language. Because of the strong repression structures and systems such as wit/jokes and dreams (mechanisms employed to escape repression) have a particular relationship to *trieb*/drive. They operate as manifestations of the *trieb*/drive in a distorted presence as well as actually demonstrating its interplay with the subject as he/she is being determined. This is also the operation that occurs between *trieb*/drive and certain processes of hysteria. The forceful nature, and ramifications, of this combination of *trieb*/drive and sexuality leads Freud to distinguish it from other forms of *trieb*/drive. Freud designates these sexual and ego based *trieb*/drives as primal.

Following on from this Freud argues for two classes of *trieb*/drive—the sexual and those connected to death. The death drive is most often represented in sadism, although with both types there is a fundamental grounding in the reflection of the self. The destructive drives are managed by being directed towards objects external to the body, which then become the assertion of the self as subject-presence by the negation of others and objects. In this way this form of *trieb*/drive is part of the destructive absence. When the destructive *trieb*/drive is directed towards the self the result is masochism. Both the sadistic and masochistic can be seen as part of the interplay between the desiring subject and absence/presence. These manifestations of *trieb*/drive are assertions of the self (that is, attempts to make present) through the objectification of others (sadism) or the objectification of the self (masochism). This is related to the *Ichspaltung* and the subsequent objectifying of the self in fantasy: "It is the subject who determines himself as object, in his encounter with the division of subjectivity" (Lacan 1986: 185). Freud's division of three types of maso-chism—erotogenic, feminine and moral—operates precisely within this context of absence. It is essential to acknowledge the cultural and historical contexts that formulate these three types (as well as the sociocultural and historical frame of the formulation itself), which must include the production of masochism by the cultural suppression of *trieb*/drive.

The urgency and pervasive nature of *trieb*/drive strengthens the connections that can be drawn between it and desire in terms of absence and subjectivity. A directly synonymous correlation between desire and *trieb*/drive needs to be avoided however. Desire, like *trieb*/drive, is compulsive and inescapable—it is a potential difficulty that must be managed. However, whereas desire is founded on absence, *trieb*/drive is a manifestation of presence; this does not make it a system of presence however. It is this junction of presence and absence which establishes the relational context of desire and *trieb*/drive.

Lacan allocates a more central position to desire in the function of *trieb*/drive than is found in Freud. He infers that *trieb*/drive is the manifestation of hidden desires (Lacan 1986). This suggests another category of ab-sence—when something appears absent but is in fact hidden rather than missing. This large category would include actions such as sublimation, repression, censorship, seduction and parapraxis, formations such as the uncanny and fantasy, and a large order which is designated here as part of the semiotics of absence, and is closely aligned to what has been termed non-apparentness as an absent type. In these terms the relationship between *trieb*/drive and desire is made sense of through absence—the desire appears to be absent but is only hidden, or at best disguised. *Trieb*/drive, and its manifestations, becomes the focus because it is symptomatic. The reverse of this formula also holds—*trieb*/drive is hidden, made absent, and the desire (or object of desire) is manifest.

An important connection between the *trieb*/drive, desire, and the subject is what Lacan refers to as "the treasure of the signifiers" (Lacan 1985: 314). To understand this it is necessary to acknowledge the significance of language and the desire for language, which also includes the function of desire in the structure of language itself, in Lacanian theory. This desire for language is based on the drive because language is seen as a key to the resolution (partial and ongoing) or abatement of desire. This is language as a part of the Symbolic, and as part of the desire for the Symbolic. It is in language that the desiring subject finds an outlet for the rigors produced by desire and the *trieb*/drives. The treasure here is not simply the capacity to manipulate and utilise the signifiers as a form of institutionalised discursive practice (for example, the *sujet supposé savoir*) which must ultimately be an exercise that ends in futility. This is the actual engagement of the signifiers through language (the Symbolic), the voice (the speaking/enunciating subject), the gaze (the subject of the gaze).

The actual object utilised has no direct relevance to *trieb*/drive. It is significant that in the formula "*la pulsion en fait le tour*" (Lacan 1973: 153), *pulsion* is given a central role. Lacan, in effect, is positioning Freud's *Objekt* in terms of the *objet petit a*. The significance of this in terms of absence is twofold. Firstly, it demonstrates the sense of absence in Freud's schema of *trieb*/drive—the object is made absent, which emphasises the *trieb*/drive rather than detracting from it. In this way the status of absence, its critical recognition of the object, defines it. Without such a sense of absence the object could not operate within the interpretative frame. Secondly, because of the strong connection between *objet petit a* and desire the *Objekt* can be seen as an object of desire, and so ordered through absence.

For Lacan the central aspect of *trieb*/drive is its relationship to the attempts to satisfy desire. Because of this *trieb*/drive must always operate within a context of absence—*trieb*/drive works for an absent desire, towards an always absent satisfaction. The one loophole in this relationship is sublimation: "sublimation is nonetheless satisfaction of the drive, without repression" (Lacan 1986: 165). To the statement: "Hence sublimation opens up the expedient of satisfying this demand without involving repression." Lacan responds: "That is successful repression" (Lacan 1988a: 134). However this is not to argue that there is a clause which permits the satisfaction of desire or, for that matter, even the *trieb*/drive. This is an indication of how sublimation enables the avoidance of repression. Even the idea of satisfaction must continue to be questioned, largely through the action of the return of the repressed and repetition. Ultimately this is the critical issue that separates the operation and function of desire from *trieb*/drive in terms of absence. Sublimation is a process for managing absence because it acts as a diversion from the absence created through repression. This diversion channels *trieb*/drive into socially accepted structures (e.g., sexuality into art/text). Significantly Freud also argues that art is a form of sublimation as it leads from phantasy (that is, connected to the unconscious) to reality. J. Hyppolite (1956) goes even further than this by suggesting that all intellectual activity (especially the philosophical) is a form of sublimation.

The subject is lacunary in the drive, reduced to the status of apparatus: "The subject is an apparatus. This apparatus is something lacunary, and it is in the lacuna that the subject establishes the function of a certain object, *qua* lost object" (Lacan 1986: 185). The lacunary nature of the subject creates a unique classificatory status and suggests two types of objects in absence: the object of the drive (e.g., Freud's *Objekt*); and the objectification of the subject through the lacunary processes. In both senses *trieb*/drive is further tied to absence, in particular in the absenting of the object of desire (the *objet petit a*). This is connected to the paradigm of subjectivity and the threat of objectification, as a form of absenting subjectivity, as it is the subject reducing itself (or being reduced) to the status of the object.

The lacunary subject operates in terms of partial drives, which in themselves suggest a form of absence—that there is something missing from the *trieb*/drive itself. These partial drives are a combination of the psychical and physical manifestations of the *trieb*/drives and include, for example, the oral and the scopic. Partial drives and the Other are inextricably tied to the notion of subjectivity not only in this sense of the lacunary subject, for Lacan goes so far as to suggest that their intersection provides a site of subjectivity. This intersection, and the subsequent formation of a site of subjectivity, is derived, in part, from the notion that subjectivity is based on sexuality and hence the sexual *trieb*/drive. The interpretation of this dynamic structure is desire as it is formulated through absence. This lies at the heart of the desiring subject. Desire, the Other, the *objet petit a* operate because of the intersection of the desiring subject and the sense of the self (the speculative subject) and the absence of those things desired, which are located in the Other. The partial drives inform the overall structure of desire and subjectivity through absence: "The drive marks the subject's attempt to realise itself in the field of the Other and to find in that field the object which is eternally lacking" (*Scilicet* Working Party 1987: 112).

Desire and Absence

In Deleuze and Guattari's complex relationship to psychoanalysis they develop the argument that desire and lack can be seen to operate in terms of production:

> In point of fact, if desire is the lack of the real object, its very nature as a
> real entity depends upon an "essence of lack" that produces the fantasized
> object. Desire thus conceived of as production, though merely the produc-
> tion of fantasies, has been explained perfectly by psychoanalysis. On the
> very lowest level of interpretation, this means that the real object that
> desire lacks is related to an extrinsic natural or social production, whereas
> desire intrinsically produces an imaginary object that functions as a double
> of reality, as though there were a "dreamed—of object behind every real
> object," or a mental production behind all real productions.
>   (Deleuze and Guattari 1985: 25-26)

They suggest that the relationship between desire and lack is an issue of
production, but not simply the flow of the production of lack through desire, or
even the production of secondary forms, as in the Platonic model, which they
so clearly reject. The psychoanalytic model, and in particular Lacan's theory
of desire, offers a defining set of ideas precisely because it accommodates this
sense of the imaginary and material productions. Deleuze and Guattari argue
that this relationship between production, lack, and desire is not invested in the
object, but in the subject: "Desire does not lack anything; it does not lack its
object. It is, rather, the *subject* that is missing in desire, or desire that lacks a
fixed subject; there is no fixed subject unless there is repression. Desire and its
object are one and the same thing" (Deleuze and Guattari 1985: 26). Lack, in
these terms, becomes associated with the abject and the formations of positions
of power (institutional, discursive, Symbolic). Desire and lack, tied to the
determination of the subject, are structures of meaning and existence. For
Deleuze and Guattari this is part of the social production of *manque*—lack as
well as need, and that the nature of this desire is always part of the social
production: "The order of desire is the order of *production*; all production is at
once desiring-production and social production" (Deleuze and Guattari 1985:
296).

Of course Deleuze and Guattari are not developing this sense of production
strictly within a psychoanalytic frame—in fact the opposite is more often the
case. They select and reject parts of the psychoanalytic concept of desire and
lack, adding to it this essential interpretation of desire as production. The
strength of this interpretation, even with its attacks and rejections, provides a
further dimension to the theorising of absence and desire in terms of the
subject. The subject is, after all, firmly located within a social context—the
social production of desire is also part of the social production of the site of
subjectivity and the subject. The centrality of lack—of a type of absence in
effect—to desire is given, but the order of this relationship is what is at stake.
It is an issue of the location of the absence in the social production, or the

definitional feature of desire to subjectivity, and so absence, that rocks back and forth here. Alexandre Kojève can be seen as a mediating position when he states: "If the human reality is a social reality, society is human only as a set of Desires mutually desiring one another as Desires" (Kojève 1969: 5). Kojève, within this Hegelian frame, argues that desire is a "revealed nothingness, an unreal emptiness" (Kojève 1969: 4). Absence and desire operate not only in the determination of the subject, but also the social context of the subject, all subjects, and subjectivity itself. Furthermore, they go "beyond" the notion of status and operate as modes of production—desire produces absence, absence produces desire, absence/desire produce the site of subjectivity. This set of relationships can be explicated through two of Lacan's most important models of subjectivity and desire - the "Schema L" and the "Bottle Opener" graph. The idea of absence as a hermeneutic process, can be distinguished from the processes of absence. Absence as hermeneutic means that concepts such as desire and subjectivity can only be made sense of through an interpretative model of absence.

Desire and Schema L

The essential point of Schema L is to demonstrate the relationship between the subject and the Other. It is a primary model in Lacan's work and reappears in different guises. One such configuration has already been considered in terms of subjectivity, absence, and fantasy. This shifting quality of the schema is important because it ties together a great many of the themes of this analytic process. The common thread within these adaptations and transformations is the model's central concern to locate the concept of the subject as it is determined by the Other, which includes the operation of the Other and the formulation of desire. This is the defining of the subject (including the position of the subject in relation to the formation of sites of subjectivity) in terms of desire and absence—which includes the operations/status of lack, lack/need (*manque*), as well as other forms of absence, including Deleuze and Guattari's modes of production. One of the most important developments in these terms is the motivation of the subject through subjectivity as absent/absence. It is worth listing the key points of the schema before considering in more detail the applicability of the model to the hermeneutics of absence:

I. The subject is in some way constructed and continually determined by the Other.
II. The "telling" of this ongoing construction/determination is a type of discourse which is positioned within a set of discursive practices.
III. This discourse is a discourse of the unconscious.
IV. The demonstration of this discourse—these "privileged moments" as Lacan calls them—occurs in processes such as dreams, parapraxis, etc.

V. The subject is inextricably linked to this discourse because it is a reflection of the self (the speculative self) and also because the subject participates in it. VI. There is a strong "internal" link within the schema through this participation of the ego and the subject's objects. (This refers to that sense of the subject making all else objects in terms of the self, measured against the self.) This is also part of the interplay between the subject and the social production of absence as desire.

VII. The Other represents a fundamental position of existence and subjectivity.

Schema L is made up of four points connected by the Z line. This line provides what appears to be a continuous flow between the points, although, as has already been seen in a more complete version, this line is intersected by the operation of the unconscious and Imaginary relations. The Z line is continuous, but it is also made up of a series of points that make it bend sharply. In this sense the connections between S—o, o—o' and o'—O can be distinguished, but more importantly the model is about the relationship between S—O; that is, the subject and site(s) of subjectivity and the Other and Otherness. The two bends at o and o' allow the representation of the stratification of subjectivity and Other so they do not appear on a continuous plane. This suggests that there is a differentiating typology operating, and this is precisely the point of desire in the schema.

The S (Subject) is the complex interplay of those processes of the subject. Lacan describes it as "ineffable and stupid", as a questioning subject, and as a subject which, through the gap, is capable of "imagining himself as mortal" (Lacan 1985: 194-196), and so filled with self-reflection because of the finite nature of his/her existence. These qualities add up to produce a subject position constructed and surrounded by absences. These are absences of the sense of the self, of what is desired, of desire itself, of gaps, of a sense of purpose, of the text and representational systems. These are the initial indicators that allow Schema L to be read as a schema of absence.

The o—the "objects"—are multifarious, operating as a type rather than any set of specifics. This o is one of Lacan's open signifiers—it carries with it a metaphoric thrust. They are designated as objects only to distinguish them from the sense of the subject. This means that their objectness is defined not by an inherent quality, but by the assertion of their objectness by the designation of the subject position as an order of subjectivity. The meaningful sense of the object in o is difference, and in particular difference to the subject.

The relationship between S—o can also be seen in terms of aphanisis, which Lacan designates as the fading of the subject. Lacan argues: "Now *aphanisis* is to be situated in a more radical way at the level at which the subject manifests himself in this movement of disappearance that I have described as lethal. In a quite different way, I have called this movement the *fading* of the subject" (Lacan 1986: 207-208). It would be more accurate to say that aphanisis represents the fear, the abject sense, of this fading, which is the fear of the absenting of subjectivity. Such a fear can be manifested in a number of different ways; however, the significant detail about this is that aphanisis involves the investment of the sense of subjectivity in the signifier. Aphanisis is the fear of losing subjectivity (i.e., the fading of the subject) through the loss of the signifier into which the sense of subjectivity has been inserted. This signifier can be partial or full, attached to the self or part of the self, textual and/or representational, loved or hated. This investment must always be read in terms of desire and how such an action is fundamentally about absence. This order of absences includes the politics of the absence of subjectivity (the fading subject, as articulated in feminist theory, postcolonial theories, and others), absence of the signifier itself, absence and desire for the signifier. Lacan points out that "the function of desire is a last residuum of the effect of the signifier in the subject" (Lacan 1986: 154). This also connects with the third part of Schema L. The o' is the imposition of the ego onto the objects, and this action is directly tied to processes such as aphanisis.

The O—the Other—in Schema L is important to this discussion for a number of reasons. Lacan defines it as the locus of the signifier, and as such it connects the other three elements of S, o, and o'. It is the traditional Lacanian Other as well as containing a number of distinct elements. Schema L and its construction of O/Other indicates that what determines the subject and site(s) of subjectivity is what is enacted in the Other. This means that even though the Other is constantly defined as distinct and separate from the subject, it provides a constant and overriding determination of the subject and his/her processes of subjectivity and operations in the world. In other words, the structure of Otherness (and its interpretation in such things as the unconscious) is both a determining presence and absence in subjectivity. It seldom is experienced directly and yet defines the condition of the subject. It is important not to read the Other simply as the unconscious in these terms, for it goes far beyond this. The Other is the discourse of the unconscious, but it is also the relationship of the unconscious to the subject, the dimension between the subject and desire, the various processes of manifesting the Other via a particular discourse. Furthermore, it is in the Other that additional defence can be made for the concept of reading presence and absence not in terms of opposition or binarism. The Other offers an example of this sense of absence and presence co-existing on equal terms but not necessarily in equality. The Other represents an absence which is present, and a presence which is absent. This status can be seen as a further model of absence, which we shall call *absentation*, or the making/production of absence via a sustained presence. Absentation negates the need for a binarism of absence and presence because it recognises the possibility of the sustaining of one in the operation of the other.

Schema L operates like two triangles: the relationship of S (Subject) to o and o'—that which the subject feels is possessed or controlled, in a very precarious manner—and the order of O (Other/Otherness) to o and o'—that which the realm of the Other dominates and makes sense of. It is because there appears to be two triangles wedged together—an abutment rather than a binding—that there is a structural tension within the model. The tension of splitting is overcome by the *pulsion* of desire—the subject's desire for the Other. Absence, and in particular the action of absentation, plays a major role in any sense of adhesion which occurs in this desire. To understand this more fully it is necessary to note an essential quality of this schema and then compare it to another schema. This quality is the sense of *"d'un Paradis perdu ou futur"* (Lacan 1971: 63)—which has a surprisingly Heideggerian sense of the ecstatic-horizonal about it.

What is important to note in this is that it is not simply a desiring for a lost past or a possible utopian future but something which is always "present" and constantly changing—that is, is a heterology which becomes specified according to the situation at hand. This capacity of desire to change, or more correctly the manifestations of desire to change (because desire rather than being a set of signifiers—in effect a paradigmatic concern—is more closely related to a coding process, so that what operates as desire as code determines the signifiers of desire), is important as it relates not only to the development of the subject and sites of subjectivity, but also to a wider cultural sense of what is permitted and what is censored and repressed, and fundamentally the nature and type of desire in production. This second aspect also relates to the nature of law and the idea of the Name-of-the-Father. In Schema R, Lacan (1971) combines the corner of the Other with the Name-of-the-Father as it determines subjectivity in the designation of reality. The Other as law constitutes both the nature of desire and the determination of the subject in terms of absence.

Desire and the Bottle Opener
De quel flacon est-ce là l'ouvre-bouteille? Lacan 1971: 171.

Schema L and the associated Schema R are significant models in terms of the relationship of the subject to the Other. The schema demonstrates the operation of absence as absentation specifically in terms of desire. This idea can be carried over to another of Lacan's important schemas, this one more directly concerned with the relationship of subjectivity, the subject, and desire as they operate in terms of the signifier. The "Bottle Opener" graph is indirectly based on the concept of the enunciating subject. Lacan's idea of the enunciating/speaking subject is related, but distinct from, Kristeva's "Speaking Subject", Derrida's "Subject in Language", Foucault's "Enunciating Subject", and Benveniste's social construction of the enunciating subject. Each of these models shares the common directive of the subject defined through his/her relationship to language and discourse. However, the idea of the subject, the definitional construction of language and discourse and the complex interplay between the two, provides a significant number of differences to each of the interpretations.

The enunciating subject for Lacan, if only in terms of his Freudian and semiotic negotiations, is always going to prove of central importance. It forms part of the theory that the signifier must exist prior to the subject. However, it is a propositional system not simply based on Freud's "talking cure". In Lacanian thought (as with a number of other theories) the enunciating subject is definitionally the human subject—the subject in the mirror stage. Once this developmental point is reached, the step taken, there is a more problematic subject produced, for language both articulates human subjectivity and introduces a complex interplay of difficulties, among which desire is central. This is in keeping with Kojève's (1969) specification of desire as defining human subjectivity. How this interplay of human subjectivity and desire operates in terms of absence can be demonstrated in terms of the Bottle Opener graph.

The status of the enunciating subject in the Bottle Opener graph includes a gap, which is an absence. What is significant in terms of absence is not so much the enunciation itself, but that this is founded on an absence. This is the absence contained in the subject's relationship to the Other, the frustrating processes in the Symbolic as encountered by the subject. All of these clearly indicate that the subject operates in terms of gaps, fissures, splits, or absences once the imperfect operations of language/discourse are entered into. The reading of the Bottle Opener graph here is centred on the ways in which these absences operate in the constitutive and functional dimensions of the subject, or, perhaps more correctly, the enunciating subject derived from the gaps of language/discourse and/in the act of enunciation.

There are at least three fundamental ways in which the subject and desire can be constructed in a relational context to one another: i) that the subject exists and desire becomes a consequential part of that existence; ii) that desire exists and the subject enters into the realm of desire via language/discourse and the Other, as well as the social production of desire; iii) the subject's desire—heterogeneous and dynamic—swells in complexity as subjectivity develops via processes such as language, discourse, and the social production of desire. These three models (and they are neither mutually exclusive nor the final word of all possible models in this regard) share the idea that the subject and his/her desire(s) are definitionally and operationally linked. That is, that the status of subjectivity and desire rely on each other to be defined and operate within a hermeneutic set of actions. This is a concept which has been at the centre of this entire examination so far, along with the qualifications that the relationship between the subject and desire (mutually defining though it may be) is ultimately based on absence; and, in addition, there is a sense of sociocultural force and production which qualifies, through certain types of absence (e.g., censorship, repression), manifestations of desire. This sense of absence is figured differently according to which of the three forms, and the possible combinations, is utilised.

Lacan builds up the complete version of the Bottle Opener graph through a series of four stages. One of his aims in doing so is to interpret desire as a dialectics of desire and the dialectisation of desire. In order to reread the graph, and its stages, more directly in terms of absence, the subject, and desire, it is important to acknowledge the dynamics of these stages of development. What this graph ultimately provides is a series of gaps and absences. Indeed, its overall layout (including the gradual putting together of the parts) indicates lines of tension and *pulsion*. But even more significant are the large absences that these lines glide around and over, highlighting them and their actions. Like the bottle opener itself, the graph functions through the absences and because of them.

The first aspect is the position of the subject in relation to the Other. This is a relationship which recalls Schema L and the interplay of S—o—o'—O. The graph commences at a seemingly simple enough level—the interplay between the desiring subject and meaningful signifiers. In another sense this can be read as the subject who is subverted via the dialectic of desire, and the ensuing and continual struggle with desire by that subject—part of the dialectisation process. This is the *necessity* of desire which is produced in both an attraction for and abjection of desire and absence. This is the "very darkness of my desire" that Barthes speaks of (Barthes 1990: 171). Part of this darkness is the inability to know about desire, its operations and manifestations. This is the setting up of the *sujet supposé savoir*, the operation of transference, the desire to know desire. Yet even this knowledge is founded on absence and substitution. This is so even when desire is positioned as love—to love, to be loved, to determine love in another or object.

The opening graph is made up of the *Ichspaltung* and the metaphorical indicators of that split, which are primarily desire and language. The subject is split on one level through the impossible desire, and on another through the inadequacies of language for the enunciating subject. The very points of intersection form dynamic sites—the treasury of the signifiers at one point and punctuation at another. This forms the second stage of the graph. What is particularly noteworthy are two qualifications: "Observe the dissymmetry of the one, which is a locus (a place rather than a space), to the other, which is a moment (a rhythm rather than a duration)" (Lacan 1985: 304). This sense of place rather than space may seem problematic in this reading of absences, but in fact two supportive aspects are revealed by this. The first is that Lacan imbues presence within that very point of the treasury (signifier not code) and punctuation - it is the denial of absence relative to that point which exists outside of it. For all the presenting in these points there exists an equal number of significant—perhaps even more significant—absences. There are, for example, the absences/gaps between the subject and his/her desire (S— < >), and the absences between the treasury and punctuation and back again (O—S[O]), which is "the subjection of the subject to the signifier" (Lacan 1985: 304) and is linked to the absences of aphanisis. These are all absences formed by the insistence of the presences, that is, the places and the rhythms. These insistences can also be seen as an operation of absentation.

The second aspect revealed by this is of a different order of absences and space/place. Lacan's defining rule of "place" rather than "space" can only really make sense if it is read within the context of surrounding absences and gaps, and if these places rely on, and are derived from, spaces for their operation. The treasury is established as a place because it is surrounded by absences, and within its very "placeness" is a further set of absences. Catherine Clément (1983) points out that the treasury is the source pool of signifiers. As such it is in some ways the equivalent of the semiotic paradigmatic, and in this sense the punctuation is the syntagmatic. The "place" is an absent order still to be completed, but is already indicated through (at least in psychoanalytic terms) parapraxis, dreams, jokes/wit, denial stretching the line from the potential to the actual, from the latent to the manifest, even if these presences are distorted, polysemic ones hiding more than they expose. The actual, the presences, in this model—the sector dominated by punctuation—contains the "locus of speech" (Lacan 1985: 305).

The second stage of the Bottle Opener graph denies the simplicity of the initial crossing of lines and evokes a number of concepts regarding the subject and the site of subjectivity. Here Lacan makes some amendments to the positions within the graph. Because it is neither strictly synchronic nor diachronic the graph alters its shape according to how it progresses. There can be no final graph, even if there are lines and symbols on a page which seem to indicate some form of completion.

In this stage I(O) replaces the barred S ($\cancel{S}$) which has moved across to the "starting" point. The barred $\cancel{S}$ ($\cancel{S}$)—the *Ichspaltung* of desire and absence—has now become the site from where all of the subsequent actions and positions are defined. The movement is now through the paradigmatics of the treasury and the syntagmatics of the rhythm of punctuation to I(O), which is the Imaginary, the unconscious, the Other. This I(O), in its unknowable, indescribable essence, has the same propensity for absence as desire and the treasury. In fact, these three points operate precisely in terms of absence. Furthermore, the arrows and cycles of flow must be read as points of absence, and it is because they are absences, known only in terms of the abstract and within the context of the desire to know about desire (and the nature of its absences), that the process operates as a dynamic. Lacan only goes part of the way in articulating this when he speaks of a "play of presence" (Lacan 1985: 307), and spends more interpretative energy on the idea of *méconnaissance*.

Lacan introduces the idea of the ego operating not as the I but as a metonym of signification. This is further support for the idea of the split subject and the centrality of language/discourse, formed in a context of absences. A metonymic ego torn from the discursive practices of the I will always be determined within the dual tension of desire and the fragmented self. It is precisely for this reason that the engagement with language by the enunciating subject is never a total satisfaction of desire, but more often quite the opposite.

The metonymic ego, contextualised through the split subject, can be linked to Benveniste's enunciating subject in the social world, and as social identity: "Language is possible only because each speaker sets himself up as a subject by referring to himself as "I" in his discourse. Because of this, "I" posits another person, the one who, being as he is completely exterior to "me", becomes my echo to whom I say "you" and who says "you" to me. This polarity of persons is the fundamental condition of language" (Benveniste 1971: 225). This situation includes the social contextualisation of the subject and the attendant processes of self-reflexivity, and the inversion of this, that is, the contextualising self-reflexivity and the attendant processes of social actions. This polarity in the social operation of the subject through language/discourse is part of the desire and split of the metonymic ego and the metonyms of the ego's operations. Further, it is this metonymic ego which necessitates a rejection of the defining qualities of consciousness to the Cartesian *cogito*, which is the transparency of the I.

The next phase of the graph introduces the concept of demand, used here in a different way from both desire and drive, although there are connections between all three. Demand is uniquely tied to the signifier: "there is no demand that does not in some sense pass through the defiles of the signifier" (Lacan 1985: 309). This demand in terms of the desiring subject who is linked to the operation of the signifier in the realm of the Symbolic as determinant of subjectivity. This phase of the graph (as well as the next one) develops through the distinctions made between desire and demand. Lacan states: "Desire begins to take shape in the margin in which demand becomes separated from need: this margin being that which is opened up by demand, the appeal of which can be unconditional only in regard to the Other, under the form of the possible defect" (Lacan 1985: 311).

Two levels operate here: the level of d—S < > o, which is the line of desire; S(O)—S < > D, which becomes the line of demand in the completed graph. Lacan's model is derived partly from Freud's analysis of the butcher's wife and the desire/demand for caviar. It is also part of the aphanisis of the subject whose subjectivity is invested in the signifier because of the configuration of S < > o. In this sense the fading subject and the *Ichspaltung* are aligned as the split of the subject from the signifier (of the Other, of Otherness, of knowing) becomes the fade. The link to absence is emphasised even further by the central operation of primal repression (*Urverdrängung*) in the formation of this subject type and position. In this alignment there is also to be found one of Lacan's clearest indicators of the synonymous signification of discourse and desire when he speaks of *discours de l'Autre* and *désir de l'Autre* (Lacan 1971). The link is made, through the play on *de*, between the action of desire (in the enunciating subject) and the determination of the subject in the Other. *Méconnaissance* is connected to the aphanisis of the fading subject and the *Ichspaltung* because when the self-reflexive acknowledgment of the subject split from desire creates a demand/need, an attempt is made to manage these desires in terms of the ego. *Méconnaissance* then incorporates the desire to know the Other, but the failure to be able to. This is part of the idea that there is no Other of the Other, in other words no transcendental signifiers. Lacan qualifies the S < > o by reaffirming this. This issue of the transcendental signifier is of central concern to the critical formulation of the enunciating subject.

Demand operates as a form of *pulsion* in the lines which connect sections in the graph. This is why it initially appears to be one of connecting lines and flows. However, the lines hide the true nature of the graph, which is the absences and spaces produced from these lines. It is precisely in the operation of demand that this becomes particularly noticeable. The absences developed through the drives of the lines are further complemented by the absences held in the circles of points of connection. Points such as the treasury of the signifiers are organisations of absences. Such a treasury cannot actually exist (cannot be realised) so they are always held in paradigmatic readiness.

A further example of this is encountered in the realm of S (O), which is the "signifier of a lack in the Other" (Lacan 1985: 316). The lack referred to is the motivational properties of the "no Other of the Other". This logarithm is an essential feature in the formation of the subject and lack/absence. In effect this is to argue that the subject (type as well as site) is defined not by what he/she is, but what is lacking. S(O) is "the signifier for all other signifiers [that] represent the subject" (Lacan 1985: 316), which is a signifier of a double absence—of the lack and of the Other. The effect of this is represented in the Bottle Opener graph as -I.

The -I is the subject of the lack, and it is in this equation that Lacan can be seen to be further challenging the Cartesian *cogito* in both its philosophical and psychological senses. Fundamental to the -I is the quality of the subject who does not know, has an absence of recognition—of the signifier, the code, the site of subjectification, etc. The combinational effects of *méconnaissance* and the forces of lack and absence constitute the unknowing subject. As Lacan puts it: "This is what the subject lacks in order to think of himself exhausted by his *cogito*, namely, that which is unthinkable to him" and "we cannot ask this question of the subject as "I". He lacks everything needed to know the answer" (Lacan 1985: 317). The unthinkable becomes the abject, and this in turn is transformed into the subject of abjection. Abjection becomes a part of *méconnaissance*, where the failure to know and recognise becomes the absence of the capacity to know/recognise. One of the most compelling forces behind this signifier of a lack/absence in the Other is *jouissance*, located here in the movement through the S(O) and the fragmented subject desiring the Other (S < > a).

It is the Law that constructs the split subject in the signifier because of the denial, perhaps even refutation—which is a sense of the absent in both cases—of *jouissance*. However it is important to note that Lacan argues that the Law does not bar access to *jouissance*, rather it contributes towards the construction of the barred subject. The subject becomes torn between *manque-à-être* (want-to-be) and *un En-Trop* (Too-much-of-it) (Lacan 1985: 323). It is the movement from the Imaginary to the Symbolic (from one side of the graph to the other), and of the utilisation of the signifier in representation (of *jouissance*). This is a tension of the same order found in the pleasure of the text and the act of reading. The interplay of *jouissance* and Law leads to the refusal (castration) through absences, but this does not mean there is an abolishing of Law. *Jouissance* is returned to, and returns, through the Law of desire.

4

"That Perilous Necessity": Towards a Metaphysics of Subjectivity and Absence

Reflexivity, Subjectivity, and Absence

The notion of self-consciousness—reflection and issues of reflexivity—as a crucial process in the formulation of a modern metaphysics of subjectivity is critically well supported. This sense of self-consciousness as reflexive process has lead to a diverse number of inquiries on the nature of subjectivity as well as examinations of the analytic process itself. Reflection has become orientated to the very nature of subjectivity and forms part of the critical methodology for its investigation. Foucault's argument that the critical sense of the subject only develops in the post-classical reflexive age is based on the same set of principles. The Freudian subject—especially as it is interpreted and formulated by Lacan—marks a further stage in the development of this critical sense. Although the idea of the subject as *bricolage* is not new (Plato's charioteer can be read in this way), what marks the Freudian model in particular is that the divisions of the subject (and the conflictual nature of these splits) are seen as definitional to subjectivity and primary to any interpretative activity. In earlier, similar models this was often posited as a corollary to the central points of defining subjectivity. Lacan places even greater emphasis on the subject's critical bind to language, paving the way for the conceptualisation (at least in psychoanalytic terms) of the enunciating subject as defining subjectivity. This paradigm of the split subject, its basis in language and the Symbolic (and, as a consequence, an ideological positioning) and self-consciousness of this ideological, enunciating position, forms the basis of a particular analytic sense of the subject and the nature of subjectivity.

A metaphysics of subjectivity entails a consideration of that particular set of philosophical enterprises which attempt to define subjectivity through the formulation of the apodictic quality of self-consciousness. This line of thought is connected to the transcendental idealism of Kant and the investigations of a priorism found in *The Critique of Pure Reason*. It should be noted that these concerns do not aim for a formulation of a metaphysics of absence and/or subjectivity, rather it is the *systems* of metaphysics as they have developed absences and have been developed by absences.

Part of the phenomenological exercise is based on formulating seemingly apodictic points which can then be used as a basis for analysis and interpretation. Absence plays a vital role in the formulation of the apodictic. Any real sense of the apodictic in the assertion of the self-conscious subject needs to be avoided in terms of an absence. The critical frame may certainly posit the centrality and existence of the subject, but this does not negate a sense of doubt that usually exists as a qualification of this frame. The Cartesian revolution stems from this certainty of the (critical and methodological) dependence on the self-reflexive, self-conscious subject. Eidetic reduction is precisely a system of absence and presence, for it involves working towards a "pure" presence, which is derived from a sustained elimination of verifiably suspect configurations. This is the essential feature of Husserl's methodology, particularly as it is articulated in *Cartesian Meditations* (Husserl 1960). In these configurations subjectivity is determined (often in an antithetical fashion) by the collocated signifiers of the body. The signifiers of the body may be collocated initially in the process of eidetic reduction, but then must be made absent in terms of the critical methodology. Veracity in this exercise exists in the absenting of the body from the formulation of subjectivity:

> When the method is followed, the certainty of sensuous experience, the certainty with which the world is given in natural living, does not withstand criticism; accordingly the being of the world must remain unaccepted at this initial stage. The meditator keeps only himself, *qua* pure ego of his *cogitationes*, as having an absolutely indubitable existence, as something that cannot be done away with, something that would exist even though this world were nonexistent.
>
> (Husserl 1960: 3).

Such a need, or critical desire, to parenthesise the body is found in Descartes's First Meditations. As was pointed out earlier, Freud both inverts and retains this schema: he inverts it by registering mental and physical manifestations as overdetermined signifiers (e.g., Dora's cough) and therefore essential and meaningful structures; he retains it by repositioning the body signifiers as part of a different semiotic register.

This suggests that the Freudian model, in this particular issue, is not as far removed from Husserl's basic premise as first might appear. In analysing the very nature of the apodictic Husserl offers the following definition:

> An apodictic evidence, however, is not merely certainty of the affairs or affair-complexes (states-of-affairs) evident in it; rather it discloses itself, to

a critical reflection, as having the single peculiarity of being at the same time the absolute unimaginableness (inconceivability) of their non-being, and thus excluding in advance every doubt as "objectless", empty. Furthermore the evidence of that critical reflection likewise has the dignity of being apodictic.

(Husserl 1960: 14-15)

This "dignity" has a number of implications for a theory of absence, not the least being the political (hidden) agenda of presence over absence. The connection with Freud's interpretation of subjectivity here lies in the apodictic nature of *eidos*, which can be read as the Platonic ideal as fundamental signifier(s) of existence. Doubts may surround and qualify every aspect of any construction of the idea, but that it exists is seen as certain. Notions of veracity become secondary as the factors of certainty and existence are highlighted. This is precisely the structure that Nietzsche challenges, thus making him a theorist of absence. Lacan in particular is concerned with how such a signifier is produced, and the implications of this production, in terms of language and cultural systems. Prior to this, however, is the potential development of the apodictic evidence for the signifier. It is for this reason that Freud's analysis of dreams, for example, is often more concerned with the actual recounting of the dream than the materiality of the dream itself. The relatively indulgent symbolism devised by Freud was never intended to replace the evidence of the signifier of the dream, and it would be a critical error to read it as such.

Because of the historical superstructure, to speak of a metaphysics of subjectivity is, invariably, to speak of the idea of presence as part of the formulation of the subject. The issues of presence in these terms has been fundamental to the methodology of a metaphysics of subjectivity, thus producing what Derrida describes as a metaphysics of presence. This urgency of presence finds at least one strand of its beginnings in the Cartesian quest for apodictic certainty. This is the methodology which seeks to make absent all that can be doubted, to leave a signifying position which is heavily invested with presence. Presence becomes not simply a sense of existence, but the evidence of existence, the defining quality of existence, a politicised epistemic order, a set of ideological practices, etc. Such a signifying position gains extraordinary density because, as Husserl puts it, subjectivity becomes an issue of claims and counter-claims: "Instead of simply existing for us—that is, being accepted naturally by us in our experiential believing in its existence—the world is for us only something that claims being" (Husserl 1960: 18). That is, all orders of being have *claims* but do not possess beingness, and so cannot have certainty about being and all its attendant qualities. This sense of the claims towards existence—in effect, because of the operations of metaphysics, claims to presence—have a particular ideological dimension which is comparable to a number of ideas generated in various Marxist readings and schools of thought, in particular Althusser (1971). Husserl designates the action of the claims as the radical development of the ego *cogito* in terms of the position of transcendental subjectivity. The density—its quality of presentness—of the transcendental subject's signifying position is derived (in these Husserlian terms) in part from the action of phenomenological *epoché*, which can be seen as both a methodology and a particular subject position and/or site of subjectivity.

This would seem to create a type of binarism of a subject type, consisting of a heavily inscribed presence (which is usually ideologically privileged) and an otherness based on systems of absence. However, it is possible to recoup some of the ideas within this phenomenological (Husserlian) model so that they can be read in terms of the non-binarism of absence and presence indicated in this semiotic reading of the onto-epistemological basis of subjectivity. What Husserl describes as transcendental phenomenological reduction does not produce absence ("[it] does not leave us confronting nothing" [Husserl 1960: 20]) but, ideally, a "purity" of presence from which to judge everything else, which is clearly not the elimination of everything else. This is an example of how absence is not simply nothingness, for the transcendental-phenomenological reduction "absents" the world but it does not eliminate it and all its objects. Husserl requires us to accommodate this mid-ground between world and subject: "neither the world nor any worldly Object is a piece of my Ego, to be found in my conscious life as a really inherent part of it, as a complex of data of sensation of a complex of acts" (Husserl 1960: 26). Being and beingness—-that is, the Ego and the particular sets of relationships that are developed between this interpretative order and all else—is one of the first apprehensions in the interpretative gaze from the ideal position of the *epoché*. This positionality of presence has become the cornerstone for metaphysics: "This privilege is the ether of metaphysics, the very element of our thought insofar as it is caught up in the language of metaphysics. We can only de-limit such a closure today by evoking this import of presence . . ." (Derrida 1973: 147). From this Derrida develops the concept of *différance* and so the deconstruction of the subject in/of language, and of the relationship between the formulation of presence and meaning/signification.

An essential feature in this reading of the ego *cogito*'s relativism to the world and its objects, and the figuring of absence within this, is the intentionality of consciousness and its processes. Intentionality represents a key link between the ideological density of the signifying practices of apodictic certainty and the absenting of everything else. The intentionality of conscious processes necessarily dismisses the notion of binarism because in intentionality both presence and absence exist. Intentionality is a necessary part of consciousness—that is, it is a presence—and yet it is not part of the same order as the apodictically determined presence of the ego—that is, it is an order of absence. It is because the *cogito* always contains its *cogitatum* that intentionality can be read as an intermediary of presence and absence. Husserl's insistence on a distinction between "natural" and "transcendental" reflection within this sense of intentionality supports this reading of having the status of presence and absence at the same time.

This investigation of a metaphysics of subjectivity as it developed into a metaphysics of presence is particularly evident in Heidegger. *Being and Time* is based on the three presuppositions on the necessary investigation of Being: the universality of Being, the indefinability of Being, and the self-evidence of Being. These three combine to make the issue of Being "the darkest of them all". Heidegger attempts to analyse this darkness with his formulation of the concept of *Dasein*. The ideas of *existenz, existentiell*—these "ontical affairs" of *Dasein*—reflect Husserl's notion of the primary intentionality of self-existence to the Ego. It is not so much self-consciousness that determines *Dasein*, but the continual reflections on the issues themselves. The self-consciousness of *Dasein* means that it "is an entity for which, in its Being, that Being is an issue" (Heidegger 1973: 236). This leads to the ontico-ontological construction of *Dasein* and the reflection of being in the world.

Kristeva argues that Heidegger's methodological construction of subjectivity is based precisely on this emphasis of the "presence of consciousness" (Kristeva 1984c: 184). Ostensibly the emphasis stems from Hegel and Kant, particularly in terms of Heidegger's reading of Kant's essay *Der einzig mögliche Beweisgrund zu einer Demonstration des Daseins Gottes* and a section from *Critique of Pure Reason* in *The Basic Problems of Phenomenology*, and finds an essentially critical quality in the developing metaphysics of subjectivity and the issue of presence. Heidegger takes up the centrality of presence to the (Western) philosophical activity. At one point he argues:

> For since the beginning of philosophy and with that beginning, the Being of beings has showed itself as the ground (*arche, aition*). The ground is from where beings as such are what they are in their becoming, perishing and persisting as something that can be known, handled and worked upon. As the ground, Being brings being to their actual presencing. The ground shows itself as presence. The present of presence consists in the fact that it brings what is present each in its own way to presence.
>
> (Heidegger 1972: 55)

The sense of such a statement as to whether or not it is a descriptive passage on philosophical discourse or part of that discourse is the issue that Derrida takes up in the deconstruction of the philosophical enterprise. Perhaps it is not so essential to decide here the line between philosophical description and prescription, rather to consider the implications of temporality, presence and being for theorising absence.

The Heideggerian exercise in *Being and Time* is, essentially, to determine Being as it is positioned in Temporality—that is, *seine temporale Bestimmtheit*, which is not Being in time, but a reading of the Temporality of Being. Heidegger aims to develop a completely distinct interpretation of time as it applies to Being, which is inextricably linked to the formation of subjectivity.

This temporal determinateness (*seine temporale Bestimmtheit*) becomes a definitional axis for *Dasein*, especially in terms of phenomenological *cura*, and so has both quantitative and qualitative dimensions. This temporal determination leads Heidegger to read Being as infused with the issues of time at all levels, from the potentially hermeneutic activities in the idea of anticipatory resoluteness to the negotiations of absence and presence in *praesens* as determining features of particular types of horizonal *ecstasis*.

Temporal determinateness is significant to metaphysical subjectivity and absence because, like Husserl's configurations of intentionality, it is neither presence nor absence. For Being to be determined in *seine temporale Bestimmtheit* concepts such as past and future, anticipation, potentiality-for-Being must be read in terms of issues of absence. The past and future are phenomenologically intentional, and can only make sense within this idea of the temporally determined Being.

Etymologically presence shares ground with temporality and being. Heidegger employs *die Gegenwart* as a conterminous for presence and the present—*praesentia* shares both meanings. Heidegger sees the combinative function as an essential one in this process: "presence (*Anwesenheit*) . . . entities are grasped in their Being as "presence"; this means that they are understood with regard to a definite mode of time—the Present" (Heidegger 1973: 47). That Being is temporally determined in Heidegger's scheme demonstrates further the development of a metaphysics of subjectivity based on presence. Derrida comments on this aspect in terms of the intractable quality of this philosophical positioning: "As soon as being and present are synonymous, to say nothingness and to say time are the same thing. Time is indeed the discursive manifestation of negativity, and Hegel, *mutatis mutandis*, will only make explicit what is said of *ousia* as presence" (Derrida 1986: 51). Presence is much more than just a prerequisite—even at its most complex—for *Dasein* as first might appear to be the case, especially in the works of Heidegger. His analytic division of the phenomenological method as derived from *phenomenon* and *logos* is significant in terms of subjectivity and desire; *phenomenon* is based on the manifesting propensity. Derived from the Greek meaning "to bring to light of day" (cf. *Being and Time*, p. 51), Heidegger distinguishes between this *phenomenon* and appearance: "*Phenomenon*, the showing-itself-in-itself, signifies a distinctive way in which something can be encountered. Appearance, on the other hand, means a reference-relationship which is an entity itself, and which is such that what does the referring (or the announcing) can fulfil its possible function only if it shows itself in itself and is thus a *phenomenon*" (Heidegger 1973: 54). Such a distinction immediately refutes any homogeneous sense of presence, just as any homogeneous sense of absence must be refuted. The typological grid that Heidegger is suggesting enables an ordering of types and forms of *phenomenon* (that is, manifesting itself) and appearance, and so becomes part of the larger phenomenological process.

Logos is privileged by Heidegger (1973) as "discourse"—it lets something be seen. This double reflection of manifestation and emphasis in *phenomenon* and *logos* as discourse indicates a particular line of investigation which is instrumental in the development of a metaphysics of subjectivity in one sense and metaphysics of presence in another. A number of these issues of presence and Being are dealt with by Heidegger in terms of *cura* or phenomenological care. "*Dasein*'s Being reveals itself as *cura*" (Heidegger 1973: 227) and as such the whole concept of *cura* is important here for a number of reasons. *Cura* becomes the insistence of *Dasein*'s Being in the World as it provides an ontological presence accorded the definitional sense of *Dasein*. As such it indicates the unique and particular relationship that Being has in terms of itself and in the World. *Cura* must then be seen as an important feature of presence in the context of subjectivity.

Cura offers a critical point for measuring the phenomenologically orientated sense against the Freudian and Lacanian ideas of wish (*Wunsch*) and *pulsion*. Heidegger insists that wish and urge are derivatives of *cura*. Crucial to this is the status of *cura* and wish in terms of absence and presence, and the relation to subjectivity and desire. For whether or not we accept Heidegger's point—and there is room for doubt in a number of issues, especially in the way wish and *pulsion* are isolated from a number of other processes and actions—the basis of the idea is revealing in terms of absence. Wish is figured as manifestly absent from the mechanisms of Being in both Heidegger and Freud. However, Freud, and then Lacan, sees it as a significant and inescapable force on the subject and by the subject, most notably in the construction of desire. This is different, although not necessarily contradictory, to Heidegger's locating of wish and *cura* in relation to each other and to the formulation of subjectivity. Positioned as a subtext of *cura*, wish is anchored as an ontological necessity of *Dasein*.

In terms of absence and presence—motivated and hidden forces acting on the subject through the compulsion of desire, as well as the compulsion to repeat and the return of the repressed—the concept of wish fulfilment and the operation of *fort/da* can be compared to the ontological issues of *cura*. In such a comparison it becomes evident that the organisation of wish as a qualitative subtext to *cura* for Heidegger is ultimately untenable in the Freudian and Lacanian schema. This is largely because of the communal quality that *cura* has, whereas the (Freudian) wish can be, and often is, oppositional to such a quality. This can be read as an issue of the ideological formation of the Symbolic, read through the interplay of the individual's relation of the self (the Imaginary) to *cura* and desire. Linked to this is the absentation of the wish and its location in the parergonal or thetic. Significant to this is the sense of presence and the action of absence that *cura* brings to wish. Kristeva argues that desire is "the praxis of phenomenological care" (Kristeva 1984c: 132). This praxis is not the essential feature of desire, but a functional realisation.

Gasché argues convincingly that the post-Cartesian concerns for the subject are based on variations of reflection. Heidegger features prominently in the meta-critical deconstruction of this tradition—a lineage which continues to Derrida. Gasché states: "By freeing the structural articulations of Being, Heidegger paved the way for Derrida's even more effective accounting, beyond traditional aporetics and speculation, for the problem of reflexivity. Concerned with demonstrating both the possibility and essential limits—that is, ultimate impossibility, of self-reflection—Derrida's approach aims neither to dismantle nor to annul reflection in a skeptical, empiricist, or positivist manner" (Gasché 1986: 86). The reflexive quality of Being demonstrates the fundamental issue of (Heideggerian) concerns here—that even though the emphasis of Heidegger's philosophical works are directed towards distinguishing the ontico-ontological differences of Being, it can be seen as a process based on the interplay of presences and absences.

A philosophy of reflection ties in with the sense of a metaphysics of presence because reflection implies presence. In order to reflect, in order for reflection to take place, there must be at least three primary elements: something to reflect with; something to be reflected (the presence of Being, whether it is positioned as ideality or as some form of manifestation and representation); and the process of the active reading (the gaze as language/discourse or semiotic). In this sense Lacan's schema of the inverted bouquet forms part of the same critical order of reflection. These three elements are the fundamental orders that constitute a metaphysics of presence and subjectivity—that is, the presence of Being, the presence of self-consciousness (of that Beingness), the mobility of the gaze (that is, the reflection of the self for the self), the reflection of the self in the Symbolic (a variation of Being-in-t- he-world), and the self-reflexive nature of these reflections. Vital to a sense of absence is that this insistence on presence through reflection is a highly politicised process and does not simply exist in an isolated state. It cannot be seen as an order of existence, rather there is a need to acknowledge this whole activity as a process, and a particular political one at that.

In a number of Derrida's works there are to be found two interconnected interpretations of presence as it operates in terms of the above examination. These two sets of issues can be loosely divided into issues on subjectivity and presence and the construction and operation of language and the sign and presence. The reason why the two are so strongly connected is related to an interpretative model already encountered in Lacan. The subject is read much less as a determining process of language and more as a determined process. The subject, in these terms is created by the sign. There are significant differences between the ways in which such a formula is developed in various contemporary critical thought, notably here Lacan, Derrida, and Kristeva, as well as Benveniste and language, Foucault and social institutions, including discursive practices, Deleuze and Guattari and social production, Althusser and the ideological prescriptions which are allowed for the subject to take up.

Ousia, *Parousia*, and the Metaphysics of Presence

It is noteworthy that the field of inquiry into subjectivity, particularly in terms of what has been called the metaphysics of presence, historically carries with it a whole set of attendant issues of presence. Derrida's writing is as much about revealing this philosophical agenda as it is changing it, engaging in it, and, perhaps, sustaining parts of it. Derrida's examination of Western philosophical traditions is construed through a critical frame directed towards uncovering not principle themes or exercises, but the very foundation of the processes themselves. So when he comments on metaphysics he directs our attention to its basis in presence. Of the many comments along these lines the following is indicative: "The history of metaphysics, like the history of the West, is the history of these metaphors and metonymies. Its matrix . . . is the determination of Being as presence in all senses of this word. It could be shown that all names related to fundamentals, to principles, or to the centre have always designated an invariable presence—*eidos*, *arche*, *telos*, *energeia*, *ousia* (essence, existence, substance, subject) *aletheia*, transcendentality, conscious-ness, God, man and so forth" (Derrida 1978b: 279-280). Derrida argues that one of the main ruptures in this metaphysics of presence is in the conceptual developments of the sign. There are some obvious difficulties with such a claim—compare this to Kristeva's positioning of the sign as classical for example—but it does offer a number of important insights into the relationship between a (determining) subject position and the sign. It is noteworthy that the list of signifiers utilised by Derrida here runs parallel to those employed by Heidegger to argue for the significance of ontological investigations in philosophy. It is precisely this list, connected to an extensive and fortified conceptualisation of subjectivity as presence that needs to be radically reconsidered in terms of absence. The subject types, and the influential models, of the subject of desire and the subject of abjection are examples of how such a tradition misses essential features of absence in the figuring of subjectivity. Heidegger's and Husserl's constructions of subjectivity and presence are primary examples of this.

Connected to a metaphysics of presence is originary processes and, by implication, the notion of transcendental signifiers. Both of these will be examined in due course, but it is necessary to note here that Derrida uses the questions of origins to deliberate on and problematise this issue of metaphysics: "Where and how does it begin . . . ? A question of origin. But a meditation upon the trace should undoubtedly teach us that there is no origin, that is to say simple origin; that the questions of origin carry with them a metaphysics of presence" (Derrida 1976: 74). Derrida goes on to describe an investigation of a metaphysics of presence as "that perilous necessity" (Derrida 1976: 74). He is, of course, not the only one to point out the centrality of presence in Western thought—in "Kant on Enlightenment and Revolution" Foucault argues that it is Kant's investigations into the Enlightenment that form a historically significant moment in the foregrounding of presence. It is at this philosophical point that there is a direct "problematising [of] its own discursive present-ness", and "Philosophy as the problematisation of a present-ness, the interrogation by philosophy of this present-ness of which it is part and relative to which it is obliged to locate itself: this may well be the characteristic trait of philosophy as a discourse of and upon modernity" ("Kant on Enlightenment and Revolution"). This sense of the present becomes, during and after the Enlightenment, a focal point for philosophical reflection. Furthermore, this sense of the present/presence in the philosophical tradition leads Foucault to posit progress in the sign of *rememorativum* (things represented by the sign as they have been), *demonstrativum* (things represented by the sign as they are) and *prognosticon* (things represented by the sign as they will be). The issues that Foucault raises form part of the larger schema of reflections on reflections on the presentness of major frames of reference.

It is almost a given that Derrida will locate Heideggerian processes and investigations within this metaphysics of presence. However, what is not so obvious is that he does so in terms of the question of presence and the signifier. The rupture of the sign discussed in various essays in *Writing and Difference* is also examined in sections of *Of Grammatology* and *Speech and Phenomena*. In these texts Derrida establishes a direct link between the metaphysics of presence and the structure of the sign as it is critically determined by Heidegger (among others). This transgression and the subject's relation to the sign (as process and product) can in some ways be compared to the way Lacan argues for the compositional frame of the subject in the Symbolic, as well as Kristeva's sense of the operation of the Symbolic, *sémiotique* and thetic. The fact that Derrida attempts to distance his work from these other models, and even oppose them (particularly Lacan's), by aligning them with other referencing frames does not negate outright some of the common points. This is particularly true of the relational context of subjectivity and the politics of absence and presence. Part of this political agenda rests in the interplay of presences and absences of *ousia* and *parousia*.

It has already been noted that the issue of a metaphysics of presence carries with it certain tacit groundings of the originary nature of the sign. This originary feature is also part of the concept of *ousia* and *parousia*—presence becomes imbued with a sense of origins. This is true of both subjectivity and a certain semiotic reading of the sign: ". . . but one could no longer call it originary or final in the extent to which the values or origin, *archi-*, *telos*, *eskhaton*, etc. have always denoted presence—*ousia*, *parousia*" (Derrida 1986: 9). From this point Derrida makes note of a concern which is central to the issues of absence at hand: ". . . thereby one puts into question the authority of presence, or of its simple, symmetrical opposite, absence or lack. Thus one questions the limit which has always constrained us, which still constrains us—as inhabitants of a language and a system of thought—to formulate the meaning of Being in general as presence or absence, in the categories of being or beingness (*ousia*)" (Derrida 1986: 10). Derrida's positioning of absence as a "simple, symmetrical opposite" to presence must be questioned within the current interpretation, and ultimately must be dismissed as untenable in terms of primary absences. However, the essential point remains constant even within a dialectic of absence—which is, that the deconstruction of the positioning of being requires it to be figured in terms of a fundamental questioning of the issues of presence as they have been privileged. Extending this to issues of absence, or even of combinational systems, is not simply to invert either the critical model—of deconstruction, metaphysics, ontology, etc.—or the focus of attention—from privileged presences to privileged absences. The concern here is not to replace the centrality of presence with absence, to unscrew presences to insert absences, for this would contain the same order of difficulties that post-structuralist theories have worked to expose. Absence is not the inverted transcendental signifier of presence—even primary absences cannot be seen in this way. Absence has the one clear advantage over all other signifiers in this sense, for by its very nature it cannot be erected as originary, transcendental, uniform.

It is clear that from the manner in which Derrida utilises the concepts of *ousia* and *parousia* (often synchronously as critical/analytic terms and as points of analysis) that he sees their critical construction as powerful signifying practices. He describes the system in which they have developed as the "ontology of presence" (Derrida 1986: 21), which is not part of a philosophical methodology, but rather a qualifying aspect, a synecdochic paradigm of subjectivity. This sense is demonstrated in a number of ways in Derrida's texts, but two are of central concern here. These are the definitional sense of presence in the metaphysics of subjectivity, and the connection between this and the operation and construction of language. The conjunction of these two is central to the idea of the speaking/enunciating subject.

The first sense of *ousia* and its contingent reformulation, *parousia*, covers the broad metaphysics of subjectivity as it is determined in presence. Derrida concentrates much of the time on Heidegger's use of *ousia* and *parousia* as definitional properties of subjectivity, which means not simply the status of being (and Beingness) but also the way in which meaning itself has been constructed from this ontological positioning, which now also becomes a signifying position. This is the issue of time as a principle process in "the determination of the meaning of Being in the history of philosophy" (Derrida 1986: 31). It needs to be remembered at this point that Heidegger's use of *ousia* is measured against the sense of *substantia*, and that it denotes a double sense of presence—substantiality and substance. Derrida attempts to "confirm" the force of *ousia* and *parousia* by compressing them within the Heideggerian sense of presence: "This chain of interdependent concepts (*ousia, parousia, Anwesenheit, Gegenwart, gegenwärtigen, Vorhandenheit*) . . ." (Derrida 1986: 32). This is a chain of privileging the present (*Gegenwart*), of maintaining presence (*reinen Gegenwärtigens*), of being present and having presence at hand

(*Vorhandenheit*)—"that is, they are conceived as presence" in that "entire differentiated *system*" of Heideggerian language (Derrida 1986: 32-33). This becomes a "will to *parousia*" (Derrida 1986: 88)—a will which connects to two essential formulations of speculative dialectics—negativity and *Aufhebung*. The will to *parousia* is the subject of desire, in absence, when the absentness quality of that desire is turned towards a configuration of subjectivity as determined and qualified in presence. Similarly, it is possible to read the fear of the loss of this will to presence as producing one particular manifestation of the subject of abjection. This centrality of presence for subjectivity—in desire, in fear of its loss, in the politics of gaining it, and the articulation of it in discursive practices—is ideologically determined and sustained. What is not so readily accommodated, but is nonetheless equally possible, is the idea of absence as a desirable determinant of a subject position.

From the critique of Heidegger, and in particular the centrality of temporality (recalling that the present carries with it the dual sense of presence and a specification of duration in time) to the determination of meaning in Being, presence has become an almost universal and apodictic concept in Western philosophical thought: "From Parmenides to Husserl, the privilege of the present has never been put into question. It could not have been. It is what is self-evident itself, and no thought seems possible outside its element. Nonpresence is always thought in the form of presence (it would suffice to say simply in the form) or as a modalization of presence. The past and the future are always determined as past presents or as future presents"(Derrida 1986: 34). What this line argues is that even if it were possible to separate the concept of presence from subjectivity in Western thought, one would still be left with a critical imperative which has ordered the essential features and devised the frames of reference for thousands of years. In the tradition of Western thought absence itself cannot exist, but can only be measured against orders of presence, it can only ever be a modalization of presence. The two counters to this frame argued here are primary absences and, as will be discussed later, a semiotics of absence. In order for such a semiotics of absence to be a viable critical concern, absence itself must be seen outside of this modalization process.

As has already been indicated, *ousia* is not merely *a* factor of a metaphysics of presence and subjectivity, but it is *the* determining factor. In phenomenological terms it supplies a sense of eidetic operation to the conceptual practices. As Derrida puts it: "To participate in beingness, in *ousia*, therefore is to participate in being-present, in the presence of the present, or, if you will, in presentness. Beings are what is. *Ousia* therefore is thought on the basis of *esti*" (Derrida 1986: 40). What is also so significant about this is the sense of participation—*ousia* is argued in terms of a dynamic process of subjectivity and, often, as self-reflexive and self-conscious. It shares certain critical features (especially in terms of a hermeneutics of subjectivity and ontology) with the subject of the Symbolic and the process of the mirror phase. This is true of the reflexive qualities involved as well as the positioning of the subject positions as desired presences, and the sense of lacks and absences in the subject of the Imaginary and Real.

Seine temporale Bestimmtheit dictates a particular relational context of Being to time and this confluence of presence, the present, and participation. It is a definitional frame which links—in fact critically binds—subjectivity to presence and temporality. Such a frame determines subjectivity as a metaphysics of presence and, because of the inextricable ties developed, time has come to be seen as a form of presence, and of a determining presence. In effect time represents a formal feature of *ousia* as a category. However, the presentness of time is indicated by time as absence. This is not a binarism of presence and absence, however, and the reason why it can be read in these terms lies in what Derrida calls the composite nature of time. Composite time, like a sense of composite subjectivity, sustains the oppositional forces within a unitary framing paradigm. Compositional framing does not completely dissolve the issue and implications of binarism, but it does suggest one possible alternative. What is needed so that absence may take precedence over presence, to be thought outside of presence, is that the compositional frame of absence and presence originate from absence rather than presence. In this way absence can be seen as holding all variations of presence, rather than the reverse. However, not all issues of absence and the relational context of presence can be resolved simply through a sense of compositional framing.

The (largely) Heideggerian reading of subjectivity in terms of temporality and presence (in particular the double plays, the duplicity, of presentness) as *ousia* is an important feature in the metaphysics of presence. Further aspects which need to be indicated here are the development of a particular type of presence in subjectivity (self-presence) and the relationship between the subject, presence, and the signifier. Both of these operations are part of what has been seen as the subject of desire and the subject of abjection. In other words, the operation of absence is fundamental to any interpretative system of subjectivity, presence, and/or the nature of the sign.

The political and critical investment of presence in the determination of subjectivity, as process, as praxis, as interpretive model, with its long and sustained history, has become a feature in a great many discursive practices, and almost certainly in the privileged ones. The concept of discourse itself operates precisely in terms of this political investment of the subject determined through presence, as presence and in presence. Similarly, one of the central features of the enunciating subject is how this subject type is based on the presence of the self within a set of discursive practices. This presence is complicated in its materiality because of the necessary combination of the conceptual features of being as presentness (*Anwesenheit*) and the temporality of that beingness in the present (*Gegenwart*). The subject, represented in its presentness by the articulation of the sign, will shift according to the temporality of the utterance (for example, speaking as distinct from having spoken, or even the use of recorded speech). This is an interplay between combinational features of presence and the present, and absence and the past. It must also take into account the non-present, which is not necessarily absent as it is held in readiness—the *Vorhandenheit*. The enunciating subject in these terms becomes organised around a subjectivity of presence, even though the very sense of the signifier is a configuration of absence. A number of recent (largely feminist) theorists have investigated the political absenting of certain groups of subject types within a patriarchal discourse, which is ultimately an issue of presence and absence as defining the status of the subject. Similarly, Foucault's orders of discourse and the hegemonic managing of language systems, such as madness, sexuality, the body, are dealing with the denial (absence and lack) or privileging of a site of presence or absence. Before all of this takes place, fundamental to the political—essentially Symbolic—orders of presence and absence of the subject is the initial ideality of the subject as construed in a subject position of presence and, perhaps consequentially, self-presence.

It is on this point of the investment of (political) presence as process for the determination of subjectivity that we find a rare convergence of ideas between Derrida and Lacan. This occurs largely through the conceptual framework of Freud. Derrida utilises Lacan's distinction between subject and Being to position the centrality of presence to the notion of Being: "Of course this is what "Freud tells us": "The purest relation," "presence," is in relation to a "Being" and it is felt all the more "vividly" in that this "Being" (this subject-being) is "less qualified", that is, obviously, more indeterminate. The presence of Being is all the more pure in that the ontic determination is less" (Derrida 1987a: 477). There are of course many tensions in this display of referentiality, parenthetic gestures, and resistance; however, the issue of the metaphysics of presence and its sociocultural and ideological power holds true. For this reason alone Lacan and Derrida can be described as principle figures in the deconstruction of the systems of presence determining subjectivity in its metaphysical hegemony. This is not to argue that, simply put, Lacan and Derrida undertake systematic and deliberate operations in such a deconstruction, but rather that a number of their critical formulations can be made sense of outside of the rigid paradigms of subjectivity as presence and presence as subjectivity. This is not even to argue that either Lacan or Derrida offer working alternatives, but they can be seen to be engaging in the very processes of this determination. The subject of desire is influenced and even motivated by a certain type of presence, but it is ultimately made sense of in terms of absence. *Fort/da* is the mediating step between a metaphysics of presence and the possibility of a deconstruction of it through a quasi-metaphysics of absence. Central to this is that presence and absence, and the figuring of subjectivity, can only ever be made sense of fully if signifying practices are taken into account.

The especially strong position that this metaphysics of presence occupies in Western philosophical thought is related to a large extent to the logocentric nature of the (philosophical) discourse. A particularly important issue in such an analysis is the connection between self-presence and *logos*. The Derridean notion of *logos* is based in part on Heidegger's use of it as discourse and yet, like so many of Derrida's texts, is also a departure from this use. The common ground with Heidegger is the collocating nature of *logos* in the operation of discourse. Kristeva's development of the enunciating subject and Lacan's idea of the subject's attempts to enter into, and in doing so gain control of, the Symbolic are pertinent here. *Logos*, read in terms of discourse, draws attention to itself and its operations. There is, of course, a significant difference between this Heideggerian sense and the ways in which both Foucault, in, for example, *The Order of Things*, and Kristeva in *Revolution in Poetic Language*, read the nature of discourse as part of a more ideologically overt schema.

Of particular concern here is the dynamic connection between *logos*, presence, and subjectivity. This is the "absolute *parousia*" which indicates "the presence to the self of the *logos* within its voice" (Derrida 1976: 89). We must be constantly aware that Derrida attempts to deconstruct what he sees as one of the absolute and fundamental issues of Western thought, particularly in this post-Cartesian sense. Derrida argues this in almost formulaic terms in his examination of certain works by Rousseau: "the history of metaphysics is the history of a determination of being as presence [and] its adventures merge with that of logocentrism" (Derrida 1976: 97). This relationship between the presence of being and the critical investment in and of language is not as clearly demarcated as first may appear. Part of the method involves a reading against certain fundamental ideas, isolating them and then positioning them in such a way that the sustaining argument itself is brought into question, or, at the very least, highlighted and revealed. Which is not, it must be added, a sense of arriving at truth through its unveiling.

The concept of logocentrism does not stem from an issue of linguistics, rather it is a question related to the issue of being, of *ousia* and *parousia* and, in particular, of the systemic interplay between the subject and writing. In a Hegelian sense, for example, the relationship between being (beingness as well as being itself) and language is part of the history of *Geist*. It is "the development of the concept as *logos* and the ontotheological unfolding of *parousia*" (Derrida 1986: 95) which contributes a determining factor in writing as presence for the subject. The Hegelian teleological interpretation of the *logos* and the subject compounds the logocentric nature of philosophical discourse and, ultimately, the metaphysics of presence. This same line of thought can be utilised to trace the political agenda of logocentrism as absenting process, and phallogocentrism as further specification of absenting processes.

This historical superstructure has meant that subjectivity has always been spoken of in terms of presence—the concept of subjectivity has come to be seen as part of the frame of actuality, truth and presence. Any notion of absence is used to denote a failed sense of presence (such as aphanisis, parapraxis, schizophrenic discourse, absurdism, the carnivalesque, rupture, disjunction), as part of political/ideological positioning (women absent from phallocentric discourse, ethnicity outside the ruling cultural perspective, the post-colonial agenda as negotiations of presence/acceptance and absence/denial, the interplay of speech and writing), or as a signification which is measured against the completeness of subjectivity—as ideality—of the self. The teleological positioning of *logos* in relation to the subject can occur precisely because of these two demarcations of absence. However, as was noted in the discussion of subjectivity and desire, the subject as presence is an unattainable ideal status. Complete, whole presence in subjectivity cannot exist, and this sets up the need for the construction of mediating systems to attempt to fill the discrepancies between the conceptual formations of subjectivity as presence and the subject who is constantly experiencing forms of absence.

Subjectivity has become a signifier of presence through *logos* (as discourse) and the concept of self-presence entailed in this. What happens to the conceptual basis of subjectivity (and subjectivity itself) based on a metaphysics of presence if the whole nature of that presence is brought into question? Can there be such a thing as a subjectivity of absence? Is there any sense of a subjectivity not based on presence that can be seen as positive rather than negative? To a certain extent Lacan's *manque-à-être* can be read as a form of a subjectivity of absence, although it is not necessarily positioned as a desirable subject position. However, what gives it a sense of desirability is the nature of desire and seduction and the attendant qualities of access, control, and the subject's interplay with the signifier. This is the powerful position of a subjectivity of absence based on the capacity to desire—to be able to want, rather than having these absences (desire, want, etc.) denied. Given the essential nature of absence in desire it becomes an attractive—perhaps even imperative—site of subjectivity to be able to have the absences of desire, to have the desire to desire, and so to formulate the paradigmatic registers of desire itself. To desire is to desire absence, and a subject position based on absence. Similarly, the mirror stage itself is based, at least in part, on the absent subject and the compulsions and obsessions for the Symbolic. Abjection can be read in terms of an absent subjectivity as distinct from an absence of subjectivity—although, once more, these examples are largely negative interpretations with some potential for positive interpretations. The desiring subject's relationship to absence is largely a positive one, mainly through the *jouissance* of absence. It is because of this that a semiotics of absence must address the act of reading in terms of subjectivity and absence. The concept of *différance* can be interpreted in terms of such a subject position.

Différance brings into question the quasi-apodictic nature of the metaphysics of presence: "it is the determination of Being as presence or as beingness that is interrogated by the thought of *différance*" (Derrida 1986: 21). Such an interrogative propensity operates because *différance* is inherently connected to absence. *Différance*, Derrida states, is not. This aspect of *différance* relies heavily on its meaningful sense and definitional frame including the idea of the trace: "one cannot think the trace—and therefore *différance*—on the basis of the present, or even of the presence of the present" (Derrida 1986: 21). Even if *différance* was to be pared down to difference the non-binarism of absence and presence is retained: "difference (is) itself other than absence and presence, (is) (itself) trace, it is indeed the trace of the trace that has disappeared in the forgetting of the difference between Being and beings" (Derrida 1986: 65-66). Not only the non-binarism but also the oppositional sense of an ontology of presence are negated. Clearly it is not just an issue of philosophical tradition for it also engenders a subjectivity of absence through the trace and *différance*. This necessarily includes the operation of *Aufhebung*.

Différance, the trace, *logos*, and writing all indicate the closeness to which the attempts to make the subject present (to have presence and to be present) through language, in all its guises, operates. An example of this has already been considered in terms of Freud's case study of Dora. Dora is made so totally absent throughout the account that when she does speak, that is, when her subjectivity is "presented" in "language" and not "re-presented", these moments are continually contextualised by Freud. These utterances reinforce the idea that a metaphysics of presence is devised through logocentrism. The sense of being as presence is produced through and in logocentrism. Dora represents a certain type of absent subjectivity, but not a particularly desirable one, particularly in terms of the idea of having the capacity to desire through absences. This is true even in the subsequent rereadings of her status as political subject. Depoliticised, speechless, marginalised—in short ordered through multiple political absences—she only regains any sense of subjectivity (and even then it is a secondary subjectivity) through the explications of others at another set of critical crossroads. This is a process similar to what Lévi-Strauss articulates in terms of the erasure of the subject through the name, and what Derrida attributes to the interplay of *différance* and difference and subjectivity. Derrida argues that this theory of the name is necessarily tied to issues of ontology.

Another possible model for the figuring of absence and subjectivity is the subject as hole or gap. Freud's *construction* of Dora and Lévi-Strauss' *construction* of the Nambikwara are primarily subjects that are made absent through erasure, but the subject as hole can be seen as conceptually approaching the Lacanian sense of absent subjectivity. The subject as hole, read as a combination of the desiring subject and the logocentric subject, is the subject located in the signifier as the *lettre en souffrance*. Failure to deliver means that the letter is absent from its intended reception—in effect this becomes a binarism of absence/failure and presence/delivery. However the *lettre en souffrance* is not destroyed, rather it is positioned within a particular type of *epoché*. It is placed in a paradigm which distinguishes it from the binarism of either/or and so what is designated as the meaningful point of reception and reading proves to be only a single point, even if it is the point of the dominant hermeneutic paradigm. Once this occurs—once the subject becomes the *lettre en souffrance*—there is a *meaningful* hole: "This is not a subject, but a hole, the lack on the basis of which the subject is constituted", this is the "truth of Being as non-being" (Derrida 1987a: 437; 439). Derrida's critique of Lacan leads him back to the logocentric nature of subjectivity and the domination of presence in Western thought. However, Derrida's argument rests on a reading of subjectivity as represented by the letter—the *propre lettre* as it may well be called. Greater consideration needs to be paid to the desiring subject and the interplay of absence and desire in the formation of subjectivity, not as an ideal but as a conceptual and operational frame of reference.

A third alternative for absent subjectivity as a positive or desirable status is the divided subject position. Absence in this sense rests in the divisional sectors of the subject. The *Ichspaltung*, especially in terms of the $\cancel{S}$ < > D, is the fragmented subject *par excellence*. Fragmentation such as this indicates a further issue—the doubling of the subject as a form of fragmentation. The doubling of the subject, the *Dopplegänger*, or, perhaps more correctly, the conceptual *Unheimlichkeit* if we are to speak in terms of parergonal abjection and/or desire, returns us to the idea of the self-reflexive nature of the subject.

There are two main difficulties in reading fragmentation or doubling (that is, variations of the *Ichspaltung* and *Unheimlich*) as indicators of a subjectivity of absence. Firstly, they both rely on a sense of presence to begin with. The fractured or doubled subject is so only within a relational context of wholeness and/or singularity. Secondly, and this is related to this sense of the originary position, the *Ichspaltung* and *Unheimlich* are seen as problematical qualities of subjectivity and as such will always be read in a comparative way, against an ontological order of subjective presence. What is suggested by positing these possible subject types of absence is that the investment of presence in subjectivity should not be argued as obligatory or a methodological given, but as part of a particular and effective set of critical processes.

5

Desire and the Voice: Speaking Absences and the Absence of Speech

The speaking subject is determined by the dynamic relationships of the subject position/type to the sign and its articulation. The term *speaking subject* designates a particular type of determination through this relationship between the subject, the formation of subjectivity, including the processes of this formation, and a set of signifying practices. All variations—the accepted and the aberrant—of the engagements with the semiotic systems by the subject are part of this order, although such contextualisation will determine a paradigmatic range of reflexive model(s). The central concern here is how this relational context is based on, and can be understood through, absence.

The significant aspect, in terms of establishing or recognising the frame of reference which defines the speaking subject, is that a particular and distinct relationship exists between the subject position/type and the operation of the sign. The essential feature of Kristeva's reading of the enunciating subject or Lacan's subject of the Symbolic is that the subject reads and is read by the sign in the articulation to (an)other. This becomes particularly evident in the politicisation of speech and its related subject position—which does not necessarily mean access to the dominant signifying practice(s), but rather access to a signifying practice. What all of these share, however, is the common feature of directing and defining the position of speech and the intention to be heard. To be heard is the qualification of subjectivity in the formulation of both primary and secondary absences.

A significant aspect of the operational processes of the speaking subject (and so ultimately the basis of that subject type itself) is the self-reflexive relationship of subject to sign, and the recognition of this in others: "the subject (in its identity with itself, or eventually in its consciousness of its identity with itself, its self-consciousness) is inscribed in language, is a "function" of language, becomes a speaking subject only by making its speech conform—even

in so-called "creation", or in so-called "transgression"—to the system of the
rules of language as a system of differences, or at very least by conforming to
the general law of *différance*, or by adhering to the principle of language"
(Derrida 1986: 15). Prior to creation or transgression, even prior to language
itself, there is self-consciousness (a self-reflexivity of the sense of subjectivity)
in the subject. It is at the point of this development of self-reflexivity that the
subject engages in the perils of the sign. This would seem to parallel the
pre-Symbolic subject's passage through the mirror stage. Indeed, the two
theories share a number of comparable features, and yet there are also
significant differences. An examination of how the self-conscious and
self-reflexive speaking subject of *différance* differs from the reflexive—and
ultimately frustrated—subject in the mirror stage, reveals certain issues
regarding the relational context of absence.

Reflexivity and the Subject's Relationship to the Sign

The subject's relationship to language as a determining factor of subjectivity
and desire has been interpreted largely through the qualification of reflection.
There is a sense of *mise-en-abyme* in the philosophical, psychoanalytic, and
textual processes here. Speculation is the critical examination of reflection, the
"philosophical concept of language" (Gasché 1986: 45). As methodology,
speculation enables "the overcoming of the major antinomy of reflection, that
between the empirical, formal, or transcendental self-reflection of the subject
of cognition (the thinking being) and the reflected object of this epistemological
endeavour (what is thought)" (Gasché 1986: 45). The process within the process
is emphasised further through the speculation on speculation (speculative
reflection), hence the *abbau* and *destruktion* so essential to the deconstructive
enterprise and methodology. To understand the particular relationship of
speculation as methodology and the positioning of the subject in relation to
subjectivity and language as formulative processes of the speaking subject as
type on the one hand, and subjectivity/language and absence on the other, we
can compare a concept of the subject's relationship to language, which is
derived from different origins.

Lacan asserts that there is a heterogeneity of language (of the Symbolic, of
the unconscious/the Other) in terms of the subject. In critical concerns this has
become a form heterological functioning. This heterogeneous set of qualities is
based on the premise that subjectivity is determined, qualified, sustained by and
destroyed in the dynamics of the subject's relationship to language. Fundamental
to such a system is the protreptic adjunct of absence. Lacan's two extremes of
full and empty speech are indicators of just such a relational context. Full
speech is the self-reflexive realisation of subjectivity as determined by and
through language, while empty speech is the *loss* of not only this realisation but
also the subjective basis of determination. Empty speech is when "the subject

loses himself in the machinations of the system of language" (Lacan 1988a: 50). Full and empty speech are only the two extremes, and there are multiple formulations of the different modes in the processes of speech between these two poles.

Part of the difficulty with this idea of heterogeneity is to articulate a common ground, or even a unifying principle, for comparison, particularly within the context of primary and secondary absences. Full and empty speech, and the various degrees between them, yield comprehensively different subject positions in terms of language. The notion of full speech suggests a closer sense of self-reflexivity to the language system, but this position is always located in a Platonic idealism rather than any actual working model or manifestation. The same can be said of speculative investigations as they clearly operate outside of non-reflexive discursive practices—that is those utterances that are usually conceived as "everyday", the phatic and communicative rather than the poetic or even metalingual. Yet there are points in the everyday use of language where speculative discourse enters and the speech becomes reflexive either of itself or of the speaking subject or, as is more often the case, a combination of the two. This is an important aspect in the structure of the sign and how it operates in terms of the semiotics of absence.

This requires us to examine the correlation between Lacanian full speech and speculative discourse, particularly as a Derridean concept. Is full speech a form of speculative discourse—and does this mean that Lacanian psychoanalytic theory must be read, at least in part, within the terms of this philosophical system? And if full speech is seen as a form of speculative discourse then what is the particular relationship of this form of discourse to the determination of the subject position? Clearly these are issues which relate to specific points of reference as well as the larger order of critical investigation.

Full speech, Lacan argues, is "speech which performs (*qui fait acte*)" (Lacan 1988a: 107). As such it transforms both the language (speech, gaze, the body, articulations of desire) and the subject who utters it and who is uttered by it. Such a dichotomy is an essential feature of a theoretical paradigm which is constitutive of the speaking subject as type. This is not to imply that full speech is always speculative, rather that this quality is a particular and powerful manifestation filled with the potential of speculative heterology as both a critical sensibility and a point of subjectivity. It is this held-in-readiness quality that provides a substantive link between a typological configuration of discourse and the subjective position. It is important to note at this point that Lacan's primary concern is with "speech" as distinct from "language"; however, such a distinction is not implicit in speculative/absolute reflection. The fact that deliberations on Lacan's distinction occupy a central point in parts of Derrida's work provides a further link.

The heterogeneity of language, and its articulation in speech, means that the extremes of full and empty speech are never realised. Speech designated as imbued with fullness (or "fuller" if such a quantitative measure be allowed) is not necessarily speculative until it reaches a point where the communicative property is displaced by another function. Metalingual speech is a permutation of "full" speech, but only in the sense of highlighting the organisational code systems, in this sense a demonstration of aspects of extra-coding. Similarly, the poetic function is "full" speech not because it has a greater sense of "depth" or "complexity", but because it has a speculative quality that collocates the operation of the signifiers (in this example the linguistic units). However, speculation as a philosophical activity is "full" speech under a different typological system, where a convolution of analytic styles and content occurs. This is the transposition of speech onto the speculative heterology through the philosophemes of deconstructional critiques or the psychophemes of Lacanian analysis. In both cases what is eventually revealed is critical absences that constitute a function of speech, of the critique itself, of discursive practices.

Lacan distinguishes full speech from empty speech through *méconnaissance*; empty speech continually "fails to recognise" at a number of levels, thus making the intentionality of this failure an open-ended structure. In many ways *méconnaissance* of everyday speech is an essential feature of its operation, for the failure is an absenting and absentation of devices, constructions, and organisational principles, which then locate the speech—the sign—to be understood outside of the formal features of the code system. This is the speech competence which operates in an unconscious manner, unless it is collocated via one or a number of structures. Examples of this include the poetic (as *sémiotique*), humour/wit (especially in the number of ways it is analysed by Freud and, in a different way, Bakhtin's idea of the carnivalesque), and parapraxis. Within such a paradigmatic it is significant that in Lacanian terms the unconscious is always "spoken" by way of absences.

Thus it can be claimed that speculative discourse is a type of full speech. Part of the legitimation of such a typological ruling is that both speculation and full speech have the propensity of reflection. This type is based on the directing of the discursive practices towards the issues of reflection. This alignment allows us to consider how the subject of cognition and the reflected object of epistemological endeavour are dealt with in a particular fashion by Lacan. It can be argued that central to the Lacanian project is his extensive examination of desire, and the viability of this as an epistemological issue.

It would be incorrect to suggest that the concepts of full and empty speech are contiguous with the (deconstructionalist) analysis and utilisation of speculative discourse in the investigation of the relationship between subject and the signifier. However, Derrida's notion of the trace—the differences in and of the sign as meaning—should not be seen as a negation of full speech. The conceptual frame—its ideality—can continue even if the nature of the sign must necessarily be based on a deconstruction of the determination of meaning itself. There is enough left to continue the comparison, and there is considerable energy in this to continue the deconstruction of presence and the theorising of absence. Speculative reflection in full speech and the unhinging of the sign in the trace share a common feature in terms of the relational context of absence as a system of meaning.

Derrida's notion of the speaking subject may well have a number of comparable key aspects with other contemporary models of this subject position, for example Kristeva's reading of the enunciating subject. However, the speculative discourse that is so crucial to the conceptualisation of this particular type of subjectivity infiltrates all levels of analysis, and in doing so shifts the emphasis considerably. In negotiating a potential problem regarding the position of the speaking subject as ontological issue, Derrida argues that the definitional properties of the speaking subject have been located within a sense of *ousia*. This centrality of *hypokeimenon* and *ousia*, as analysed by Derrida, is derived largely from a number of the key texts of Husserl and Heidegger. Derrida is particularly concerned with deconstructing the central philosophical idea of presence as *hypokeimenon*, a strategic position from which he investigates the self-reflexive nature of subjectivity—that is "the subject as consciousness has never manifested itself except as self-presence" (Derrida 1986: 16). In *différance* Derrida puts some of the difficulties with this construction quite emphatically: "Just as the category of subject is not and never has been conceivable without reference to presence as *hypokeimenon* or *ousia*, etc., so the subject as consciousness has never been able to be evinced otherwise than as self-presence" (Derrida 1973: 147). It is part of Derrida's aim to challenge precisely this historical bind. This is why *différance* is the antagonistic opposite of presence—the productive external that disrupts any sense of settling a sign/signifying chain in terms of presence.

Heidegger, in "The End of Philosophy and the Task of Thinking", argues that *hypokeimenon* is linked to substance, that is a materiality of presence. It is significant that he employs the same term and conceptual (or certainly comparable) frame to speak of the transformation of objectness into the materiality of the subject in the essay "The Origin of the Work of Art". Heidegger points out that it is a far from innocent movement from the Greek to Roman-Latin which establishes this connection: "*Hypokeimenon* becomes *subiectum*; *hypostasis* becomes *substantia*" (Heidegger 1971: 18). This is part of the larger order of a metaphysics of presence, which has become so rigid that it is almost impossible to think of subjectivity outside of the determinants of presence. The emphasis of presence, as both definition and operation, in this determination of subjectivity and self-consciousness needs to be shifted to include the idea of the unconscious so that an alternative perspective becomes thinkable.

The unconscious always "speaks" through, and is spoken by, absence. With the idea of *ousia* and *hypokeimenon* there would seem to be a complementary set of readings by saying that consciousness is always spoken through presence. Such symmetry should make us uneasy, however. It is tempting to look for such inversions (particularly such symmetrical ones) so that the unconscious/absence and conscious/presence schema will accommodate each other. To a certain extent the model does hold true, and a whole series of points can be made utilising this. One example of this is how repression as an agent of absence operates precisely in these terms of unconscious/absence and conscious/presence. The difficulty with such an equation is when it gains a sense of rule-governing. What happens, for example, once an absence passes into, or is transformed into, a presence? What happens to its fundamental properties of definition? Once part of the unconscious ceases to be absent, or spoken of/through absence, does it then also cease to be part of the unconscious? If consciousness is not spoken of in terms of presence, but rather in terms of absence, does it cease to be consciousness? Is the non-self-conscious subject non-present, and does this mean it is necessarily an absence? Clearly, in terms of absence and presence, it is far too reductionist to see consciousness and unconsciousness as two sides of the same coin. Just as it is an error to see being and subjectivity simply as a matter of presence.

One alternative—and it is significant that this is specifically related to the concept of the speaking subject—is to apply the idea of *différance* to subjectivity. In *différance* the speaking subject engages in both the conscious and unconscious, presences and absences, because each one necessarily contains the other. This process can be seen as the operation of *Aufhebung* in *différance* as subjectivity, for in these we find both a questioning of the centrality of presence and the operation of a binarism of presence and absence in the constitutive processes of subjectivity: "In this way we question the authority of presence or its simple symmetrical contrary, absence or lack. We thus interrogate the limit that has always constrained us, that always constrains us—we who inhabit a language and a system of thought—to form the sense of being in general as presence or absence, in the categories of being or beingness (*ousia*)" (Derrida 1973: 139). Thus, presence can no longer be seen as an absolute of being and subjectivity, but rather as a (political) determinant. In these terms the speaking subject's relationship to language is based not on integration, but on difference and deferral. Difference entails absence because it suggests that the difference of the signifier is the absent, non-selected others. Similarly, deferral is constructed through the selection of the signifier and the deferring of others. *Différance* is a unifying point of syntagmatic and paradigmatic operations. The otherness of the sign in relation to the speaking subject is particularly evident in structures such as metaphor and metonymy. This idea of the speaking subject as *différance* is particularly relevant to the discursive practices of desire and the insertion and development of subjectivity. There is a triplefold of absences in this sense: the absences and lacks which constitute desire; the absences of *différance* (and the subtexts of difference and deferral); and the absences formulated as necessary to subjectivity. These folds and connections do continue—the absences of language, for example—and each permutation produces different configurations of absence, subjectivity, and desire. Before continuing with this line it is important to consider further the tradition of being/subjectivity as presence which Derrida goes to such lengths to deconstruct.

Derrida returns often to this idea of the powerful and pervasive metaphysics of being/subjectivity as presence. In these various returns he posits the connection between self-presence, presence and consciousness. Furthermore, in a considerable number of these returns Derrida parallels the "Being as presence" construction with the Western metaphysical tradition dominated by the idea of presence. Logocentrism is the forceful structure of presence which this tradition sees as articulating the subject and the whole idea of subjectivity, and so can be seen as part of the construction of the speaking subject as subject type within a larger order, for it indicates that the subject is bound to the representation of the self through language as presence. This concept must be read as radically different from Lacan's description of the subject's movement into the Symbolic, even if at first glance there seems to be a common ground. The subject's movement in the Symbolic is not the determination of the subject as presence in the field of logocentricism. The subject of desire may well desire the signifier, but it is still motivated and defined through absences. This also ties in with the self as presence to the self, which forms part of the speculative heterology of discourse.

The manifestation of subjectivity in terms of presence has so far been viewed on essentially two levels—the self as presence as presented through the consciousness of the self to the self, and the self as presence as manifested to others. This second aspect is linked to the idea of the speaking subject as social process. The speaking subject is a particular type of subject which, although not strictly tied to the exteriority of subjectivity, is often critically bound to it. The Lacanian idea of a language of the unconscious (and the unconscious as a language) is, in many ways, a concurrent system of a presence of subjectivity, although it is not necessarily based on external representations (that is, to the self or to others in the social praxis). Speech, then, forms one of the fundamental issues of the self as presence: "speech is *par excellence* that which confers existence, presence (*Dasein*) upon the interior representation, making the concept (the signified) exist" (Derrida 1986: 90). It is significant that Derrida chooses to specify the Heideggerian idea of subjectivity in this context. *Dasein*, with all its incumbent qualities (the idea of Unauthentic existence, which can stand for the sense of presence without the qualification of language), requires a particular notion of subjectivity as presence in which to operate. *Dasein* is a substantiating concept which can be seen as part of the "self as presence" typology. The ways in which speech (including the signifier and its articulations in all guises) is specified are being aligned here with the concept of *Dasein*.

Speech can be neither owned nor possessed by the subject, even though efforts are constantly made to do exactly this. This is one of the fundamental reasons why absence is such an essential concept in the understanding of subjectivity and discourse. The speaking subject possesses an estranged relationship to speech and orders of discourse—a critical idea which has been crucial to the contemporary definition and deconstruction of the subject position:

"This speech, which constitutes the subject of his truth, is, however, forever
forbidden to him, outside the rare moments of his existence when he attempts,
however confusedly, to grasp it in sworn faith, and forbidden in that the
intermediary discourse condemns him to misconstrue it. Nevertheless, it speaks
everywhere that it can be read in his Being, that is at all the levels it has
formed him. This antinomy is the very antinomy of the meaning that Freud
gave to the notion of the unconscious. But if this speech is nonetheless
accessible, it is because no true speech is only the subject's speech, since it is
always toward grounding it in the mediation of another subject that it operates"
(Derrida 1987a: 475). This is not as contradictory as it first appears. It is
important to remember that self as presence operates on the recognition of the
conscious mind. Self as presence to others—that is, the idea of subjectivity
formulated external to the self and therefore dependent on a set of (social)
processes—is a presence through mediating systems. One of the most important
of these systems is language and, in this particular instance of the speaking
subject, speech. We can refer equally to the gaze as language, and therefore the
centrality of the gaze to the determination of the subject. It is the problematical
bond of subjectivity as presence based on language, and the absented system of
this language system, that leads Lacan to deal so extensively with the
Ichspaltung and the tension of the drives. It is for this reason that subjectivity
may well be critically invested with a metaphysics of presence, but the essential
features of understanding it, determining it, and representing it lay in the
analysis of absences. To engage in this further we can compare Derrida's notion
of the estranged subject from speech to Lacan's treatment of *Vorstellungrepräsentanz*.

The very essence of *Vorstellungrepräsentanz* is embedded in *fort/da*, that
is in the tensions of absence and presence yielding the *Ichspaltung*, or as Lacan
puts it *Je me deux* (the rent subject) (Lacan 1987: 123). *Fort/da* itself is based
on alternating absences and presences in this construction of the split and
fragmented subject: "It is aimed at what, essentially, is not there, qua represented—for this is the game itself that is the *Repräsentanz* of the *Vorstellung*.
What will become of the *Vorstellung* when, once again, this *Repräsentanz* of the
mother—in her outline made up of brush-strokes and gouaches of desire—will
be lacking?" (Lacan 1986: 62-63). The structure of *fort/da* is coded within the
triple configuration of repetition (which in turn becomes the pleasure of repetition), representation of the self in the Symbolic, and alternating presence and
absence. This *fort/da* structure of *Vorstellungrepräsentanz* can be carried over
to the idea of the speaking subject who is both a part of language and apart
from language. Subjectivity—which is both a subject position and type—is
invested in discursive practices (it is in both these practices and constitutes
them), but the subject is continually reminded of the estrangement of the subject
to subjectivity. This is why subjectivity is based as much on absence as it is on
presence—the self strives for the representation of the self to itself and to
others, but is constantly located outside of the desired presence in a mediating

and frustrated system of presence and absence. The subject is always under erasure, located as *brisure*. This is precisely why desire continues to operate with the very same sense of the *fort/da* of subjectivity and language systems. This is the most Oedipal of notions—but Oedipus read from a different perspective. For Derrida sees Oedipus's destruction of the Sphinx as clarification of the position of the subject in terms of the object and writing: "With the answer to the riddle, Oedipus's words, the discourse of unconsciousness, man destroys, dissipates, or tumbles the petroglyph" (Derrida 1986: 99). This is also why language must be read as neither subject nor object, absence nor presence, determinant nor determined—but as all of these things at once.

Silence, Absence, and Presence

The idea of absence indicating an absented subject position, and the political implications of this—the repression of speech, the denial to discourse, the speech of the mad—became one of the central issues in post-structuralist theories. Before dealing in more detail with this political agenda it is necessary to consider how such a conceptualising of silence can be included in the idea of the speaking subject as type, particularly in this reassessment of presence and absence. To begin with we can return to Derrida's evaluation of logocentrism.

Derrida argues that one of the dominant Western philosophical systems has been the privileging of the spoken over the written. The examination of this system is one of the fundamental aims of grammatology. For this critical *method*, as an activity, sets up an antithetical paradigm of absence which ultimately must question the systemic presences of fundamental ontotheological and metaphysical issues. Central to this questioning is the analytic sense of logocentrism. The difficulty in this idea and process is that so much of the grammatological activity is directed towards the types of issues that these very infrastructures have devised, and so risks becoming part of the structure that is being examined.

The conceptual frame of logocentrism, specifically in terms of discursive practices, is based on the assumption that the written word is seen as subordinate to, and is subordinated by, the spoken word. From this Derrida connects logocentrism to the metaphysics of presence: "logocentrism would thus support the determination of the being of the entity as presence" (Derrida 1976: 12). This suggests a double register of absence: an absence based on the negation of subjectivity through silence; and an absence based on the negation of discourse through the privileging of one set of signifiers, and codes, over another. Both of these absences rely on a sense of preferential presences to exclude, and in doing so produce absences. This can occur through the desire to produce specific presences and consequential absences, or the desire to produce specific absences and consequential presences. In the first action the primary motivation will be on the types of presences, while in the second it will be based on the types of absences.

Both of these absences rely on a sense of preferential presences to exclude, and so produce an absence. Derrida demonstrates both these absences in *Le Facteur de la Vérité*: "First of all, what is at issue is an emphasis . . . on the authentic excellence of the spoken, of speech, and of the word: of *logos* as *phonè*. This emphasis must be explained, and its necessary link to the theory of the signifier, the letter and the truth must be accounted for. . . . For even when he [Lacan] repeats Freud on rebuses, hieroglyphics, engravings, etc., in the last analysis his recourse is always to a writing spiritualized (*relevé*) by the voice" (Derrida 1987: 462-63). Part of what Derrida is attempting to establish in this analysis is the logocentric positioning of the voice in terms of subjectivity. There can be no denying that speech is of central significance to Lacan, who clearly argues that the analysis of speech, in its operation in the determination of the subject, is a methodological necessity to psychoanalysis. However, this centrality of speech should not be construed as part of the logocentric tradition—certainly not in any sociopolitical homogeneity. Lacan specifically argues against the *logos* as a, or even the, definitional quality of subjectivity, instead seeing the unresolvable issues of doubt and certainty, what is represented and what is "missing", as far more significant. Derrida misrepresents Lacan's conceptualisation of speech, placing the centrality of speech in the psychoanalytic/semiotic model into a definitional frame directed towards subjectivity, which is not necessarily there. A significant part of Derrida's argument is based on devising a particular aspect of logocentrism—that is, that a subject position based on speech does not fully accommodate the written word, so silencing the letter, writing, and text. This grammatological line is orientated towards the investigation of the metaphysics of presence, which is seen to contribute substantially to the development of logocentrism. But Lacan also critiques this same tradition which posits the centrality of presence in the determination of being. The difficulty develops when this idea is read against Lacan's methodology as distinct from an actual definition of subjectivity and the subject position as it is constituted in the modes of production.

One of the main points Derrida makes in his examination of logocentrism, and in particular his positioning of Lacanian theory, is the emphasis of the relationship between speech and presence. Derrida takes up this same issue at various points throughout his works, a notable example being "The Supplement of the Copula", which is a critique of the connection between language, thought, and Being. At a number of points Derrida compares Benveniste's ideas to their Aristotelian roots. Of particular relevance to this study is the relationship between thought and language systems as part of that tradition dealing with language and presence. There is a tradition of thought which sees language not simply as speech, for it emerges from a site that ultimately determines Being, which is the central importance of the function of simultaneity. Furthermore, this indicates that Derrida's actual position does share more with the Lacanian notion of speech and subjectivity than what is initially indicated in *Le Facteur de la Vérité*. It is not simply the juxtapositioning of being, speech, and presence, but a complex interplay between these three and absence, yet an interplay nonetheless. This is not to argue that Derrida is simply accepting the Aristotelian position; rather, the sense of the dynamic is being acknowledged.

The language/thought couple as the site of Being parallels the idea of the mirror stage as process and the *Je me deux* of the Symbolic order. Furthermore, the *legetai* of Being is further demonstration of why desire must be positioned in terms of absence, why it is so difficult to articulate and why it becomes a crucial issue for subjectivity. It could be argued that Derrida is not, in fact, supporting this system, but deconstructing it, and so any alignment with the Lacanian fragmented subject in the Symbolic cannot take place. This in turn would mean that Lacan's ideas must instead be placed within this very schema that Derrida speaks of, with all its Aristotelian roots. This, however, is not strictly speaking the case. Derrida is neither dismissing the connections outright or accepting all of them totally. He is certainly not accepting the centrality of presence—but then nor does Lacan. The issue at stake is subjectivity in the matrix of thought and language. By positing absence as primary to this a connection between what Lacan does and what Derrida wants to do can be made. Desire to "speak" Being creates a sense of frustration in the self which, ultimately, becomes a definitional point of subjectivity itself. There is not a single articulation of Being, but of particular concern here is the relationship between language and thought as processes of Being. Cassirer points out that "the unity of *physis* and *logos* appears in Aristotle's system not accidentally, but necessarily" (Derrida 1986: 188). For Derrida the crux of this is not that there is a relational context of language, thought, and Being, but rather what are the implications and qualities of that context. This incorporates the idea of the transcendental value of Being and/in language. This transcendental value leads back to the idea of silence.

Up to this point silence has been positioned as an absence indicating at the very least a deficit in subjectivity as read by others/the Other, and in the social praxis. Silence, then, can represent in varying degrees and combinations: negated subjectivity to others (silence as politic); negated subjectivity to the self (silence as negation of the self to the self); a constructed absence of language or the denial of language; language determined exogenetic to the subject (and in this externality exists absence), etc. The transcendental is transcategorical (Derrida 1986), which is also the very status of "to be". The transcategoriality of "to be", that which allows it to be both within the categories of language and thought and also beyond them, is a quality shared by silence as absence. Such a qualification is significant because silence—the absence of subjectivity through the denial of speech, which is a definitional aspect of presence of being/Being—is not an absence of the transcategorial signifier "to be" but the denial, negation, suppression, etc., of a politically and/or ideologically orientated ontology. To be condemned to silence is not simply to be denied access to language, but also to have subjectivity—Being—itself threatened, denied, suppressed. The re-reading of Freud's case study of Dora indicates the various ways such an absence has been constructed. Her silence has been read variously as a symbol of repression, revolution, dependence and independence, passivity and activity. A great many of these readings (Freud's included) are based either implicitly or explicitly on questions of subjectivity and language as they operate as presence and absence.

Subjectivity asserted and/or confirmed through speech, and by implication language, carries with it a further consequence which is also connected to the overall issue of the speaking subject and absence. The idea of the voice implies the imposition of the body within the signifying process. The voice is the presenting of the body as subject in a particular metonymic arrangement. This is also part of the process of the body as desiring system. The exteriority of the body as subjectivity is directly tied to the voice. As such it forms part of the articulation of the "internal" (self-reflexive) processes: "writing of the soul and the body, writing of the interior and exterior, writing of the conscience and of the passions, as there is a voice of the soul and a voice of the body. "Conscience is the voice of the soul, and the passions are the voice of the body" (Derrida 1976: 18). The relationships of the voice of the body and the voice of the soul contain a number of important concepts relevant to the theorising of absence. It is worth comparing some ideas of internal and external positionings of the body and soul (within the deconstruction of the metaphysics of presence) to a similar analysis by Foucault, particularly in terms of absence. This will also allow further discussion of the representation and theorising of the body as structure of desire and absence.

From the Speaking Subject to the Inscribed Body

It is clear that the subject who "speaks"—that is, the exclaiming and claiming of subjectivity to others and to the self—has largely been seen as an operation of presence. Silence as the antithetical absence of this position is only one possible interpretation however. Silence can be seen as an alternative subject position which is demarcated by a different set of absences, just as the speaking subject necessarily contains a set of absences within itself. The speaking subject is an insistence of presence through the voice. The silent subject can be equally insistent, but through a different set of signifying practices. For such a definition (and distinction) to operate it is necessary to see how the site of the voice and the site of silence operate in terms of desire.

The insistence of the voice, either through speech or silence, is based not on the articulating subject, as first may appear to be the case, but within a site of discourse. Foucault's sense of discursive practices illustrates just such a site: "Discursive practices [are] . . . a body of anonymous, historical rules, always determined in the time and space that have defined a given period, and for a given social, economic, geographical, or linguistic area, the conditions of operation of the enunciative function" (Foucault 1986: 117). Silence and speech as discursive practices indicate that silence is not the absence of the voice or noise, etc., but the inability to be heard. This is a subtle but essential distinction—Derrida links the effacement of the signifier in the voice with the determination and formulation of truth and the very history of truth. If the speaking subject's presence and if, within the definitional paradigm, subjectivity is indicated through the voice, the question then arises as to how the silent subject is indicated. The answer is through a set of signifiers articulated in a system which is not heard within a certain paradigmatic and syntagmatic register. Such a reading shifts the property of absence—the silent subject is absent because the voice, the system of articulation, is not heard and not necessarily because the voice itself is absent. Similarly, Lacan picks up on the difference between making oneself heard and making oneself seen: "In the field of the unconscious the ears are the only orifice that cannot be closed. Whereas making oneself seen is indicated by an arrow that really comes back towards the subject, making oneself heard goes towards the other" (Lacan 1986: 195). This distinction is important in terms of the presence and absence of the self to the self/for the self and to others/for others.

With this notion of the definitional context of absence it becomes necessary to further clarify what is meant by voice here. Discursive practices are the clarifying frames which establish within the sociocultural and spatio-temporal (including the synchronic and diachronic) paradigms what is understood and, even more importantly for the issue at hand, what is heard—the *J'ouis/Jouissance* configuration. As such they carry with them the full hegemonic potentiality and ideological mechanisms normally ascribed to politicised language structures. Voice is one of the principle operating systems of discursive practices, largely because it has this connection with the determination of subjectivity and politicised subjectivity. Althusser's investigations into the subject and ideology have obvious connections here.

Because of the complex interplay between presence and absence and the fundamental role that Voice plays, it is important to recognise that Voice does not simply indicate a presence of subjectivity through articulation. "Voice" is used here to designate a particular (ideological) state of presence, and this presence is specified as such through its recognition via discursive practices. Being heard is, of course, distinct from being understood—and such a distinction yields a multiple set of absences. These absences are important to the overall constitution of the speaking/enunciating subject.

The interplay of presences and absences which formulate Voice and the speaking subject as presence can be represented using a concept from Heidegger and Husserl and developed, and digressed from, by Derrida. This is the concept, or critical action, of erasure or *sous rature*. Heidegger notes that his crossing over of ~~Sein~~ is not a negation of Being—rather it is quite the opposite. The crossed lines operate as indicators of ~~Sein~~ as a focal point of existence, here transposed to read as subjectivity within the qualifying sense of presence.

We can replace ~~Sein~~ with ~~Voice~~ to observe the interplay of absence and the speaking subject in terms of a subjectivity of presence.

Within a metaphysics of presence the desired subject position is formulated within a sense of the ~~Voice~~, that is, within a particular set of discursive

I

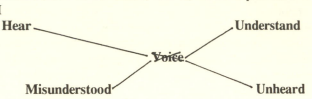

Hear — **Understand**

~~**Voice**~~

Misunderstood **Unheard**

II

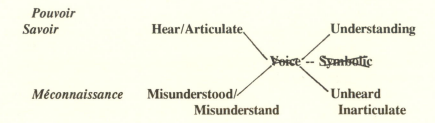

Pouvoir
Savoir   **Hear/Articulate** **Understanding**

~~**Voice**~~ -- ~~**Symbolic**~~

Méconnaissance   **Misunderstood/** **Unheard**
                   Misunderstand **Inarticulate**

practices. Some of the points of this model need to be clarified within this context. The insisting ~~Voice~~ is crossed over/out (*sous rature*) as in the Heideggerian ~~Sein~~, which indicates a complex site of interaction(s) of subjectivity. It also indicates the potential for exclusion from that site—in this sense comparable to the *Ichspaltung* and the splitting and barring functions. ~~Voice~~ is as much an ideological process as it is the individual's articulation. The crossed lines include and exclude because they indicate a point of intersection and a crossing out. As such they allow a reading in terms of absence and presence, which is comparable to the way in which Lacan positions the subject in terms of the Symbolic. If we were to transpose the Symbolic onto the position of ~~Voice~~ in the diagram (cf. part 2), the principle difference would be that the exclusion is emphasised through the mechanisms of desire. The Symbolic and Voice are desired sites, and become even more so when determined as essential features of subjectivity.

Strictly speaking ~~Voice~~ as discursive practice is not the same as the Symbolic. However, the two share a number of common features, especially within this context, which allows them to be positioned in a sense of equivalence. Of particular note in this equivalence is the shared quality of exclusion—*sous rature*—and the complex process of establishing a desire for the excluded site. The four axes of diagram 1 indicate notional features of the crossing over. It is significant that an opposition is set up in terms of active and passive processes—the upper stratum is an active process (to hear and to understand), whilst the lower stratum is passive (misunderstood as opposed to misunderstand, and unheard as opposed to not hear). The upper stratum can be seen to contain Lacan's interpretations of *pouvoir* and *savoir*, and hence the phallic sense of presence—it is tied to the *Bedeutung* of the Phallic order. With the convolution of the Symbolic with ~~Voice~~ the three strata become *pouvoir/savoir*; ~~Voice~~/Symbolic; and *méconnaissance* (diagram 2). The excluding and including lines of *sous rature*, connecting and disconnecting what are ultimately not binary opposites but points necessary to each other, can be usurped. This can only happen in a limited fashion within the epistemic operations of the systems of signification. Cixous's (1986) concept of *voler*—to fly and to steal the voice is one such possible action of usurping the order. *Voler* will always attempt to disengage the *Sein*/Voice lines, and in doing so operate to disrupt the strata themselves.

There is a real temptation to read both these schemata as being devised of an upper stratum of presences and a lower stratum of absences. However, this is not always the case. Within certain contexts of absence such a reading does operate and offers a number of significant insights. But, there are other absences in operation here that are not based solely on this idea. Crucial to one such absence is that of desire. It has already been noted that within certain discursive practices of subjectivity ~~Voice~~ is figured as a desired presence—it carries with it a sense of a surety of presence and an external confirmation of being/Beingness. This suggests that subjectivity is constantly positioned in terms of, and operates as, an absence—it is a site to be filled rather than already existing as occupied. This goes some way in explaining the polymorphic and heterogeneous nature of both desire and subjectivity. This is also why Foucault's notion of discursive practices must be seen in both synchronic and diachronic perspectives. Discursive practices may well interact but they are also dynamic and socio-temporally fixed and undone, created and destroyed. Within such typological frames both subjectivity and desire are orders of discourse.

The overriding absence of the ~~Voice~~/Symbolic conjunction is exclusion. Because desire operates within a similar sense of exclusion what develops is a sense of desire for a certain position, and the larger order of desire itself. This duality is supported by the idea that desire must always operate in terms of a lack, that is, an absence. Desire cannot be achieved, only engaged in and postponed. In these terms ~~Voice~~ is an *objet petit a*, and must always be retained as an absence. There can be no subject to occupy the upper stratum, to hear and understand, no *sujet supposé savoir*—to make sense of the nature of signification itself, for it is a site of heterogeneous absences which operate in a declaratory frame of presences.

Voice is one of the key discursive practices through which the body is inscribed as a (possible) presence within the desired site of subjectivity. As such it can be seen as part of the attempt to fill or occupy this site. ~~Voice~~ is part of the presenting of the body within this site, and so is comparable to the abjection of the *corps propre*—voiceness and the abject foreground the body in the

determination of subjectivity. Because of the dynamic, heterogeneous nature of
this site, all attempts to fill/occupy it will meet with only limited success, and
this holds true of ~~Voice~~ as well. The double absences of the site itself and the
subject position of absence provide a considerable amount of the impetus for
these attempts to occupy the site—and impetus which is comparable to desire
and the lack, and, more specifically, the *manque-à-être*. In this sense it is like
Derrida's reading of the Saussurean sign—sound is "what is heard, not the
sound heard but the being-heard of the sound" (Derrida 1976: 63). Bakhtin
argues that the status of being heard is a dialogic relation: "The word wants to
be heard, understood, responded to, and again respond to the response, and so
forth *ad infinitum*"; and earlier: "This follows from the nature of the word,
which always wants to be *heard*, always seeks responsive understanding, and
does not stop at *immediate* understanding but presses on further and further
(indefinitely). . . . For the word (and, consequently, for a human being) there
is nothing more terrible than a *lack of response*" (Bakhtin 1987: 127). This is
the desire from the ~~Voice~~/Symbolic *objet petit a*, as distinct from the desires for
this site and its manifestations. The "third party" in Bakhtin's dialogic system
then becomes of the same legitimising order as Freud's absent listener in the
telling of the joke.

A further, but connected, sense of ~~Voice~~ and the body is the voice as
metonymy of the body. To understand how this operates it is necessary to
consider the body as it is inscribed by ~~Voice~~. It should be noted that it is
beyond the direct concerns here to engage in the extensive ontotheological
relationships between the body and soul. The non-binarism of this relationship
and the subsequent issues of the representation, and manifestation of the body
under such a rubric, have become one of the major issues in philosophical,
textual, and sociocultural theories. The examination here will be limited to a
specific sense of the body and absence, and how the voice is positioned as
metonym, particularly in terms of its synecdochic functions. Note will also be
made of the reversal of this arrangement and how the body is sometimes seen
as metonymic of ~~Voice~~. For sake of clarity ~~Voice~~ refers to the development of
specific types of discursive practices related to this issue, and *sonare* will be
used to refer to the manifestation of Voice through the body. *Sonare* is part of
the inscription of the body through the site of discursive practices.

Sonare and ~~Voice~~ are part of the presenting body as subject. The *sous
rature* of ~~Self~~-~~Voice~~ forms a basis of the genotext of the body as subject,
operating as absence to the presenting body in much the same way as the
Ichspaltung lies against the Symbolic, and the Kristevian Speaking/Enunciating
subject lies against discourse through the *sémiotique* and Symbolic. Both *sonare*
and ~~Voice~~ are reactions against the absence (threatened and actual) of
exclusion—even though both can be seen as part of this very absenting system.
As such they can be measured against what Foucault has termed the archaeology of silence.

This archaeology is based on absence through exclusion and silence read as a form of absence. The exclusion specified by Foucault is madness, and the silence is the utterance of the mad. A central point for Foucault is this idea that madness is defined as an absence, and hence is why the silence of madness is also in turn read as an absence. This does not exclude the reading of silence (and therefore madness) as a presence, as has been noted above, rather it indicates that the archaeology of silence operates on a different register to other archaeologies. This distinction is crucial to how silence can be read within the discursive practices and not simply ignored. For an archaeology of silence, like an archaeology of absence, is crucial to the existence, understanding, and operation of all other systems of discourse that are figured as present, presenting, and (re)presenting.

Sonare and Voice often operate within a context of attempts to avoid the silence which incorporates the subject's condemnation to an absence of self and subjectivity. This silence is ideologically determined, often hegemonic and restrictive. The *sonare* as phenotext is the production of noise (both meaningful and meaningless), and Voice as genotext is the "translation" of that noise into presence. However, within the archaeology of silence, *sonare* and Voice do operate, but both the genotext and phenotext are radically different from the translatory process and the articulation which is heard. It is for this reason that the silence is read as an absence. The "madness" of a dream condemned it to silence until Freud devised a different genotext system for its interpretation. The absence of silence stems from it being a closed system, and it remains as such until it is positioned within a different genotext.

The discussion so far has implicated both Voice and *sonare* as manifestations of the body. This metonymic process is essential to the understanding of the speaking subject as presence and absence. It is not the only manifestation, but it does occupy an important position in the determination of the subject and subjectivity through enunciation. It would be incorrect to align the speaking/enunciating subject solely with Voice and *sonare*. The obvious, almost denotative, connection between the two must be acknowledged, but should not be seen as the total set of issues. The speaking/enunciating subject is not simply a subject who speaks, just as Voice is not simply the system and manifestation of sounds. Voice and *sonare* have been specified as metonymic of the body in terms of presenting subjectivity both to the self and external to the self. This metonymic structure is also applicable to subjectivity and the body.

The inscribed body (that is, the body as presenting subjectivity) must be inscribed onto something. A double layer of presence operates: the inscription of the body as signifier of subjectivity (Voice/*sonare* and phenotext, etc.) and the inscription of the inscribed body. This *mise-en-scéne* of the inscribed body against something operates on multiple levels as many diverse combinations occur with different inscriptions and bodies. The principle example developed here has been selected because of the connection with absence, although, as previously noted, the whole enterprise of inscription is always linked to the metaphysics of presence and, if by implication alone, also to absence. Accentua-

tion of the body through inscription will be examined in terms of the eroticisation of the body as absence. Such a positioning is reminiscent of the way in
which Lacan describes desire as "the furrow inscribed in the course; it is, as it
were, the mark of the iron of the signifier on the shoulder of the speaking
subject" (Lacan 1985: 265). This mark of the iron becomes an ideal metaphor
for the central themes that Foucault develops in *Discipline and Punish*. This
example of the inscribed, eroticised body and the related concerns of the voice
will not be a complete agenda here, for it must be seen within the larger context
of the issues at hand.

The eroticisation of the body as inscription shares a number of features with
the abject body. Certainly the idea of the *corps propre* is central to both
configurations, with a sense of inversion operating. The eroticised body
represents the discursive practice of desire, often in archaeological terms, as
partial manifestations of the *corps propre*, largely because of the inherent
Ideality of this. Eroticisation and abjection are inscriptions of the body and on
the body, synchronically, socioculturally and ideologically located. Both are
constructed through absence, although of different types. The eroticised body
is a primary signifier of desire and so is always based on a lack through
acquisition. The abject body is seen as lacking aspects of the *corps propre*, or
of possessing elements that distinguish it from the *corps propre*. The inscribed,
eroticised body in terms of absence can be read in what Foucault called the
mode d'assujettissement—the mode of subjection: "that is, with the way in
which the individual establishes his relation to the rule and recognises himself
as obliged to put it into practice" (Foucault 1986: 27). This particular *mode
d'assujettissement* is how the subject sees himself/herself in terms of sexual
practices and identities, and, significantly, how the subject himself/herself is
determined by these constitutive ideological systems.

Foucault's history of sexuality project is not "a historical survey of the
theme of desire" but a study of "the hermeneutics of the self" (Foucault 1986:
6). One of the unifying principles of these histories is that of the Western
tradition of speculative processes in the determination of the subject as a subject
of desire—a concept that ties in with many of the central arguments in Deleuze
and Guattari's *Anti-Oedipus*. This is fundamental to a concept such as *mode
d'assujettissement* because the site of subjectivity is historically located in
reflexive desires. The inscribed, eroticised body exists in this way because of
the construction of subjectivity in terms of reflexivity, which is the speculative
quality of subject positions, and, in particular, when the speculation (as
heterology) is directed towards the desired and/or desiring body. This
establishes the ideal of the *corps propre* as a desired lack/absence, and
important discursive practices are developed to construct the site of the absent
corps propre and the constitutive processes of desire. The *mode d'assujettissement* is the subject position and its relation to the discursive practices and their
absences.

The inscribed, eroticised body is part of *aphrodisia*—the "ethics of the flesh and the notion of sexuality" (Foucault 1986: 42). *Aphrodisia* locates the inscribed, eroticised body within the discursive practices of morality, sexuality, the taboo, etc., in terms of pleasure and unpleasure, and desire. However, *aphrodisia* is not simply the processes of the pleasures of the flesh as they are made to fit within the established (or establishing) sociocultural and ideological paradigm. *Aphrodisia* operates as a dynamic, moving between desire, act, and pleasure, and then back to desire. It can be further argued that fundamental to this dynamic, and so to *aphrodisia* itself, is absence. For the inscribed, eroticised body the absences of *aphrodisia* are desire as lack, the act as incomplete, and the pleasure as leading to further desire, and so further lack. The basis of Foucault's reading of both the Platonic and Aristotelian models can be seen as one of absence: ". . . for the Greeks there could not be desire without privation, without the want of the thing desired and without a certain amount of suffering mixed in; but the appetite . . . can be aroused only by the representation, the image or the memory of the thing that gives pleasure; he [Plato] concludes that there can be no desire except in the soul, for while the body is affected by privation, it is the soul and only the soul that can, through memory, make present the thing that is to be desired and thereby arouse the *epithumia*" (Foucault 1986a: 43). The implications for absence and the inscribed and eroticised body here are that there can be no inscription or eroticisation simply of the body, for this would lead to a complete absence. Absence, in these terms, would become a negative and destructive process. The soul is the inscriber of eroticisation of the body because of the absences circulating and sociocultural, ideological, and Symbolic demands for presence—which includes that site of subjectivity based on enunciation. In many ways this has critical similarities to what Derrida discusses in terms of the aligning of *Bedeutung* to the body/soul formation.

These terms are not simply a subscription to the idea of the soul as imprisoned in the body—in fact the opposite is the case. The "anatomy", as Foucault describes it in *Discipline and Punish*, of the body as political system means that the two orders of power and knowledge are invested in the body itself. Because the "soul is the prison of the body" (Foucault 1987a: 58), the erotic inscription of the body can be seen as part of the larger order of things. The anatomisation of the body to the body as politic is part of the determination of the subject and the site of subjectivity, and as such incorporates the eroticisation, punishment, torture, exclusion, purification, putrefaction, etc., of the body and the soul.

Aphrodisia as subject site (or part of the formation of this site) involves two central positions—*aphrodisiazein* and *aphrodisiasthenai*, which Foucault designates as largely "masculine" and "feminine", "active" and "passive", "subject" and "object". The centrality of absence to *aphrodisia* means that this dichotomy can be read as presence (*aphrodisiazein*) and absence (*aphrodisiasthenai*). Part of the reason why such a division operates is because of the presenting nature designated to subjectivity—the insistence of subjectivity within

Western metaphysics is presence, whilst absence is to objectify the subject. The essential feature in this process is that *aphrodisia* operates as a code system, allowing the establishment and development of certain combinational features to occur within the discursive practices. The active/passive and the subject/object qualities of *aphrodisiazein* and *aphrodisiasthenai* are essential features in the inscription of the body in terms of desire.

This particular inscription of the body—the eroticised *aphrodisiazein* and *aphrodisiasthenai*—operates in a fashion comparable to Voice and *sonare*. The (ideological) urgency of presence in the formulating and sustaining of subjectivity, even at the most tenuous of levels, and the interplay of absence, forces the production of methods of presence. The combination of the speaking subject to the eroticisation of the body is not the only manifestation of these production processes, but it is, however, a significant one. In this combination there is the intersection of two powerful systems of inscribing subjectivity based in presence—eroticisation and speech. The ideological dimensions of the transformation of the body through *aphrodisiazein* and *aphrodisiasthenai* (active/passive, presence/absence) are also to be found in the systems of Voice and *sonare*. Beyond such a connection are the actual combinations which occur in the determination of particular types of subjectivity and sites of subjectivity. The eroticised body as speaking subject positions the site of subjectivity in terms of speech as inscriber of eroticisation (*aphrodisiazein*) and the inscribed body as erotic (*aphrodisiasthenai*). It is noteworthy that even with the ideological superstructure none of these categories are fixed and as a consequence there is always the underlying potential for the dismantling of the site of subjectivity. This is the revolutionary spirit of absence in the determining systems of presence(s).

It is possible to merge two of the fundamental issues of subjectivity at this point—that of speech/language and desire. The subject is made present—and has presence, and therefore a sense of subjectivity—by "speaking", through desire, and by speaking desire (*aphrodisiazein*) and by being spoken through desire (*aphrodisiasthenai*). What has been argued so far is that all these systems of the production of presence in subjectivity (and subjectivity in presence) are in fact based on absence, largely through the dual operations of lack and exclusion. This is the *mode d'assujettissement* to the rule of absence. Desire and speech are connected at a number of significant points in the determination of this absent subjectivity. Such connections operate in juxtapositional relations and through dissection, each case producing a different combinational set in much the same way as a code organises and selects signifiers and their signification. The very nature of desire as absence leads to the demand to speak it, whilst the excluding nature of the discourse leads to a desire to obtain it. *Différance* can be read in precisely these terms.

Central to the operation of *différance* is the subject: "Differences, thus, are "produced",—deferred—by *différance*. But what defers or who defers? In other words what is *différance*?" (Derrida 1986: 14). Answers to such a question become less important than the fact that the question is asked at all. For in such an asking rests the centrality of the subject position in *différance*. Derrida picks up this idea: ". . . being present to itself, as consciousness, eventually would come to defer or to differ: whether by delaying or turning away from the fulfilment of a "need" or a "desire", or by differing from itself. But in neither of these cases would such a present being be "constituted" by this *différance*" (Derrida 1986: 15).

The subtlety of Derrida's argument must not be misread here. Derrida is continuing his critique of the metaphysics of presence—a metaphysics that seems to invite the initial question posed. What is being indicated here is that the restrictive nature of such a critical position cannot adequately deal with *différance* and subjectivity, *différance* as subjectivity founded on absence. *Différance* can thus be seen as part of the methodology to examine the relationship between absence and subjectivity, and also as a designatory register of a subjectivity based on absence(s). Such a critical alignment can take place largely because the interconnections between subjectivity and absence are constructed through exclusion from the Symbolic order, and because of the operational similarities of desire and the *mode d'assujettissement*—that is, desire as institutional processes of absence as well as the revolutionary qualities of desire external to institution.

The desiring/speaking subject position as absence can also be connected to *différance* in another way. This connection lies in the idea that *différance* is fundamentally about desire in the speaking subject as it attempts to engage in signification, and that this speaking subject is, ultimately, a political agenda. In a passage crucial to the definition of *différance*, Derrida positions it in terms of Freud's Pleasure Principle. The Pleasure Principle, argues Derrida, is comparable to *différance* because it is essentially about the deferral of pleasure by the Reality Principle. It is only in such comparative terms that sense can be made of either the Pleasure Principle or the Reality Principle. However, deferral is not abrogation, and so there is always a returning to the pleasures that have been deferred, which is, in many cases, the return of the repressed. The pleasure is made absent because of the foregrounding of the processes of the Reality Principle—in effect "reality" as it is determined in the Symbolic rather than the Imaginary or the Real—and is a sociocultural paradigm. These absented pleasures and desires are read as *différance* because they are different from the regime of the Reality Principle—which has come to occupy a position of presence—and are deferred. As with Dupin, desire is set in motion by something other than the subject: "Like all the others he has perfectly doubled, he is set in motion by the desire of the Queen and by the pact which contracts itself in this desire" (Derrida 1987: 455)—so the definitional nature of the desiring subject is always one of *différance*. Within this *différance* of desire, constantly reminding of the difficulties of possession and satisfaction, is the dialectic of presence and absence. Derrida reminds us that "*Le désir est désir de la présence*" (Derrida 1972: 59), but we must add that this is always based on absence.

Absence, Desire, and the Subject of Enunciation

Beyond the kind of description offered by Kristeva, there can be little doubt that the enunciating subject position must be seen as inextricably connected to other types of subjectivity. The abjecting subject may be overwhelmingly concerned with the particular fears that currently manifest themselves, but the articulation of such fears and threats (external or internal articulations) links this subject type to practices of enunciation. Similarly, the desiring subject in Lacanian terms is also a subject of enunciation, for desire, subjectivity, and language act as cornerstones to many of Lacan's theories.

The desiring subject and the enunciating subject share a number of common features in their conceptual frames, their ideational nature, and their operations in practice. The desiring subject engages in language in an attempt to satisfy the compelling and constant desires that define it, just as the enunciating subject is compelled by desire to enter the Symbolic. Whether measured in terms of the thetic phase or the mirror stage, clearly what is constructed is a subject "driven" by desire into language. Caught in the Symbolic, except for the rupturing effect of the transgressive *sémiotique* and *chora* in the parergonal, the subject discovers that far from producing satisfaction, the Symbolic, and its multiple and diverse discursive practices, offers only further compulsions of desire and absence. Hence the overall process is one of absences: the absence of the Symbolic in the *sémiotique*; the absence of possession and control of the Symbolic; absences produced through frustration; desire itself constantly figured as a system of absence. Added to this is the dialectic of presence and absence determining degrees of the sense of subjectivity. What now needs to be considered is how desire, signification, and absence operate as constitutive elements of, functional processes for, and, ultimately, definitional properties of, the enunciating subject. What also needs to be examined within this context are specific forms of satisfaction that might occur for the desiring, enunciating subject surrounded by these absences. It is important to recognise that the enunciating subject is not a different type, in terms of categories, of subjectivity to the desiring subject. The enunciating subject position can be located in terms of the desiring subject, with the emphasis placed on the role and function of language as a principle determinant of subjectivity through absence.

Desire operates specifically as *manque*. In terms of subjectivity and the formation of the subject this is the *manque-à-être*. However, as Lacan points out, *manque-à-être* is not simply derived from the egocentric deliberations on subjectivity, but develops out of a series of frustrations and encounters with lacks and absences. This is particularly true in the case of desire, as it is through desire that the subject becomes a subject who wants to be. Desire is not just absent, it is absence. Further to this, the status of *manque-à-être* is part of the subject position of the *Ichspaltung*, as it is the splits, gaps, and absences which construct the want. Even at the most fundamental level subjectivity in these terms is positioned as a series of presences and absences: the conscious is seen as present, the unconscious, through repression, as absent; the manifestation of the absent through texts (including the sense of the literary, filmic, painting as well as dreams, parapraxis) and the subsequent repression of conscious censorship—a process similar to the transgressive manifestations of the *sémiotique chora* and how it is determined in the Symbolic. Lacan even argues that the subconscious is not a whole but "lacuna, cut, rupture inscribed in a certain lack" (Lacan 1986: 153).

All of this indicates that subjectivity, and its extensive and inextricable connections with desire, is constituted not by a single absence, but by multiple ones. Lacan articulates two such absences: "Two lacks overlap here. The first emerges from the central defect around which the dialectic of the advent of the subject to his own being in the relation to the Other turns—by the fact that the subject depends on the signifier and that the signifier is first of all in the field of the Other. This lack takes up the other lack, which is the real, earlier lack, to be substituted at the advent of the living being" (Lacan 1986: 204-205). This is the lack of the subject—that is, an enunciating subject beyond the mirror stage and positioned in terms of the Symbolic—dealing with lacks derived from language and sexuality.

It is because desire is constituted as absence that there is a constant and productive series of attempts to fill some of these absences. These attempts will always be unsatisfactory because of the inherent nature of the desires. Some of the reasons for this dissatisfaction include: the desiring process is based on absence as a constitutive and definitional feature; desire emerges from the *Ichspaltung*, towards an Other which cannot be reached and so becomes a constitutive determinant of the production process; the *objet petit a* resists any attempt to restrict its motility; and the essence of desire, its eidetic "desireness", is that it is absent from the subject and a transcendental point of signification. Although these attempts are bound to fail, they continue to recur with vigour and in a multiplicity of forms.

It is the desire for the signifier, and the inability to possess it, that constitutes one of the fundamental and crucial features of the enunciating subject position. This desire for the signifier is manifested in a great many ways—an example will serve to illustrate this. One of Barthes's central ideas can be read as the desire for the signifier in writing. The site of *jouissance* is a space that the subject attempts to fill, but can never occupy. It is in the text, Barthes argues, that this site exists and is created. The text of pleasure is "the text that contents, fills, grants euphoria; the text that comes from culture and does not break with it, is linked to a comfortable practice of reading" (Barthes 1988: 14), whilst the text of *jouissance* is part of absence and desire—it operates in "a state of loss", and, like desire, is "the impossible text" (Barthes 1988: 14; 22). These are the modalities of the Symbolic (the text of pleasure seeks to satisfy through presence) and the *sémiotique* (the text of *jouissance* seeks to create and promote absences and give pleasure in and through these absences). Crucially, for this *jouissance* to operate, the absence must never be filled. It is the absence that gives the pleasure, not the presence, which indicates that the absence found in desire, although seeming to be a process of frustration, can also be a site of pleasure. There also exists the pleasure of consuming a text which, too, can be seen as a pleasure of absence. In this Barthesian sense of desire and writing, consuming a text can be regarded then as a deferral acknowledged within and by the reader.

Part of the difficulty for the desiring subject in the regime of enunciation is this link to the signifier. This can only be understood fully once the nature of the signifier and absence has been examined but some important notes can be made here relating to subjectivity. The *Ichspaltung* emerges from a totally different, in some ways antithetical, order into the Symbolic. Although never fully abandoned, the primary order of the drives (*chora, sémiotique*) must be managed in order for the subject to engage in the Symbolic. The emergence of the subject into the Symbolic is motivated largely by the desire for the signifier. This signifier is maintained as absent on two levels—the signifier itself is always absent from the subject because it is located in the Symbolic, and the compelling desire for the signifier strengthens the absence. One reason why the desire for the signifier is never satisfied is because even though the subject and signifier are united through absences, the registers giving rise to those absences are different. The absence typologies of signifiers and subjectivity are heterogeneous to each other, and to the overall configuration of absences, as well as acting in terms of pluralism. This is why it is essential to speak of *types* of absences as distinct, rather than in a uniform sense. The idea of a homogeneity of absence can only operate at a superficial level. Part of the reason why the force of desire is contained in the signifier, and so operates as a fundamental aspect of the enunciating subject's desires, is the desire to possess not only the signifier but also the means of production.

The enunciating subject's relationship to the signifier as desire causes this subject positioning to be transformed into the *manque-à-être*. The very fantasies of the enunciating subject are positioned and partially realised through the signifier—"In the speaking subject, fantasies articulate this irruption of drives within the realm of the signifier" (Kristeva 1984c: 49)—a signifier which is always alien, always absent. It could be argued that this is part of the reason why Kristeva speaks of the absence of amatory codes today. This relates the absence of amatory codes to the subject and desire and the positioning of these processes in terms of the social context. This is also the reason why Foucault argues that the concept of the subject only exists in a post-classical frame of reference. What alters is not the texture of the culture, but the relationship and configurations of absence in the efforts of the enunciating subject to possess and utilise the signifier.

Because desire can only be made sense of in terms of absence, the enunciating subject is constantly produced within the solicitation of the *manque-à-être*. There is a triple articulation of absences at this point: the absences created by the split subject (the *Ichspaltung*); the absences created from the lacunae of the signifying practices (and the subsequent engagements with these by the enunciating subject emerging from the *sémiotique*); and the absences which constitute desire itself. These constitutive absences are devised in a multiplicity of practices, but the fundamental core remains consistent. Kristeva, via Hegel, argues: "desire organises its logical structure on what can be called nothingness or the zero in logic" (Kristeva 1984c: 130). The notion of desire's absence as nothingness or the zero relates to the distinction between Freud's negation, Hegelian negativity, and *Aufhebung*.

The correlation between desire, language, and absence is extended beyond a simple synchronic collision within the enunciating subject. The concept that desire is the desire of the Other operates through the very essence of language—it is because of language that such a dictum can make sense. All desires are produced and manifested from the position of the enunciating subject, and so all interpretations of those desires must take this into account. The Other operates in terms of a sensibility of language and absence. Similarly the desiring subject is someone "who lives at the expense of his drives, ever in search of a lacking object. The sole source of his praxis is this quest of lack, death, and language, and as such it resembles the praxis of phenomenological *care*" (Kristeva 1984c: 132). This is the inmixing of the individual drives with their sociocultural features.

Connected to this idea of the enunciating subject and desire are the fears and threats inherent in such a structure. Lacan speaks of this in terms of aphanisis and alienation, Freud in terms of parapraxis (Signorelli is not so much forgotten as repressed), and Kristeva in terms of abjection: "any practice of speech, inasmuch as it involves writing, is a language of fear. I mean a language of want as such" (Kristeva 1982: 38). This is not a unique or aberrant type of subjectivity. Due to the ubiquity of the various absences involved, this is "typical" of the site of the enunciating subject.

Part Two

Absence and the Gaze

6

Absence and the Scopic Drive

The Scopic Drive

"*Comme eux mon oeil est vide et comme eux habité/De l'absence de toi qui fait sa cécité*" (Lacan 1973: 21). This is how Lacan commences *Seminar XI*—a quotation from Aragon, a contrapuntal sense of gazing at and gazed at, of presence and absence. This is also the relationship between the subject and desire, subjectivity, and being as it is caught in the specular. The gaze is the mediating principle of the presence or absence of subjectivity as determined through desire. To gaze is to locate the subject as a desiring presence and to be the subject of the gaze is to be negotiated as a desired presence. Furthermore, as with other drives it is located at the hole, produced through a liminality in the negotiations of culture. Such positionality operates in the specular and speculative moments between the drive and the Symbolic. In all of this dynamic interplay is the centrality of absence—the gazing, desiring subject is located in terms of the Other, of scopic Otherness based on absences. The gazed-at subject is the Other, is the absent.

However, even a binary model as generous as this one is too simple, too limited, for it reduces many of the complexities to an either/or and suggests a homogeneity that cannot adequately describe the nexus. The need to go beyond such a model is also derived from the inadequecies of a dialectic - an *Aufhebung* without reserve still produces a drive toward the synthesis. This is revealed most clearly when the issue of gazing and gazed at is approached through absence, which in its very proffering raises a whole number of questions, including what is absent in the act of looking? how are absences constructed by and through the scopic drive? what is the absence of the gaze and how does this affect subjectivity and desire? what is the status of presence in the gaze? what fixes and unhinges the gaze?

These should not be blind spots, or something out of the corner of the eye; they are of subjectivity, language/discourse, and desire. The issues at hand are twofold—examining the relationship between absence and the gaze, and some of the principle effects this relationship has on the exchanges between subjectivity and desire. This in turn suggests that the gaze can be figured as a discursive system, or at the very least subject to the pressures and boundaries of the orders of discourse. This is true of both the gaze itself and the ways in which the gaze is figured. This discursive quality, that is its political agenda, is what transforms the act of looking and being looked at into processes of the gaze. The discursive quality that defines the gaze operates in the act of watching and being watched, but we must be wary of falling into the same trap of binarism. The discourse of the gaze (the gazing discourse) necessarily goes beyond looking and being looked at, just as speech and silence are not straightforward categories of articulation.

Augenverdreher—Eye-Twisters and the Empty Eye

A retold story—a case history where a second look is taken. A woman patient comes to Tausk's clinic, but no ordinary woman for she is a lover who has just quarrelled with her beloved. She speaks of how her eyes are not right, that they are twisted because of her lover: "She could not understand him at all, he looked different every time; he was a hypocrite, an "eye-twister" (*Augenverdreher*), he had twisted her eyes; now she had twisted eyes; they were not her eyes any more; now she saw the world with different eyes" (Freud 1987: 203). *Verdreher* is to twist, to distort, to pervert, and eye-twisters can work both ways—the gaze/eye can be twisted and what is gazed at can be twisted. But of course every gaze is twisted and every reading through the gaze is twisted. There cannot be a transcendental untwisted gaze, a Platonic ideal gaze fixed to an ideal untwisted object. The image on the cave is twisted many times but eventually it passes as the actual, the "unmediated". This passing over to seem like the actual or the real is part of the transformation of the gaze into an order of discourse. This discourse, linked to power, is also part of the relationship of the Other to the figuring of the self. Lacan argues that: "If one does not stress the dialectic of desire one does not understand why the gaze of others should disorganize the field of perception" (Lacan 1986: 89). Desire becomes not simply the motivating principle of the gaze, but also the organisational structure.

Eye-twisting as a form of a dialectic of desire and the dialectisation of the sign is a fundamental part of the discourse of the gaze, so fundamental in fact that the overall processes of the gaze itself must be seen as *Augenverdreher*. The gaze puts a forced construction on all that it meets because this is how the discourse operates. When we see something totally new we rub our eyes, we blink rapidly, we twist our head to one side to try to assimilate the unfamiliar, the uncanny, the defamiliarised. But what we really try to do is draw the new into the old twist, the established discourse, the familiar pattern. But the old twist does not seem like a twist because it is the ordering principle, a hermeneutics rather than just an act of perception. Narrative doesn't seem to twist the gaze, and yet this is precisely what it does in a constant and highly formulated fashion, so much so that events, histories, acts of interpretation become twisted into narratives so that they fit more easily into the act of gazing. Some "narratives" twist back so that the gaze becomes aware of the act of forcing constructions.

Eye-twisting is part of the discursive practice of presence. The forced construction privileges one set of presences over any other, and this is often because of the ideological basis of the twist. Presence and absence here often translates to the active and passive, to Foucault's *aphrodisiazein* and *aphrodisiasthenai*, to that binary choice of either gazing or being gazed at. Yet even though there are many senses of the present and the absent the twist of presence is limited and the range of absences veiled from the gaze. This is the Foucauldian shift from archaeology to genealogy so that eye-twisting is epistemic in its genealogical function. The dual interplay of power over the body and the body's power is the twisting of the eye by the object/event and the eye twisting the object/event. Foucault, in dealing with the relationship between power and knowledge, speaks of the body in a similar way: "But the body is also directly involved in the political field; power relations have an immediate hold upon it; they invest it, mark it, train it, torture it, force it to carry out tasks, to perform ceremonies, to emit signs" (Foucault 1987a: 25). If the body is twisted and twists then its parts are also liable to the same types of actions, and the gaze, as one of the fundamental processes of subjectivity, is no exception.

In these terms the gaze is not simply the act of perception, or even the individual subject metonymically referenced. It is the powerful discursive order that has direct connections, via the epistemic operations, to power and knowledge. Once more we can refer to Foucault to contextualise this point: "In appearance, or rather, according to the mask it bears, historical consciousness is neutral, devoid of passions, and committed solely to truth. But if it examines itself and if, more generally, it interrogates the various forms of scientific consciousness in its history, it finds that all these forms and transformations are aspects of the will to knowledge: instinct, passion, the inquisitor's devotion, cruel subtlety, and malice" (Foucault 1977: 126). Historical consciousness is the gaze twisted, and the twisting that occurs to create the mask of neutrality is of the same order that positions all gazes, both literal and metaphorical.

The centrality of absence and presence to the discursive function of eye-twisting is related to another process that figures the gaze in terms of desire and subjectivity—the emptying of the eye. This phenomenon involves the distinction between the gaze and the eye which in turn has its basis in the idea of scopophilia. Freud's concept of scopophilia as the opposite of, but referentially connected to, exhibitionism is based at least in part on Jean-Martin Charcot's idea of scotomisation, of *scotome scintillant* and its *éblouissement de ténèbres*. There is the historical (and political) complicity of scotomisation and repression here, but it is possible to put to one side these difficulties and see how scopophilia relates to the notion of absence, which in part implies a connection with repression. It is significant that of the four phases of hysterical attack (epileptoid, large movements, *attitudes passionnelles*, and terminal delirium) described by Charcot both Freud and Breuer concentrate on the third—the *attitudes passionnelles*—which is the evocation, by the hysteric, of a memory through the visual. The hallucination twisting the hysteric's eye becomes the defining point of subjectivity in their analytic discourse. If this is true of the hysteric it is equally true of all subjects—the type of gazing/gazed-at site occupied can define the constitutive and functional qualities of subjectivity.

The twisting of the eye and the emptying of the gaze operate through the correlative system of subjectivity and absence/presence. Eye-twisting is the interplay of presences (the instigation of one set of presences over any other set)—Cassandra's eyes are twisted to see the truth, but the paradigm of presences in operation renders her gaze unbelievable. The emptying of the gaze is akin to aphanisis, whereby the fear of losing the signifier of the self is translated into the loss of the gaze. In all these configurations it is absence that defines the order of things, and it is these absences that are determinants constitutive of both the gaze and subjectivity. These issues are centred on the action of the gaze, the subjective position of the eye, the temptation of the lure.

The scopic drive is directly connected to the action of desire, and therefore of lack and absence. The scopic drive is not about the subject's relationship to the object, as might first appear to be the case, rather it is about the subject's relationship to desire. In the scopic drive the object is relatively unimportant, for the subject is concerned with the gaze: "You grasp here the ambiguity of what is at issue when we speak of the scopic drive. The gaze is this object lost and suddenly refound in the conflagration of shame, by the introduction of the other. Up to that point, what is the subject trying to see? What he is trying to see, make no mistake, is the object as absence" (Lacan 1986: 182). It is important to recall that the movement from the domination of one set of drives to another (for example, the oral to the anal) is not necessarily a developmental one, but can be based on intervention. This occurs, when something intervenes in the field of the drive that cannot be taken into account with the existing order: "the intervention, the overthrow, of the demand of the Other" (Lacan 1986: 180). The scopic drive is part of the desire for the Other. To this extent drives are systems of meaning for the subject—they make something meaningful because of their centrality to the formations of subjectivity.

It is for this reason that the gaze can be aligned with anatomical marks (trait) of gaps and holes. In the "Bottle Opener" graph the gaze, the voice, and nothing are positioned as operating in the same manner in terms of the partial. Freud's work on the unconscious (as well as the earlier work on hysteria) indicates that scopophilia and exhibitionism are concerned with the scopic drive (watching/being watched) and not the object of the gaze. Lacan extends this point when he argues that the object is absent in the scopic drive—it is the drive itself which is the key. The intervention of the scopic shifts the emphasis from the object to the act of looking/being looked at. The scopic drive is primarily concerned with the gaze as it functions and operates in terms of the subject and desire: "At the scopic level, we are no longer at the level of demand, but of desire, of the desire of the Other" (Lacan 1986: 104). The function of absence in desire returns us to the issue of activity and passivity.

Clearly the scopic drive's connection to desire cannot simply be equated to a sense of an absence of the gaze—this is quite another configuration. All considerations of the scopic drive must accommodate the idea of the centrality of absence in terms of the gazing subject's relationship to the Other. To this end the scopic drive must not be mistaken as a mechanism of self-consciousness—the centrality of the drive ensures its continuation, not necessarily self-reflexivity. The scopic drive contributes significantly to the splitting of the subject, which is the difference between the eye and the gaze: "The eye and the gaze—this is for us the split in which the drive is manifested at the level of the scopic field . . . must we not distinguish between the function of the eye and that of the gaze?" (Lacan 1986: 73; 74). In other words the translation of the *Ichspaltung* to the scopic drive produces the differentiation between eye and gaze. But what is this difference besides a furthering of the split, an accentuation of absence in subjectivity? It can be read as an essential aspect of absence and the scopic.

The difference between eye and gaze is based on the tension of the drive. Drive is *pulsion* or *trieb* and the scopic drive—*la pulsion scopique*—is part of this same order of demand and absence. Lacan also uses the term *champ scopique*, which is related to the scopic drive but is distinguishable from it. The scopic field contains the drive and so includes the actions of both eye and gaze, gazing and gazed at, or the scopic subject and its objects.

This distinction is important for a number of reasons, primary amongst them is the emphasis placed on the *pulsion* of the scopic within the wider context of the field—the eye is part of the field but the gaze is a demonstration of the drive. What is also evoked in the pulsative absence is the desire to satisfy the gaze, and this sense of scopic satisfaction hinges on understanding the relationship between the drive and the field. The gaze is the more active process—it is spoken of as seducing, as having an appetite, as a right or law, as an act of insertion, of penetrating, of piercing, etc. This active quality stems from desire and the Other, of the lack and absence.

A crucial issue in the scopic drive is the relationship between the gaze and the *objet petit a*, for it is here that Lacan positions the possibility of scopic satisfaction. Lacan ties the scopic and its potential for the *objet petit a* directly to the collapse of subject status. This idea can be traced back to Sartre when he states: "My original fall is the existence of the Other" (Sartre 1957: 263). This is not the fall to knowledge, self-reflection even, it is the fall to ignorance of anything that exists beyond appearance. This, according to Lacan, characterises all progresses in thought and in this we find one of the clearest indicators that what is at issue here is not simply the processes of perception, or even the operation of the observing subject, but the core of subjectivity itself, of the operation of language, of textual systems, of power and institution through desire and absence.

The gaze—the scopic drive—is part of the larger order of drives as well as this configuration of desire and the subject. Lacan formulates the following to detail this: "The *objet a* in the field of the visible is the gaze $\{$ in nature
as $= (-\phi)$'(Lacan 1986: 105-106). Beneath this is constructed the intersecting triangles of the gaze and the subject of representation, with the image/screen forming the mid point.

Lacan is demonstrating here the configuration of the desiring subject within the scopic drive and field, where (-o) is the "*manque central du désir*" (Lacan 1973: 97). It is the centrality of this absence that determines the gaze as *objet petit a*. It is noteworthy that Lacan constantly refers to *objet petit a* here as *evanescent*, which symbolises this quality of absence in desire and the gaze. The first part of this equation is the reiteration of the scopic drive, manifested as the gaze, as *objet petit a*—this is the drive motivated by absence. The section after the bracket indicates the operation of the Symbolic in terms of the gaze and its lacks. In this sense this is the transformation of events into ideological paradigms. This action takes place through the gaze in two fundamental processes: the transformation into the Symbolic and the operation of absence through desire. The triangles overlap and Lacan describes the first as that "which, in the geometral field, puts in our place the subject of the representation, and the second is that which turns *me* into a picture" (Lacan 1986: 105).

This even more clearly indicates the ideological function of subjectivity and absence through representation. The concern here is with the subject as he/she is represented and represents, with the primary function of the drives (in particular the scopic) within this interplay, and with how the subject negotiates the self in terms of the scopic drive and scopic positioning. The two apexes can be seen to represent the division between scopophilia (gazing) and exhibitionism (gazed at), and the intersection of screen-image the mediating ideological apparatus. Both scopophilia and exhibitionism are extreme ideals which suggest a binarism, but such an interpretation misses a crucial issue in the figuring of the gaze. For scopophilia and exhibitionism share the same function in terms of subjectivity and desire, which is the centrality of the drive as absence, and absence to the centrality of the drive.

The associated pleasures of scopophilia and exhibitionism is not what is looked at (the object) or the occupation of the site of the observed (objectification of the subject/self through the visual), rather in both cases it is the process of the gaze. It is the activity of the gaze as subjectivity and/or ideology that is the issue and the (possible/potential) pleasure. This is, in part, the reason why the gaze is positioned externally, and the subject, as *Ichspaltung*—split again through the scopic drive—becomes the picture.

The outside gaze and the representation of the self in the scopic field can be read as part of the wider sense of the gaze as discursive practice. Lacan's (1973) anecdote of the fishing trip with Petit-Jean illustrates precisely this point. That the sardine can could not see the young Lacan signifies that he has no meaning within that context—the outside gaze cannot register him as a picture so subjectivity is absented. The sardine can, as focal point for the scopic drive, absents the individual's subjectivity—it becomes a blind-spot in the discursive praxis of meaning and existence. This whole structure of meaning and seeing is connected to what Lacan calls *je me vois me voir* (seeing oneself see oneself), which is not the self-reflexive process, but the self's negotiations with the recognition of the gaze as drive, as institution. This is the translation of *méconnaissance* into the scopic field, that is, scotoma. Scotoma is visual *méconnaissance* through lacunae and the self-reflexive quality of *je me vois me voir*. It is not difficult to see here the mirror phase phenomenon theoretically transposed, through a type of eidetic reduction, to essential features of subjectivity and the gaze. This phenomenological *epoché* is "seeingness", or what Lacan calls *voyure*, and this is the desire of the scopic drive.

The gaze as *objet petit a* is the gaze figured as the central point for the subject—*voyure* is to see the gaze, to be observant of the discursive practices of the gaze as it positions the subject in terms of what is absent from the self, the speculative absenting. What is absented in this dynamic is precisely what would normally thought to be highly presented—the object. The scopic drive, operating through the scotoma, shifts the emphasis to the gaze itself—and, perhaps ultimately, the status of *voyure*—and in doing so highlights a different set of absences. This other set we have observed before—it is the *Ichspaltung*, motivated through desire, organised by absences. This is the shame that Lacan speaks of, via Sartre, in the rediscovery of the object through the introduction of the Other.

The Shame of the Gaze and the Operation of the Imaginary

The shame of the gaze is the relevation of awareness of looking. It is the moment where the act of looking is revealed to the subject and the action of the gaze disappears. But this is not simply the self-conscious process of looking, or even the creation of a blindspot in the register of what can be seen/observed. It is, significantly, the positioning of the subject, and the realisation of this position, in terms of the Other: "The gaze sees itself—to be precise, the gaze of which Sartre speaks, the gaze that surprises me and reduces me to shame, since this is the feeling he regards as the most dominant. The gaze I encounter . . . is, not a seen gaze, but a gaze imagined by me in the field of the Other"(Lacan 1986: 84). Lacan's point here is not to establish the intersubjective operation of the gaze as ideological function as may first appear to be the case. The concern is with the relational context established for the subject as a function of desire. The gaze, as drive and as part of the Other, is both a system of interaction with the world (in essence the "eye") and a complex link with the Other with all its attendant qualities of absence and desire. The idea of this shame originates in the same work that yields the division of *pour soi/en soi*, that engages in the distinction between the noumenon and phenomenon and seeks to outline the moral structure of existence and, perhaps most significantly, develops the idea of nothingness or nihilation (*néantisation*). *Néantisation* is the consciousness exercising the power to make things absent and of the full responsibility for the decipherment of the sign. The key to all of this is responsibility—the existentialist reading of being condemned to freedom.

But why shame? For Sartre it is not so much the essential quality of "shameness" that is the issue, but the effect of something on consciousness which becomes revelational to the self about the self. Shame is Sartre's example of the self's sense of the self in terms of the Other. It is ". . . a non-positional self-consciousness, conscious (of) itself as shame; as such, it is an example of what the Germans call *Erlebnis*, and it is accessible to reflection. . . . it is a shameful apprehension of something and this something is me. I am ashamed of what I am. Shame therefore realizes an intimate relation of myself to myself. Through shame I have discovered an aspect of my being" (Sartre 1957: 221). This relationship is centred on the Other and the subject. The person crouching down to peer through the keyhole, suddenly discovered by someone, is filled with shame—but the central point to this is not the feeling of shame but the disturbing realisation of the self in terms of the Other; ". . . it is the recognition of the fact that I am indeed that object which the Other is looking at and judging. . . . Shame reveals to me that I am this being, not in the mode of "was" or of "having to be" but in-itself" (Sartre 1957: 261; 262). Barthes (1990) speaks of the same sense of shame as the junction between subjectivity and the Other which becomes one of the central issues in the formation of the discourse of love through subjectivity.

Abjection, terror, pride, *jouissance*—the list is boundless—are of this same order of alienation and identification, of fixing the idea of the subject and consciousness to the self at that point in time and space, for the Other both spatialises and temporalises. What this boundless list shares is the ordering frame of absence—the revelation is always about something which is absent or could be made absent, the fear is for a loss, a lack. What we see as we crouch at the keyhole and then feel the gaze of the Other is absence and the inextricable bondage of desire to this.

This quality of revelation and the Other—of being watched by the Other and so having a sense of being/consciousness exposed, of marking the subject in terms of the Other—is what the gaze is all about. It is the inscription of the subject in the image. The gaze is part of the Other and because of this it shows the split subject his/her alienated position to the site of desire. The fear involved is the transformation of the subject into the object through the field of the Other—it is the absenting of subjectivity from the self. The gaze focuses not on objects but on the process of looking, of being itself, and this quality of being is the desiring subject constituted by absences and of absences.

The idea of the mirror stage stems from this whole set of issues of the negotiation of subjectivity, primarily through the operation of the gaze. In many ways Sartre's voyeur at the keyhole goes through, or more correctly is experiencing, aspects of the mirror stage at that moment of shame. The mirror stage is not simply a process of (chronological) development, but is a fundamental part of the formation of the I through the transition of the ego-centric world order into the Symbolic. As with the gaze, the significance of the mirror stage is not the mirror (or even sight) but the desiring subject in absence located in terms of the Other: ". . . subjectivity is implicated at every moment. When you see a rainbow, you're seeing something completely subjective. You see it at a certain distance as if stitched on to the landscape. It isn't there. It is a subjective phenomenon" (Lacan 1988a: 77). To illustrate and develop this point Lacan examines the experiment of the inverted bouquet as an issue of the subject (cf. Lacan 1988a: 18; 139). Lacan initially uses these diagrams to illustrate the relationship between the desiring subject and the Imaginary, and then extends it to include the Symbolic and the Real. He argues that, as with the position of the eye in this classic model of optics, the subject must be at a very specific point in order to see, that is "exist", have being: "It means that, in the relation of the imaginary and the real, and in the constitution of the world as results from it, everything depends on the position of the subject. And the position of the subject . . . is essentially characterised by its place in the symbolic world" (Lacan 1988a: 80). Here we find a cogent summary of the positioning of the subject in the interaction of the three orders of the Imaginary, the Symbolic, and the Real. The second of the two models illustrates the convolutions of the subject placed within the context of the Other. The formation of the VS (the Virtual Subject) shares many of the qualities of the voyeur at the keyhole at the moment of realising the gaze of the Other.

The gaze is not fixed here, and the position from which the gaze originates will determine what is seen and how it is seen: "this represents the uneasy accommodation of the imaginary in man" (Lacan 1988a: 140). Lacan revives the term *captate* to stress the seductive qualities and absolute fascination that the gaze holds, hence the reason why desire plays such a crucial role in the scopic drive. In as much as the first of these diagrams details the operation of the Imaginary and the subject, the second locates the subject and the Imaginary in terms of the Symbolic—this is the rent subject of absence. It is the Symbolic, and the operation of speech, which qualifies the position of the eye and, in turn, what is seen and how it is read: "It is speech, the symbolic relation, which determines the greater or lesser degree of perfection, of completeness, of approximation, of the imaginary" (Lacan 1988a: 141). Furthermore, the model is extended to include the Real by exchanging the plane mirror for a pane of glass—we see ourselves reflected in the glass and we see objects beyond this reflection. In this sense the Real and Imaginary operate at the same level, and so the subject's relation to them must be ordered through the Symbolic. It is this concept of Symbolic ordering that strengthens the rendering of the gaze as discursive practice. Whoever tips the mirror controls the reflection of the world.

7

Heterology of the Gaze and the System of Eclipse

The Ecliptic Gaze

So far the gaze has been figured as part of a larger order of operations which include the politics and economies of subjectivity as a site and position, the ideological function of meaning, and paradigms of the subject/self as discursive practices. The subject positions of the gaze—the gazing subject and the subject who is evinced to and by the gaze—are part of the larger typology of the split subject, determined by absences, gaps, and fragmentations. These factors are redirected through the operation of desire, as fundamental *pulsion*, and the scopic field to form an ontological order of the determinate self. The site of subjectivity is figured as a position invested in and with desired presence(s), although this is an ideal presence constructed on absences (through absentation and the relational contexts of secondary absences and presences, as well as the influence of secondary absences), in the context of these absences. There is an unrelenting and constant action of constructing the site(s) of subjectivity, being constructed by such a site or sites, and attempting to enter and control it or them. It is seen as a position of power and knowledge because it connects, at a number of levels, the essential discursive practices of cultural operations with processes of the psychogenesis of the subject via the Symbolic. These practices include the conceptualisation of the gaze as a formalised language system (in effect a *langue*) and as an operational system of discursive practice (a *parole*).

The discursive function of the gaze includes the transformation of the object into a sign, which also involves a sense of desire. The lektonic is part of this political transformation of the object into a sign because of its dimensions of desire, representabilities, and the operation of the specular/speculative. An important feature of this process is the insertion of the sense of meaningfulness or signification, which is not necessarily a meaning determined for the sign but the recognition of the sign in its sign-ness. The object is transformed, via the lektonic, into the specular signifier. The diagram positions these elements in terms of specularity and an interpretation based on chains of signification as they locate the structure of the sign, in its absences, in terms of the subject, and the subject (with its absences) in terms of the sign. The term *specularity* is used here specifically to indicate all these processes—especially the desiring function of the gaze in terms of the absented site of subjectivity. This is further evidence of how the construction and operation of the text is motivated through the context of multifarious and polymorphic absences.

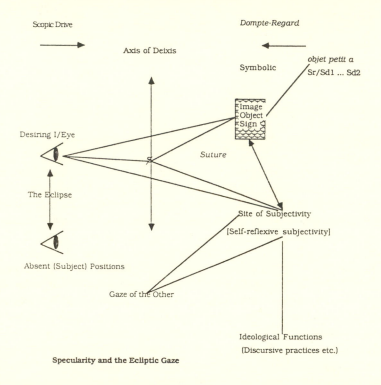

Specularity and the Ecliptic Gaze

The first part of the diagram is the construction of the gaze, and this is also the first issue of a heterological order. The gaze can be of two distinct registers, which in themselves contain multiple frames. The two specified in this context are the gaze of the desiring eye/I and the gaze constructed as the desired subject position. However, the strategy so far has been to align these two positions, while acknowledging their differences. In order to hold the two together it is necessary to see this as an ecliptic position. Eclipse is used here in the dual sense of its etymology of a *failure to appear* and to *leave its place*. Its failure to appear is the desiring eye/I because the self is not seen in this site, whilst the action of leaving its place (as process) is the absent site of subjectivity. This is because when the subject *looks*—in that action of *captation*—towards it the site shifts from its originary, transcendental, and ideational position into a configuration of the Symbolic. This is the same action of speaking the Other, of measuring the fragmented body against the perfect body of the Other, of attempts to consume the Other through the oral.

No matter which of these ecliptic positions is *taken up* (in a figurative sense—these are always absented sites of the gazing subject), the next point is the *Ichspaltung*. The subject is split (further) precisely because of operations such as the ecliptic. The diagram represents the gaze as "behind" the subject—this is because part of the gazing process is locating the self in terms of the gaze and the object/sign. In the field of the scopic drive as part of the Other, we watch ourselves watch ourselves—this is the specular/speculative, the *specula(tive)r*. This status fluctuates, but at its most powerful the lektonic operation becomes of greatest significance in the heterology of the gaze. This heterology produces a series of absences, including a range of possibilities (the paradigmatics) and some actualities (formations of a syntagmatics of absences). The subject is split at least four ways in this sense of the ecliptic and heterology—each split representing a form of absence: he/she is split from the ecliptic gaze (which includes two further splits of the desiring eye/I and the desired site for gazing); he/she is split from the pre-Oedipal site as well as the Symbolic; there is also the split from the self-reflexive positioning (the influence of the gaze of the Other) as cultural operation; and there is the split from the manifestation of the desiring site of the Other. All of these splits are interconnected and operate in terms of the subject, desire, and the gaze as constructed by, and constructing, the self.

The configuration of "Image/Object-Sign as *objet petit a*" operates through two primary functions. It represents the transformation of the object into the sign through the action of the lektonic trace, and consequentially the sign as specular to the gazing subject, that is visible and imbued with a sense of meaningness or signification. It can also represent, independent of this or as part of it, the gaze as *objet petit a*. Read in this sense the action of the scopic drive, determined by and determining the subject, flows through the image so that the process of the gaze is central to the operation, as opposed to the Image/Object-Sign. In this sense the *image* stands for the systems of representation; yet, it must necessarily include a sense of considerations of representability. It is also part of the idea of *Vorstellungrepräsentanz*. In this sense *image* means both the aspects that are used to construct a text (language, organising principles of language, its grammar, etc.) so that the reader recognises its textuality and dialogism to other texts, and the insertion of the reading act (perception and interpretation) into the text. This is why *image*, the sense of imageness as well as the image itself (including the processes which construct something as an image), becomes an *objet petit a*—that is, it is positioned in the Other and determined through absences and desire. Image, like sign, can be absent until it undergoes the configurations constructed by the gazing process.

The relationship between $ --- Image/Object-Sign is not fixed and will alter according to a variety of influences, both external and internal to the specifics of the reading of a text. Two examples of this include the development of perspective in painting and the multiple devices which operate to construct various type of narrative, including endogamous elements of specific narrational systems—literary, filmic—as well as larger orders of narrative itself. Perspective is not simply a different form of representation, but a substantial alteration in the ways in which the image and the gaze are positioned in terms of each other.

The split subject is located on a glissading bar, the axis of deixis, which is the relational context of the gazing subject to itself and/or the Image/Object-Sign. The axis of deixis holds the paradigmatics of the *points de capiton*, which operate at various levels, including the textual, cultural, diachronic. It is the manner in which the image is articulated in relation to the gazing/speaking subject, as well as the ways in which the subject is articulated by the Image/Object-Sign, that formulates the qualitative features of the axis and its interplay. It is on the operations of the axis of deixis that a connection is made between the relationship of $\cancel{S}$ --- Image/Object-Sign and $\cancel{S}$ --- Site of Subjectivity. Within this relational context a sub-triangle forms of:

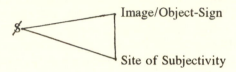

This represents the determination of the split subject's locus of the gaze through the systems of textuality and the operation of the Other in the form of an idealised, ideologically formed site of subjectivity. The configuration "Image/Object-Sign" is the textual, its materiality, the conventions of form and content, the sense of textual operations (genre, narrative, representation, space, time, etc.), and the configuration "site of subjectivity" is the discursive practices of the subject and subjectivity, the onto-theological, the metaphysics of subjectivity, the cultural operations of being, including concepts such as *Dasein*, processes of alienation, the horizontality of Being. The dynamics of the elements within the triangle, their positions and influences on each other, are directly affected by the axis of deixis. Combinational possibilities of this influence include: the Image/Object-Sign determining the position of the gaze (for example, perspective in painting, reading and narrating positions in narrative systems); the site of subjectivity determining the position of the gaze (the proposed site of desire, the ideologically determined gazing position); the split subject determining the gaze via the Image/Object-Sign (for example, the determination of the object as sign, Kleinian projection and introjection, narrational point of view in the novel); the split subject determining the site of subjectivity (for example, discursive practices, Kristeva's sense of *sémiotique* as revolutionary language, reconstructing subjectivity—for example, Irigaray's *Spéculum de l'autre femme*).

This list is far from exhaustive and perhaps hides the most essential feature of the triangle—that it is the interplay of the three elements that constitute the issue. It is also important to note that the relationship between the Image/Object-Sign and the site of subjectivity is determined in different ways in different contexts—the sign can stand for the site of subjectivity (the sign as desirable subject position), oppose it (the sign as revolutionary act against the dominant discursive practices of subjectivity), disguise it (the operation of the gaze as ideological function and as discursive practices), emphasise its desired status, particularly in terms of the gaze as the Other (desire and/or to be desired as subject position). This is connected to the glissading quality of the axis of deixis and consequentially to the splitting of the subject.

The ideological function also has the potential to operate directly in terms of the originary sense of the gazing process, which is why they are seen to be connected here. This interplay between the ideological function and the gaze can stimulate the operation of the ecliptic, in which case at least one further eclipse takes place—ideological sites can be added to the sites of desire (the desiring eye/I) and the sites of absence. It is the case with all three types that the ecliptic function reads one gazing site in terms of at least one other type and that none of the eclipsed sites are exclusive. So, for example, ideological functions can also be issues of desire, and, thus, desire becomes an issue of ideology and/or ideology operates as desire. This is the eclipse of one determining order by another to alter the sense of the gaze.

Within the triangle absence operates at a number of levels. Both configurations of Image/Object-Sign and site of subjectivity are necessarily systems of absence—the first of these because of the *objet petit a*, the second because of the Other. Jean-Pierre Oudart's concept of *suture* offers further possibilities for the mapping of absence within this model. Oudart in fact bases his concept of *suture* on the Lacanian idea developed in turn by Jacques-Alain Miller. Miller states: "*Suture* names the relation of the subject to the chain of its discourse . . . it figures there as the element which is lacking in the form of the stand-in. For, while there lacking, it is not purely and simply absent. *Suture*, by extension—the general relation of lack to the structure of which is an element, inasmuch as it implies the position of a taking the-place-of . . ." (Miller 1977-1978). The boundless absences in the pure field of absences must also take into account the non-diegetic elements of narrative, specifically all those elements that encroach on the diegesis and all those that are introduced and then held in readiness, in absence. In terms of the triangle in this model, *suture* is a determining and qualifying action of the axis of deixis because it is part of the larger order of the gaze, the locus of the gazing/speaking subject, and the interrelationship between subject, subjectivity, and the sign.

The structure of the gaze in terms of its *pulsion* (the scopic drive) can be measured against an oppositional force which flows from the Image/Object-Sign, located as it is in the Symbolic, towards the gaze. In other words, this is the gaze as it meets something which determines it and attempts to assert control over its operations, both at a perceptual and hermeneutic level. This operation can be articulated in terms of four qualities: the lure; the trap; *invidia*; and *dompte regard*. Of these it is the final one that most clearly operates in terms of an oppositional flow to the gaze. However it is important to recognise the role played by the other three in creating this situation. Unlike other elements of this model, these are qualities that determine the type and function of various parts of the scopic operation in terms of desire and absence.

The Lure

The lure operates to capture, to *captate*. It seldom, if ever, can be seen as innocent, and yet it is precisely this quality of innocence that makes the eye take the bait. Allurement is the creation of an operational absence as a desire in the gaze. It is the transformation of the sign so that it becomes irresistible to the gaze, not simply as a point of attraction, but as a focal point. The lure is an exaggeration, an excess which threatens to topple over into its own sense of sign-ness, and in doing so to lose its capacity to capture and become the tain of specula(tive)r action. The lure must draw attention to itself, and at the same time disguise this very action—this quality is lost once the eye becomes aware of the allurement. One strategy for avoiding this is to surround the sign with lures which will disguise and mask the underlying hook that catches the gaze. This is precisely the manner in which terror operates in texts and why horror can be so compelling. This complicity of lures forms part of the heterology of the gaze of the gazing subject and the site of subjectivity.

Lacan figures the lure as part of the subject's relation to the Other—not as a straightforward relationship of the Other's attractiveness to the self, but of the nature of desire and the demand of need. A gap is established between the gaze as part of the scopic drive and desire through the operation of the lure: "the relationship between the gaze and what one wishes to see involves a lure. The subject is presented as other than he is, and what one shows him is not what he wishes to see. It is in this way that the eye may function as *objet a*, that is to say, at the level of the lack (- o)" (Lacan 1986: 104). This is significant in terms of theorising the gaze as a structure of absence because it is the disjunction between the act of gazing and what is desired to be seen that figures the scopic and not just a relational context of viewer and viewed. The lure provides an attraction for the gaze within a potential context of resistance. The manifestation of the sign—its point of attraction to be read—leads to a specular seduction. This is a desire to read the sign despite any *lacrimae rerum* that might be encountered. The lure is not solely part of the operation of the gaze and the scopic drive, rather it is a polymorphic structure which sets up points of connection between the Real and the split subject. It does, however, illustrate one of the fundamental systems of absence in terms of the gaze. The lure, therefore, must be seen as a qualitative order invested in, and including, the signifier, the operation of the sign, the function of the gaze, and the feature of the scopic drive, and not simply as an order within a category of desire. It is in this sense that Lacan's connection of the lure with the Freudian idea of love (in a fundamental way the relationship of the self to the Real) can be seen to be based on absence and so permits a rereading of the crucial operation of drives. Furthermore, it is quite feasible to locate Kristeva's idea of the absence of an amatory code within such a context.

Absence operates in two ways in terms of the lure: the lure as representational presence, which takes various forms, such as the lure as simulacra (false presence); and the demand on the gaze by the lure (privileging certain presences). In both cases, which are never mutually exclusive, the lure disguises the absence by devising a point of attraction. The second operation is the lure motivated by absence, which is derived from the numerous points of absence within the structures of subjectivity and desire. In the first of these the lure operates external to the gaze, pulling it toward the point(s) of attraction, in the second the lure operates within the gaze, forcing it to determine meaningful sites in terms of the gazing subject. Such a division is mostly arbitrary and it would be very difficult to establish types of lures according to this external/internal conceptualisation. What is significant, however, is the forceful nature of the lure which is entwined in the trap.

The Trap

Lacan's discussions of the gaze as a process of subjectivity are often based on a dynamic of tensions and counteractions. The gaze is seen as playing against the eye, the gazing subject as struggling against the object. Lacan sets up a struggle for control of the gaze that operates directly in the subject's relational context to the Imaginary and the Symbolic. The struggles between the gaze and the eye are not so much about representation and perception, but fundamental models of knowledge and being. Lacan's analysis of Holbein's *The Ambassadors* is precisely about this struggle between the subject and what is gazed at—the distorted death's head is present "in order to catch, I would almost say, *to catch in its trap*, the observer, that is to say, us. It is, in short, an obvious way . . . of showing us that, as subjects, we are literally called into the picture, and represented here as caught" (Lacan 1986: 92). Earlier Lacan states: "This picture is simply what any picture is, a trap for the gaze. In any picture, it is precisely in seeking the gaze in each of its points that you will see it disappear" (Lacan 1986: 89). The underlying issue in this struggle between the gaze and the eye, between the subject and the picture (sign), between drive and action, is the interplay between subjectivity and absence—how the lack (-o) operates as a crucial point in the manifestation of desire and language/discourse.

What seems initially to be a debate on the control of the gaze through the

organisation of signifiers (those which dominate and those which are subordinated) turns out to be an examination of the function of absence in the desiring
subject. Foucault touches on these same issues—although for quite different
reasons—when he investigates the archaeology of classical discourse. Foucault
(1970) concentrates on the issue of representation and its essential features
through his analysis of Velasquez's *Las Meninas* and in doing so emphasises the
significance of invisibility—that is, in effect, absence. Representation and its
systems of production are inextricably tied to this issue of invisibility and
doubling. This concept of the instability of the superimposition is also to be
found in the formation and operation of the scopic drive. The instability exists
because the gaze, that investment of the self in the scopic, is constantly determined external to the self—it is the mediated passage from the centrality of the
Imaginary to the order of the Symbolic. The loss of control, or even the fear
of this loss, is measured against the need to operate within the Symbolic.

The invisibility of representation, which is also the absence of subjectivity
and this loss, is why the image/sign operates as a trap. Two determining
forces—the gaze and the image—vie for control over the ordering systems in an
onto-epistemological struggle. To keep the gaze active draws the action of the
Other, which already rests, *in potentia*, in the image, into the field. The
motivation for this struggle is desire and the desire for the Other—the gaze is
always towards absence. The significance of the text (the artistic text as well as
the transformation of other signifying systems into texts) is that it provides for
precisely this interplay of the trap and the active, resisting gaze. What for
Lacan is an issue of the subject's relational context to the Imaginary (the turning
of the self into a picture) and the Symbolic is for Foucault an issue of the
visible action of representation—an issue that at the very least can be connected
to Freud's examination of *Vorstellungrepräsentanz*, particularly in terms of
Lacan's own distinction between representation and the picture. This can also
be seen as a further ideological function of the text. Of course none of these are
divorced from the others—the trap is at the same time ideological, a system of
representational visibility and the demand of the Symbolic in terms of the
Other.

Invidia and *Dompte-regard*

The motion back from the Image/Object-Sign—from the configuration of
the sign in the Symbolic to the site of subjectivity through the gazing/split
subject—is the action of the managing of the gaze. Lacan coins the phrase
dompte-regard, the laying down or taming of the gaze—the "exploitation of
desire" (Lacan 1986: 111) because it pacifies the desiring gaze and its sense of
absence. The *dompte-regard* offers presence (albeit short-lived) to the hungry
eye, but implicit in this are further absences—which is also why Lacan speaks
at such length on the relationship of the gaze to the systemic order of *objet petit*

a. This is particularly important in terms of the formation of the text because there is a constant juxtapositioning of absences (desire) and presences (*dompte-regard*) in the act of reading. This is also part of the interplay of the visible and invisible in the formation of representational practices. Texts establish (historically, generically) and employ various devices for this binding of opposites.

This is the issue of the gaze, a function of subjectivity and desire as *objet petit a*, in the context of the Imaginary and the Symbolic. Lacan notes: "there is something whose absence can always be observed in a picture—which is not the case in perception. . . . In every picture, this central field cannot but be absent, and replaced by a hole—a reflection, in short, of the pupil behind which is situated the gaze" (Lacan 1986: 108). It is this negotiation of the subject in the picture as signifier—that is, the textual, the Image/Object-Sign—the externalisation of the self and the dynamics of the gaze (lack and desire) which forms a central part of the ideological function of absence and presence in the operation of the gaze, as well as the double level of signification in specula(tive)r. It is precisely within this context that Althusser's concept of determinate absences within the categories of subject and object as inversions of production and consumption operates.

When Lacan speaks of *dompte-regard*, he also mentions the process of *invidia*—the envy of the gaze. *Invidia* is not simply envy however—it is a central challenge to the point of subjectivity: "Such is true envy—the envy that makes the subject pale before the image of a completeness closed upon itself" (Lacan 1986: 116). The distinction needs to be made between the gaze engaging in desire/*invidia* and so seeking/watching the *objet petit a*, and the gaze actually figured as *objet petit a*. In the second case it is the desire for the gaze, or the envy of a gaze, that is the focal point. This is why the ecliptic gaze operates as it does—there is the determining action of the gaze from the subject (the scopic drive), the contiguous pull of the lure and the trap (the attraction of the sign, the *captated* look), the demand of the *dompte-regard* (from the sign to the site of subjectivity), and the potential act of *invidia* (the desired site from which to gaze, the desire to possess another's gaze, the desire for the gaze of the Other). *Invidia* develops from the gazing site of absence—sight is seen as lacking, as a lack—or even in the pressure of the *dompte-regard* to retain the domination of the gaze. The source of the envy is that absence which determines at the same moment in time desire and the register of subjectivity. This is the combination of the envy for the absences, the absences of desire, and the gaps in the formation of subjectivity.

This paradigm of absences in the interplay of subjectivity and the gaze—which includes *invidia*, the political agenda of *dompte-regard*, and the shame of the gaze through the operation of the Other, as well as whatever distinctions can be made in terms of active and passive processes of gaze and look—is marked by the heterology of absences in the operation of the gaze. Such an inflection results in not a single construction of the gaze, or a binarism (of active and passive, masculine and feminine, hegemonic and submissive, master and slave). It cannot even be adequately explained in terms of a triad, that is of subject, object, and the absent observer of the act. The nature of the gaze means that the system of absences articulates both the paradigmatics of gazing positions and the determination of subjectivity through desire. This is why the gaze is not a single relationship, but a multiple paradigmatics of absences based on possible permutations, including different structures, different observers, and different points of observation/gazing.

Part Three

Towards a Semiotics of Absence

8

On the Structure of the Sign and Absence

Absence and the Structure of the Sign

It is necessary to consider the sign from two perspectives here—on the one hand, the sign and its semiotic operations as it performs in terms of the relationship between subject, absence, and desire; and, on the other hand, how absence features in the sign and systems of semiosis and discourse. Essentially the first of these is the paradigm of diverse, heterogeneous processes developed because of the excesses of desire and absence in the production of the subject position. Systems of signification exist because of the forces of insatiable desire (and their absences), on the one hand, and the multitude of complex absences on the other. When we engage in signs of any type we are attempting to satisfy desires and fill the absences. That is not to deny the communicative role of signs and languages, for communication is essentially about desire: the desire to communicate something; the positioning of desire onto a signifier to communicate it; the positioning of a signifier onto desire in order to qualify, engage in, understand it; the desire to utilise the signification system and its discursive powers (the enunciating subject). It is also essentially about absence—being absented from the discursive systems, the struggle to express the desire because of the absences, as well as the sense of absence in the subject and the sense of absence in the perceived addressee.

Every signification system is motivated by desire and absence and exists solely because of these two forces and the subject apparatus. This is true of written and spoken languages, visual languages, cultural languages (the anthropological, sociological analysis as well as the actual *langue* and *parole* of the specific cultures). Even so called pure mathematical languages exist and function because of the interplay between a desiring subject and a system of absence. This fundamental property of all semiotic systems differs only in terms of the emphasis placed on absence, desire, and the subject position, and of the combinations possible.

Part of the reason for this domination is that the sign itself is based on the interplay of presence and absence: "The sign represents the present in its absence. It takes the place of the present. . . . when the present cannot be presented, we signify, we go through the detour of the sign. We take or give signs. We signal. The sign, in this sense, is deferred presence" (Derrida 1986: 9). This is the situation of the trace and erasure ("the trace is not a presence but the simulacrum of a presence that dislocates itself, displaces itself" [Derrida 1986: 24]). Simulacrum becomes an order, a typological range, of absence that typifies the operation of the sign at its most quintessential level. Because the sign is based on absence yet derives its power and authority from this sense of presence, there is a constant and extensive constructing of the sign within itself and through systems such as codes. This is the privilege of presence as it operates in the sign: "The formal essence of the signified is presence, and the privilege of its proximity to the *logos* as *phone* is the privilege of presence" (Derrida 1976: 18). It is significant that the sign and its sense of presence are part of desire, which reflects the ideological mechanisms of discourse. This sense of privilege orders the ideological dimension of the sign and its users, the relational context of truth, the operation of discourse as a system of presenting, and the operation of signification. This privilege goes beyond the constitutive factors of the sign and informs the very ways in which the sign is thought. Theorising absence is an attempt to unsettle this way of thinking about the sign and presence. However, the sign does not operate simply in terms of presence and relational absence, for this is the disguise which has operated for too long. Derrida's assertion that "the process of the sign is an *Aufhebung*" (Derrida 1986: 88) supports this. It is not just the process, but the notion—the way of conceiving the sign itself—which needs to be figured afresh in these (at the minimum non-binary) terms. Similarly, one of the central projects in *Of Grammatology* is precisely this putting of the (binary nature) of the sign under erasure, through the fundamental issue of *gramme*, which is "the new structure of nonpresence" (Derrida 1986: 84).

The creation and existence of semiotic systems through the triad of subject position, absence, and desire consequentially contribute to absences within the language systems themselves. Absence exists within the systems because of (in no sense of priority): the impossibility of closure and completion; the creative processes involved whenever the subject engages in the systems of signification; the desire for absence within the system; the inherent and necessary lacunary nature of all these systems.

The Glissement of the Bar

Putting to one side the idea of the materiality of the signifier it becomes necessary to ask what constitutes the signifier in terms of its existence, its visible legibility and legitimation. The signifier exists not because of some inherent quality of *signifierness* but because of the code structures that qualify it and the correlative nature of the devised signified(s). The "bar" is defined as that metaphoric, graphic, and critical structure which is used to designate a difference and relationship between the signifier and signifieds. The correlative nature is directly linked to the operation and function of the bar between the signifier and the signified, and it is this structure which we must now turn our attention to.

An essential and fundamental legacy of Lacan's enterprise is the reformulation of the sign structure, the questioning of the materiality of the signifier (its "materiality as well as its formality" as Derrida [1987a] describes it—the letter of the signifier, the site of the signifier in the letter) the structure of the signifieds. The capacity for overdeterminism in the sign relates to the metaphoric concept of the sign to the unconscious, and in particular to the interplay between the unconscious and desire. The bar of the signifier/signified is directly connected to the discourse of desire and the subject, for it is here that the subject, via the unconscious, negotiates desire, its manifestations and effects. This is partly the motivation behind Lacan's renaming of Freud's term *Wahrnehmungszeichen* as signifiers. Lacan sees Freud's concern that the traces of perception be read as distinct from consciousness as an anticipation of the structure of the sign, and in particular the signifier. This is also part of the reason why Lacan returns often to the concept of a language of the unconscious. In these terms language (the sign and its operations) becomes the intervention in the conflict of the unconscious.

What does the bar stand for? It is not simply a structural device, an architectural support for the signifier to rest on its signified(s). Nor can it be seen as simply divisional, although it does provide both of these (necessary) functions. At one level the bar is the site of the construction of meaning(s), that is, the site of signification or what Lacan (1985) calls the effect of meaning. This effect is the construction rather than any sense of fixing a meaning or set of meanings to the sign. This is not the transcendental signifier/signified, nor is it an agenda for the interpretation of the sign via the relational context of the bar. It is the *effect* of meaning, not some sense of meaning itself, and the effect of meaning is the subject's insertion into the interplay of the signifier as it is located in the Other. Subjectivity and desire are pivotal points in the bar because of the subject"s positioning of the self/narcissistic self to the sign. This, in turn, means that the bar can be seen as a type of operational absence.

The bar operates in terms of absence in a number of ways. It features in the sense of absence found in both desire and subjectivity, particularly in the activities of desire for the subject site. These activities include attempts to satisfy desire, attempts at a register of desires and development of a language/semiotics of desire, or attempts to assert the subject in the self. In short, any activity that involves the engagement of the signifier also involves desire, subjectivity, and absence, and one of the principle points of reference

of this triadic flow is the bar. This is not to argue that the bar contains all of
these elements and their functions in a uniform and consistent manner. Any sign
can contain within its construction a bar which has as its central feature any one
of these, or any combination of the three. However, absence must be a
necessary feature in any process or combination. So a sign which has a bar
constituted predominately by the semiotics of desire—that is, the bond between
the signifier and the signified is essentially one constructed and sustained by
desire—will still contain aspects of absence. This is due largely to the operation
of absence in both subjectivity and desire, as well as the construction of the sign
itself, specifically in the formation of the bar and the action of *glissement*.

Lacan takes up the idea of the glissading bar most noticeably in "*L'instance
de la lettre dans l'inconscient ou la raison depuis Freud*". The original place of
the paper's delivery and its intended audience causes Lacan to preface the text
by indicating the literary reference of the title. This meta-discursive tone
continues throughout the article—the significance here is that Lacan calls on the
issue of the letter and its position. "*L'instance de la lettre*" produces an interplay between the agency or the insistence of the letter, *la lettre/À la lettre*
("*Mais cette lettre comment faut-il le prendre ici? Tout uniment, à la lettre*"
[Lacan 1966:251]). The *insistence* of the letter stems from the "constitutive
moment of an algorithm that is its foundation" (Lacan 1985: 149; 1966: 253)
which is the S/s—the signifier over the signified. It is also significant to note
that insistence in the signifying chain is related to *Wiederholungszwang*—the
repetition of automatism and compulsion. This insistence is part of the
positioning of the signifier as desire in the realm of the Other, filled with those
qualities of desire. It is the history of France—perhaps all histories—outside the
toilets on the station platform because it includes not just the structure of the
sign, but the cultural, ideological, sexual, meanings, and politics. There is the
possibility of a realm of essentially non-phallocentric readings of the sign, the
subject and interpretive actions. It is the complex network of surrounding praxis
that causes the divergence of masculine and feminine, which is ". . . actually
the same country and neither can compromise on its own superiority without
detracting from the glory of the other" (Lacan 1985: 152). The overdetermined
sign, caught in unlimited semiosis, operates with a shifting bar.

This *glissement* accounts for the dynamics of meaning and the non-equivale-
nce of the signifier to a single signified, or even a limited set of signifieds. This
is not to argue that the flow of the *glissement* is totally anarchic and transitory.
Contributing to the relationship at any moment are the *points de capiton*, which
we encountered earlier in the Bottle Opener graph: "In it is articulated what I
have called the "anchoring point" (*point de capiton*), by which the signifier
stops the otherwise endless movement (*glissement*) of the signification" (Lacan
1985: 303). Much more than the operation of language at a formal level,
glissement and *point de capiton* represent the interplay between the *Ichspaltung*
and its desire for the Other. The sliding of meaning and the anchoring points
must inevitably become part of the ideological function of subjectivity and

interpretation. The forces that "fix" and "unfix" signifieds are fundamental to discursive practices because they *become* these discursive practices. The aphanisitic quality of *point de capiton* ensures that the I pays attention to the signifier and its development. It is a critical investment because this is a form of anchoring and sliding that becomes an essential feature in the subject's relationship to desire. It is also fundamentally an issue of interpretation and the ways in which the text makes sense to the subject and the subject makes sense of the text. This is the drifting (*dérive*) of the signifier as it operates within the Symbolic and constitutes the subject as a lack. Lacan argues against the explosion of meanings that *glissement* might suggest: "Interpretation is not open to all meanings. It is not just any interpretation. It is a significant interpretation, one that must not be missed. This does not mean that it is not this signification that is essential to the advent of the subject. What is essential is that he should see, beyond this signification, to what signifier—to what irreducible, traumatic, *non-meaning*—he is, as a subject, subjected" (Lacan 1986: 250-251) (my emphasis). This is the signifier located in the Other and the subject being determined by his/her desire for that Other and the series of lacks and absences which become constitutive. Yet, even this "significant interpretation" points beyond itself towards a non-meaning, an absence.

Lacan aligns the *glissement* of the signifier/signified to Freud's concept of *Entstellung*. Why does Lacan devise this? There initially appears to be a difficulty with such a schema, for it suggests the inversion of meaning and meaning-production into *Entstellung* as a specific process of repression and subsequent re-presentation/representation. Lacan does this to work towards the second part of his thesis—the unconscious as language system. If the *glissement* of signifier and signified is equivalent to a process such as *Entstellung* then the essentially linguistic model can cover more of the concerns of how the unconscious operates and how it can be read. *Glissement* significantly contributes to the polymorphic action of the sign and its interpretation. In this sense *Entstellung* carries with it the poetic/metalingual function of semiosis. Meaning is devised through these positions which locate the *glissement* of the bar. This is not to assert the universal sense—there must always be an allowance for *méconnaissance* or aberrance.

Absence and the Signifier/Signified: Lacunae, Semiosis and the Sign

Beyond the bar exists the signifier and the signified(s) of the sign, but their existence is not assured simply because the sign is devised. The essential feature of the signifier is its relationship to absence: "For the signifier is a unit in its very uniqueness, being by nature symbol only of an absence" (Lacan 1975: 54). The signifier's inextricable link to absence exerts the sense of presence—the signifier appears to have indubitable presence, but this is only because it is located against a backdrop of absence. This is the intuition of absence of the sign in Hegelian semiology. The purloining of the letter/signifier emphasises this absent quality.

In a different, yet aligned, fashion Derrida speaks of the supplementary requirement of the signifier: "The *overabundance* of the signifier, its *supplementary* character, is thus the result of a finitude, that is to say, the result of a lack which must be *supplemented*" (Derrida 1978b: 290). This supplementary characteristic relates to the insistence of the signifier: "*D'où l'on peut dire que c'est dans le chaîne du signifiant que le sens* insiste, *mais qu'aucun des éléments de la chaîne ne* consiste *dans la signification dont il est capable au moment meme*" (Lacan 1966: 260). Here Lacan is clearly emphasising the active, authoritative side of *l'instance* in the letter, but clarifies the sense of a transcendental signifying order. This is the point he makes in "Seminar on *The Purloined Letter*"—it is the relational context of the signifier against a glissading bar of signification. The chain of signification builds up tendencies not certainties, and the lacunal property of this shifts the emphasis from the consists to the insists.

The feature of the bar can be seen as the originary interplay of absence. The *glissement* of the bar reveals a more fundamental equation of absence than the simple replacement function of the sign for the concept. All signs are founded on absence because all signs deal in replacements and standing in for others. But absence extends beyond this, operating in the determination of the signifier, the signified, the bar, *glissement*, the code. In fact, at all levels and in all aspects of the sign—it is impossible to think of the sign without taking into account the fabric of absences. Absence is such a dominant feature in the sign because of the dual function that it performs—that is, that the sign is designed to negotiate absences of various types (representing what is absent, conveying ideas in order to fill an absence, producing a "presence" which is read against absence[s])—and because signs in themselves are systems of absences. This raises the question that if signs are systems of absence, then what makes them so desirable to the subject who is also constituted and determined by absence(s), given that a central rationale for possessing the sign is to "fill" the gaps and "mend" the splits of the *Ichspaltung*. The desirability of signs rests precisely in these systems of absence—it is the absence which makes the signs desirable, and it is the absent nature of the signs which increases this desire. This is not to deny the *mode d'assujettissement* process, or any correlative ideological interplay, for these conceptual operations are the linking point of subject desire as discursive practice.

In the phenomenological reading of lacunal properties of the text, the act of reading is based on the determining of the gaps as much as it is in reading what is present. Ingarden's *Unbestimmtheitsstellen* illustrates the desirability of these gaps to both text and reader. *Unbestimmtheitsstellen* operate in terms of the sign. If we were to transpose the fundamental sign structure onto this lacunal system we would find aspects of it in the signifier, bar, signified, and the overall structure of the sign itself. Far from a complete unit which, added to other units, produces *Unbestimmtheitsstellen*, the sign also needs to be constructed. It is not a uniform contributing pattern however—the signifier will appear to have fewer lacunae than the signified; the bar will seem to disappear altogether in the "utilitarian" operation of the sign. However what is common is that all facets of the sign have undetermined as well as indetermined aspects. No matter how complete the signifier appears and how apparent the signified(s) seem, and how "fixed" the *glissement* acts according to the *points de capiton*, in each of these absence will dominate. This becomes attractive to the subject, because, as the reader of the sign, he/she is primarily concerned with the relationship of the sign to the self—its material sense and the sociocultural constructions of sign and subject—and its lacks (including the self/being as semiotic system), and therefore any space for insertion and a potential for the gaining of the sign will be a space of possible control. What happens, however, is that the sign, because it belongs to the Other, is never possessed and so the attraction of constructing/reconstructing the sign for its reader is always deferred. *Différance*—and also, if by implication alone, both trace and *gramme*—originate from this fundamental aspect of the signifier's relationship to the signified. *Différance* is inherently about instability and dynamic forces, it is the critical focusing on the slippage that constitutes the sign. Derrida seeks to undermine even its status as a concept: "*différance* is thus no longer simply a concept, but rather the possibility of conceptuality, of a conceptual process and system in general" (Derrida 1986: 11). In this sense *différance* is not just about the production of specific meanings but about the possibilities of the mechanisms of signification. This is also part of the reason why Derrida introduces the concept within the critical context of Heidegger's distinction between Being and beings; for it is also about the formation of subjectivity in terms of the interplay of the sign, signification, and the subject. In this sense *différance* and absence are foundational, because without them signification could not occur.

Différance operates within the wider context of grammatology and deconstruction and as such seeks to acknowledge the historical processes of the sign as it functions in its various guises. The concept of the sign has always existed within a particular history and philosophical discourse: "the concept of the sign—which has never existed or functioned outside the history of (the) philosophy (of presence)—remains systematically and genealogically determined by that history" (Derrida 1976: 14). The philosophy of presence is bound to the metaphysics of subjectivity, to the presence of the subject and the positioning of the trace as simulacrum, that attempts to secure that presence in the face of the non-arrival of the sign. For this reason alone the *glissement* structure of the sign, which could almost be seen as a complex form of *brisure* in the sign, is invested with passionate ideological force—a force that at another level links with the pleasure principle and the sex drive because it is about existence and continuation. The ideological function of the construction of meaning and the investment of the self in the sign are connected to the process of semiosis. This is not to say that semiosis is necessarily ideological or offers assurances ("false" or "real") for the self in the sign, but it is the space where such issues continue to operate and be assessed.

Unlimited semiosis is an "inherent" aspect of the sign because of the complex and diverse interplay between representation and meaning. In this case semiosis acts like desire because it continually suggests a beyondness to any formulation of either representation or interpretation. The suggestive quality of the connotative levels ensures that the process of semiosis continues within the central frame of the sign, its connection to other signs, and also as a pressure independent of the sign itself. Engagement with the sign is ostensibly "about" meaning and communicative functions; however, the subject's necessary participation in the dynamics of semiosis at the same time produces the difficult and enigmatic pleasures of absence.

Both semiosis and lacunae in the sign operate as absent structures that are connected to the desire for the sign. However at an even more fundamental level is the subject's perception of the imperative nature of the sign to subjectivity. If for no other reason, this would provide an essential feature of the sign which guarantees its desirability through absence. The top left corner in the Bottle Opener graph constructs a significant point in these terms. It is the interconnecting site of the signifier as it determines the subject in the dialectic of desire. This determination of the subject should not be read as completion of the subject—this is after all a seminar on the subversion of the subject—but rather as the way in which subjectivity is positioned through the Other and the signifier. The algorithm $S(\phi)$ is to be read as "signifier of a lack in the Other" (Lacan 1985: 316). As discussed earlier, this produces the -I, the subject of the lack. However, in as much as this is the point of the $S(\phi)$ it is also *jouissance*, and the reason why it is both lack and *jouissance* is the function of the ecstasy in absence and the sign. We can follow Lacan through his production of the algebraic method and beyond: "What am *I*? *I* am in the place from which a voice is heard clamouring "the universe is a defect in the purity of Non-Being". And not without reason, for by protecting itself this place makes Being itself languish. This place is called *Jouissance*, and it is the absence of this that makes the universe vain" (Lacan 1985: 317). This is not the vanity that determines narcissism, but rather emptiness. The empty universe extends the absences of the subject, the defect makes certain the subject's sustained attempts to gain wholeness. The direction of the top part of the graph is powered by "the myth Freud gave us"—the castration complex (Lacan 1985). By locating the castration complex within the larger order of primal phantasies, as Freud does, it becomes much more than an issue of developments. Included in this is the subject's negotiation of sociocultural orders, the evolution of the super-ego, the managing (often repression) of desires, certain consolidations of the subject's identification, interpretive gestures towards sexuality, and origins.

Within this primal phantasy we find further evidence of the centrality of absence for the subject and the signifier, for, after all, the castration complex is founded on a sense of absence and presence. Even in its presences exists absences because of the *manque-à-être*. It is in this sense that both lacunae and semiosis operate in terms of a code structure of desire, largely because of the features of primal phantasy of the site of subjectivity. This includes the applicable, although not necessarily intended (by Freud in particular), sense of the partial object and the drive as representative of absence in the castration complex. The Freudian paradigm, via Lacan and Kristeva in particular, develops the castration complex as a central model for the splitting of the subject from language. This intersubjective discovery and subsequent separation is instrumental in the thetic phase "which posits the gap between the signifier and signified as an opening up toward every desire but also every act, including the very *jouissance* that exceeds them" (Kristeva 1984c: 47). This thetic phase and gap of signifier/signified is an order of absence that the subject attempts to operate in—it is the political gap for the possibility of the site of subjectivity for the subject. This is what qualifies the absence of the sign structure (including the *glissement* of the bar) as *sémiotique* (as thetic), Symbolic and semiotic, and adheres it all the more to the desire of the subject for subjectivity within the sign. It is the terrifying knowledge of otherness that becomes the social context for the signifier and the subject and marks the subject as absent from the signifier.

This bonding of the subject to the signifier is crucial to understanding how absence operates in terms of alterity, signification, social praxis (particularly in terms of systems of representation): "The Other is the locus in which is situated the chain of the signifier that governs whatever may be made present of the subject—it is the field of that living being in which the subject has to appear" (Lacan 1986: 203). Lacan is most emphatic here ("*qui commande tout ce qui va pouvoir se présentifier du sujet, c'est le champ de ce vivant où le sujet a à apparaître*" (Lacan 1973: 185) regarding the necessary nature of the bond between the subject, what is present for that subject and how elements of presence exist. This is the same chain of the signifier that operates in the dialectic of desire and produces the *glissement* of the bar, and it is this quintessential feature of dynamics that becomes the semiosis of the chain and the subject. This is why Lacan's definition of the signifier, which appears so odd initially, can make sense according to absence and desire. The hieroglyph-ics on the stone in the desert are rendered as signifiers not because they *mean* something in themselves but because they refer to other signifiers within a system of differential relations.

Kristeva invests this link with a phenomenological sense, particularly in terms of Husserl's *Logical Investigations*. The issue at hand is the connection between acts of signification and Husserl's configuration of the transcendental ego: "the thin sheath of the sign (signifier/signified) opens onto a complex architecture where intentional life-experience captures material (hylic) multi-plicities, endowing them first with noetic meaning, then with noematic meaning, so that finally the result for judging consciousness is the formation of an object once and for all signified as real" (Kristeva 1984b: 129). It is from this stance that Kristeva develops the operating thetic consciousness which can be seen to have a number of connections to Lacan's subject stumbling through the desert in pursuit of hieroglyphic stones. Furthermore, Kristeva's two conclusions are drawn from the critical positioning of Husserlian phenomenological concerns and modern linguistics: issues of signification must include considerations of "the subject thus formulated as operating consciousness" (Kristeva 1984b: 131) and these considerations lead to the interconnection between the subject, signification, and sociability.

An obvious difficulty appears here. If absence and splits determine the subject, then how can we correlate this to Husserl's idea of the Ego as unified and orientated through singularity? The answer lies in the categorising process that organises these processes. Singularity and unification within the category do not conflict with a split/absent subject, in fact they strengthen the concept because the greater the sense of unification in one area the greater the split from others. This is why ultimately there is a conflicting relationship between the transcendental ego and the subject in the Symbolic, or more specifically the subject in language. The relationship becomes one based on rejection as distinct from scission and separation, which clearly indicates a sense of the mirror stage and the entry into the Symbolic. It is the intrinsic rupturing gap between signifier and signified which allows the formation of the enunciating/speaking subject (Kristeva 1984c), locating this subject type within a constitutional absence. This also becomes an essential feature of narrative in terms of the subject and absence—narration and the subject of enunciation are fundamentally based on concepts such as anonymity, absences, blanks, and gaps.

The heterogeneity of language as a functioning process in relation to the subject is part of the formulation of the "questionable subject-in-process" (*le sujet en procès* and *mise en procès*). The questionable subject-in-process occupies the same relationship to the signifier (desire through absence, dependence for existence) as is articulated in the S(O) of *jouissance* and castration, pleasure and primal origins. Kristeva's notion of the *clivé* (split) in the subject contributes to both the question and the process found in the *Ichspaltung*. The *clivé* is in some ways comparable to the glissading bar that splits and joins the signifier and the signified. Most noticeably the *clivé* operates in terms of the split subject and subject-in-process which are positioned oppositionally to the unary subject. Unification/oneness in this largely Marxist/cultural context is devised through the Symbolic and the subject's utilisation of the sign. This is why the Symbolic represents both the splitting of the subject and hopes for the unary subject.

The exchange between *sémiotique* and Symbolic and the "internal" structure of the sign demonstrates further this double-edged relationship. The danger for the subject in this sense is the furthering of the split, the further loss of the signifier to the Other. Absences are emphasised. The potential gain is the disruption of discursive practices and, as a consequence, power within and above the discursive systems of the Symbolic. In many ways this is the historical context that Kristeva (1984b) speaks of with the transition of symbol-based thought to sign-based thought in Western culture in the thirteenth to fifteenth centuries.

When the subject's relationship to the sign becomes aphanistic need the issue of the existence of the sign passes into the paradigmatics of meaning/signification, being and truth. Each anticipates and requires the other: the self measures the sense of being against the sign; the sign exists external to the self with this external existence drawing attention to the sign's beingness; signification and the production of meaning for the subject and the sign become entwined with this meaning becoming a measure of truth. The difficulty with this is that there is a sociocultural/ideological context which constantly affects these processes. Truth is determined within the processes, but can never be seen as fundamental, even identifiable. Truth retains absence because this is how it can continue to exist as a concept. To fix truth with presence is to alter its essential quality because truth must always be absent. To "fix truth" is to locate it in a temporal sense, which is different from saying there is a fundamental and stable truth, although the duration of a truth will give it the appearance of these qualities.

Similarly, Derrida argues for a teleological positioning of the sign in time which occasionally comes close to a form of transcendentalism that he is, in effect, deconstructing, and becomes a central issue in the discussion of the arbitrariness of the sign and its relationship to truth and reality. This is the case with the subject's relationship to the sign and the sign's relationship to everything. Can there be a type of sign that is more truthful than others? Is, for example, the iconic sign more truthful than the symbolic sign? Such questions suggest a motivation between the sign and truth, but this is devised rather than something incorporated in the structure of the sign. The purloined letter (of the seminar and of all letters) has a special relationship to truth: "The truth of the purloined letter is the truth, its meaning is meaning, its law is the law, the contract of truth with itself in *logos*" (Derrida 1987a: 439). This is an issue of the sign and the processes of codes.

What is particularly significant about this in terms of absence is that the relative strength or weakness of truth in its signification is based on what is revealed and what is hidden, and how such revelations and disguises operate within discursive practices (which in themselves are prone to these very actions). Part of the play between the sign and truth is the indication of revelation, even if this does not actually take place. To produce "truth", to give the appearance of truth, is to produce a function of presence, which is different from any sense of truth as it appears in a teleological or archaeological process; it is absence which determines a sense of truth. Truth appears, but this appearance is the manipulation of absence, or even the manipulation of the manipulation of absence rather than an interpretative movement towards *eidos*. This is the ideological function of the discourse of truth and what is located

outside of it: "Truth—cut off from (or adulterated with, *coupée de*) knowledge—is constantly determined as a revelation, non-veiling, that is: necessarily
as presence, presentation of the present, "Being of being" (*Anwesenheit*) or, in
a more literally Heideggerian mode, as the unity of veiling and unveiling"
(Derrida 1981: 117).

This is, in many ways, comparable to Lacan's reworking of the signifier
operating in a context which is essentially one of absence but invested with
presence. This conjunction of the signifier, notably the sign itself, and
truth-as-presence order the very sense of truth and knowledge in terms of
presence. This is the *episteme* (in its permutations of knowledge, history,
discourse, ideology) as symbiotically linked to presence, to its determination "as
detours for the purpose of the reappropriation of presence", and the link
between the *episteme* and "logocentric metaphysics" (Derrida 1973: 10; 46),
which is an organising principle of presence and truth-in-presence and
truth-as-presence. Lacan's definition of truth in the closing section of "La chose
freudienne" likewise indicates a sense of truth's distance from the subject: "For
truth proves to be complex in essence, humble in its offices and alien to reality,
stubborn to the choice of sex, akin to death and, all in all, rather inhuman"
(Lacan 1985: 145). Truth's inhumanness distances it from the individual, and
its distance from a reality aligns it more closely with the site of subjectivity and
the attendant absences. In this sense truth is external and becomes part of the
Other.

Truth outside of the sign and located in the Other reflects another attribute
of truth and absence. It is only within a context of truth that something can be
hidden. Truth is determined not transcendentally but within the context of the
subject's relationship to the sign as absence. Some dimensions of truth are
located within the Symbolic, but this does not dispute reading it as essentially
Other—the Symbolic is also Other because of how the subject engages in its
structures and systems. Such a reading also enables us to understand more
clearly the category of error as it functions in terms of truth and the sign. Error
is a fundamental issue of Freudian psychoanalysis. A great deal of Freud's key
works are based on the operation of error and its relationship to concepts of
truth.

Lacan emphatically states the connection between error and truth: "It is
clear that error is only definable in terms of the truth. But the point is not that
there would be no error if there were no truth, as there would be no white if
there were no black. There is more to it than that—there is no error which does
not present and promulgate itself as truth. In short error is the habitual incarna-
tion of the truth" (Lacan 1988a: 263). Error, then, is not the absence of truth,
rather it is a point where the investment of presence in truth is revealed. An
error is truth until the signs are reread according to different code systems, and
it is this temporal sense and this temporalisation of truth in the readings of
absence that indicate the interplay of presence and absence. Truth is present and
presence is assured until that moment in time when the sign moves from truth

to error or falsehood. This is the case with all forms of signs. Magritte's painting *Ceci n'est pas une pipe* illustrates the error-truth-presence factor in both written and visual terms. The double bind of one set of signifiers against another (the visual against the written, the iconic against the symbolic, the photo-realistic against the authority of the word) engages in truth and error because the presence of one negates the other and so produces absences. Foucault's reading of the painting deals with this, in the final chapter entitled "*Peindre n'est pas affirmer*", when he speaks of the "simultaneously present and visible, image, text" and how when it is opened up "the caligram immediately decomposes and disappears, leaving as a trace only its own absence" (Foucault 1983: 54). Here the text draws attention to truth and error. But there are also whole genres of texts that play on the reader's "errors" in reading the signs to produce false truths that are revealed much later in the text. In these cases it is textually imperative that the errors of reading are sustained for as long as possible so whole clusters of signs are developed to create *truths* whose presence is demanded by the text. This is a form of textual habituation of truth through error.

Truth and the configuration of presence is the Parisian striptease of Barthes's *Mythologies*, a "spectacle based on fear, or rather on the pretence of fear" (Barthes 1972b: 84). Part of the fear of truth is that once its essential features are revealed the disclosure will disappoint. The eroticism, or even seduction, of truth lies in its feigned revealing, its assertion of presence yet always crucially, totally bound to absence. But the more significant fear of the spectacle of revealed truth is that the exchange of presence and absence is lost—the cotton reel returns and stays, always a cotton reel. Fear in this sense is the more primary notion of closure—of foreclosure—of possibilities. The shifting place of truth is not the proper because "in truth" is not "as truth" and vice versa. The overwhelming operation of presence in truth means that the epistemic, hegemonic even, operation of certain signifying practices turns the signifier from in truth to as truth, and so the place of truth—which like the body/signifier in the striptease—must never be revealed or its erotics are lost.

Truth continues for as long as it posits signs in truth, and their sense of truth, of verity, that is signs as truth, are kept absent. The veiling/unveiling of truth is truth in terms of absence and presence, of truth as presence measured against absence. But it is also the seduction of the veil, Parrhasios's veil, the burning son, and smoked salmon, in short all veils. This is "the site of the signifier, the letter. But this is also where the trial begins, the promise of re-appropriation, of return, of readequation" (Derrida 1987a: 439). The veil provides the connection to the presence of "truth", like the glissading bar sets up connections of signification and meaning. This is the site where issues of the truth of the text reside, and it is part of the seduction of truth-as-presence-in--presence in representation—the sign functions precisely at this point of seduction and re[present]ation. Once this is revealed, even before analysis, there is a movement towards a whole new system of thought—a thought that "henceforth may no longer need to be either true or present" (Derrida 1986: 38). This becomes an integral part of a theory of absence. Such a concept does not extend the deconstruction methodology so that the notion of truth is abandoned—this is quite another agenda—rather it suggests that the ways of thinking about the relational constructions (such as truth, the site of truth, presence and its validation of truth) need to be reconsidered in terms of absence. This is the construction of truth in absence as it operates in terms of the sign. This returns us to the arbitrary nature of signs, and, as Nietzsche points out in his consideration of the "philosophical illusion of truth" and of the "compliance with an order of signs which one has forgotten to be *arbitrary*" (Derrida 1986:178) this leads him to the idea of the signifier being a metaphor for the signified.

The sign, then, becomes more essential, more critical and vital, because it is not just invested with a sense of meaning and meaningfulness but also with processes of truth (and the contextualising presences and absences) and being, beingness, the ideological function and operation of truth. In this configuration we find Hegel's *Entfremdung* (estrangement) and *Entäusserung* (externalisation or alienation), although the sign can never be totally and adequately aligned with the object in terms of the subject because of its sense of the midway region of neither/nor. This is also true of the Hegelian subject which at one point Lacan describes as the legal being: "in which respect it is more concrete than the real being from which it was earlier thought it could be abstracted—as appears from the fact that it possesses both a civil status (*état civil*) and a statement of account (*état-comptable*)" (Lacan 1985: 126-127). Such a being is both inside and outside the self, social praxis, formations and representations of truth and as truth, and the sign. It is not, however, the subject of *jouissance*- —at most it is the subject of pleasure.

This is the difficulty of the sign for the subject invested in these signs, for it involves the desire for the signifier and the fear/abjection of the sign. The sign in the chora is abject because it engages in both fear and desire, repression and expression, absence and presence. This process in its widest sense is *signifiance*, the "unlimited and unbounded generating process, this unceasing operation in the drives toward, in, and through language" (Kristeva 1984c: 17). *Signifiance* is the point where *jouissance* becomes possible for the subject through language, through the interplay with the sign and its generation. The *type* (if such a classificatory sense can be employed) of absence involved here is also choric in terms of the determining factor of time (signifiers that do not yet "exist") and through the modal function of chora as *signifiance*.

9

Love and the Symphysis of Absence

Codes and Semiotic Systems

Eco seeks a return to a primary order of the conceptualisation of codes by avoiding what he sees as a metaphorisation through the various critical readings of their structures (Eco 1984: 164-188). That such a return is possible is not very likely, although the gestures towards it are useful and significant in themselves. The three orders of codes outlined by Eco—the palaeographic, the correlational and the institutional—which he then extends and adds to a polymorphic nexus, are perhaps more originary, but no less clearly organised, in part because of the systems of exchanging signs. Eco's examples of the Italian *Codice Penale* and *Codice Civile* provide illustrations of the interchangeable nature of code systems. This sense of exchange and interchange appears to be true of most, if not all, theories and categories of codes.

Codes, like signs, give all the appearances of presence, yet operate in terms of absence. Most obviously this is the excluding quality of codes—that they allow certain elements and exclude others and that they allow the combination of certain elements and disallow others. This is the issue that Foucault engages in with his conceptual development of archaeology. In this sense *Le Mots et les choses* is actually dealing with a form of epistemic codes, and this same sense of the centrality of absence in code is found here. What is knowable and what cannot be known is based on the inclusive/exclusive function of the code itself. This is why codes not only determine meaning but also determine what can be meaningful/known and what cannot. Such a quality gives codes an ideological function as well as an epistemological one. Meaning/signification itself then becomes tied to the system of the code. There is no inherent *meaningfulness* in a sign, only the positional *value* of codes gives meaning. This is part of the alterity of signification as it comes to stitch truth as absence to the sign.

Interpreted in this fashion the concept of the code seems somewhat paradoxical. It is a system that fixes meaning—a form of presentational "truth"—and yet also unfixes it; it operates as exclusion and inclusion and yet must also permit the addition of new members to the system; a code enables communication and interpretation and yet must also contribute to any breakdowns in the communication process because it cannot guarantee meaning/signification as well as the acts of reading the signs. Clearly this is not simply because the conceptualisation of what a code is and what functions it performs is inadequate. The difficulty arises when attempts are made to attribute to codes more than they are capable of, or more than they should be capable of, and also less than what they are capable of. This is precisely why Barthes's dynamic and Foucault's condition of possibilities are included as part of the definition of the codes and also of the operation of codes. Just as the sign shifts within itself and in terms of other signs, so codes build up and collapse within themselves and in relation to other codes. Any attempt to solidify a code will be resisted because of the dynamics of that system. The resistance and dynamism stems in part from the code itself and in part from the elements that the code deals with.

This may at first seem disturbing, after all a code has as its essential feature at least three primary functions: it stabilises the signs (the fixing of meaning—the *point de capiton*); it permits possibilities of interpretation(s) (through the code new signs can be included and understood, known signs can be combined to produce meaning); and it provides a structure for the interplay of signs (which often implies a distinction between the transitory nature of the sign and the permanence of the code). If a code is seen to be as unstable and as, relatively speaking, ephemeral as the signs which it governs over, then are these primary functions totally negated? It is important to note that, there can be no transcendental code, even as attached as it is to these functions, and that all these processes operate entirely within a context of absences. It is these absences which allow codes to have gestures towards hermeneutic value, fixing presences, senses of permanence; however, these can only ever be gestures towards such values.

The relative strengths and weaknesses of a code system lie in its capacity to balance the constructive and de(con)structive qualities that are an inherent part of its makeup. This is further evidence that a *code* does not exist, there are only types of codes to which various qualities or orders can be attributed. Hermeneutic codes, cultural codes, codes of desire, and others are specified as engaging in particulars, reserving their "codeness" to the ideal. This is why signs invariably belong to, and are read through, more than one code. It also contributes to the explanation as to why codes operate as both prescriptive and descriptive. It would be impossible for a single code to operate by itself and be productive and useful. The issue then becomes how do codes themselves combine and how do the combinational processes affect the sign and how does the sign affect the codes. Within this issue also lies the investment of presence in codes—a presence which is based on absences.

Part of the internal dynamic of the code is fuelled by the *glissement* of the bar and the shifting position of the signified(s). In one sense this is Hjelmslev's "connotative semiotic" (1969: 119) and Barthes's connotative signs—this and something more. The pulsative function of signs through *glissement* in terms of codes can be represented as:

$$C^{Ex} \qquad C^T \qquad C^L \qquad C^1 \qquad C^2 \qquad C^x$$

Sr

$$\mathbb{S} \quad < > \qquad Sd^{ex} \quad Sd^t \quad Sd^l \quad Sd^1 \quad Sd^2 \quad Sd^x$$

In commencing with the *Ichspaltung* the model is in keeping with the motivating forces of absence and desire. The relationship between the S and the sign represents an unsettling, yet definitional, force. There can be no stasis even at this point, which is why the chisel is both a point of connection and a barrier for the subject to the order of the Other. It is the double vel of alienation and separation which moves from the split subject back to that same site of subjectivity. This is why it is constituted of < > as well as ♢ . The subject can encounter the sign in its uncoded state, but rarely (if ever) without some process of contextualisation, which then formulates the initial basis of the reading of the sign. Often the code and signs are so familiar that expectation formulates the relational context prior to the encounter with the sign—this is the subset of "Ex" which may or may not be fulfilled. "Ex" is not necessarily a single set nor a homogeneous group, rather it is a model of interpretation that may soon be abandoned in the reading of the sign—it is the horizonality of the sign as it is figured in a socio-temporal paradigm. The signifier remains constant in its materiality, although in a sense the signifier is polymorphic, and uniformity at the formal level can be challenged. Defamiliarisation is an example of this process of seeing the components of the signifier of the sign differently. The changing of the signified through the code systems also leads to a variation of the absent signifier, whereby the emphasis is so heavily placed on the alterations to codes and signification that the signifier in effect becomes absent from the reading.

Different signifieds are produced according to the codes and their combinations, just as different codes and code combinations result from possible sets of signifieds. *Différance* forms a fundamental part of this process, with the locating of the signifieds through their differences in the code structures and the deferral of the interpretation of the sign because of the other codes. Here we see the sliding of the signified back and forth from the *Ichspaltung* to other codes. Other possible code structures specified in this example are codes of "Truth", which are in keeping with the Nietzschean idea of the forgotten fictionality of truth as it passes as apodictic; love as an amatory code; the notational "value" of codes, from a primacy to the diversity of all possibilities. There is nothing inherently truthful, amatory, expectational, etc., in the signifier or the signified—these are all absent from the sign itself. What produces such qualities is cultural coding. The designatory and hermeneutic processes of the codes are inflected in the signifieds so that they themselves become subsets of the signification patterns. This is why the model represents the possibility of a unary signifier but with inflected, multiple signifieds. What is being wrestled with when the subject encounters the sign is not some sense of a transcendental signifier, but the reading and situating of the sign as absence and presence. This is further to the model's representation of the signifier's capacity to remain constant whilst the signifieds are prone to polysemes and heterology. This is not a digital system, however, and the signified becomes meaningful both at its fixed points (*point de capiton*) within the code system and while in transition. It is for this reason that the model needs to be developed further in order to take into account the analogic production and systems of absence.

Codes Determining Absence, Absence Determining Codes: The Syntagmatic and Paradigmatic; (Syn)tactical Readings

It has already been noted that one of the primary functions of codes is to exclude certain elements and their combinations and include others. This is a model of absence and presence, of the *fort/da* process of making presences through absence, and is a further demonstration of the crucial role that absence plays in understanding semiotic theory and the operation of the semiotic as cultural systems. What the code excludes becomes vital to the signs within the code and the code itself, because, more than by any direct categorising of essential features, it is through these absences that the code is defined. Absence is more than the definitional ground rules for codes, however. It provides the central mechanism for their operation. In this sense although codes can determine absences, absences themselves determine codes.

Codes determining absences is an ideological function. At the least this is the absenting of elements from the *parole* in specific utterances and texts. At a more extreme point it is the absenting of the sign (at both its denotative and connotative levels) absolutely. *Absolute absenting* means that the closure of the text negates whole systems of (alternative) thought and representation. This repression ensures that, despite the limitations, the coding processes are seen as extensively exegetic and exemplary—it is the compulsion of completion. Freud's concept of primary and secondary processes is a demonstration of how codes operate in terms of dreams, parapraxis, etc. Foucault provides us with a further example of this in his examination of discourse: "But as long as Classical discourse lasted, no interrogation as to the mode of being implied by the *cogito* could be articulated" (Foucault 1970: 312). (His study of the discourses of madness is of the same order.) Discourse, as a highly complex system of codes, provides presence only through the operation of absence. Codes, particularly the complex types such as discourse, like signs, are not static and so even the most seemingly absolute absenting must always give way to the insertion of new presences. Because codes are defined by what they determine as presence and absence, once the qualitative changes occur the code itself alters or becomes redundant, particularly in terms of its capacity to organise, encapsulate, and determine meaning and signification. This is part of the syncretic function of code structures. It is the interplay between the presences and absences, and the determining systems, that enables or prohibits codes to combine. It is also part of the process of the exchange of signs between codes, and this exchange forms part of the construction and deconstruction, absence and presence, of the code itself. This action includes the production and dissemination of codes as well as the negation of coding processes. Such a negativity is invariably based on an operation, or operations, of primary absence.

Absence determining or constructing codes is most apparent in the drive towards the interpretation of the signs. New or unfamiliar signs demand a code in order to be read, which is the feature of performance and competence in the reading of the sign and its connotative levels. This is a complex case in its mechanisms but relatively straightforward in the light of the need to develop a code when one is absent. A further imbroglio is the determination of the code itself through absence. Codes are suspect to the very phenomena of absence and presence that they utilise to either enable and/or prevent signs existing, combining, and meaning. The lacunae of a code system becomes its strength and weakness, for it represents the capacity for the code to survive and the danger of being incapable of performing certain, perhaps essential, functions. A code must necessarily be able to incorporate a corpus of signs, but it cannot incorporate all signs—there is no transcendental code in either a synchronic or a diachronic sense. The gaps in the code enable the dynamic interplay and exchange of signs to occur, for without these gaps/absences the code would be totally sealed off, occluded, and preserved from all else. However, counter to this, too many absences within the code destabilises its hermeneutic capacity and the rule-governing principle of the code is negated. This is why new signs to the code add to the code itself, for in "shifting" from one order to another the sign provides a possible connection for the codes at a nodal point, which in turn has the potential to extend the codes.

Just as codes negotiate (to incorporate and to have at hand, in readiness, and so the syntagmatic and the paradigmatic) the absences of sign production and reading, there is also an epistemic order of absence for the code itself. This is not the deliberation on balance, and so stasis, but the dialectic of absences and presences as a determining feature of the code. This is why codes often form subcodes to provide for the diversity of the signs and their meanings and to establish typological groups of absences and, necessarily, presences. The dialectic here can operate within the code (intradialectic coding), in the formulation of subcodes (dialectic subcoding), and across codes (interdialectic coding), which also includes established codes as well as the new formation of codes. Absences in all three cases fall largely into two types: those absences that operate within the dialectic and so determine the corpus of presences which ostensibly represent the code structure and its operation; and those absences which are external to the dialectic axis. The distinction between the two sets of absences can be blurred, but is often, in its noumenal sense, crucial to the understanding of the code.

The two forms of absence in intradialectic coding operate to determine presences against the distinctive and determining absences, as opposed to other absences, for the code itself. Let us assume that there is a code dealing with letters—not the letters of word formations, but those profound and complex systems of exchanges of letters from one person to another. The intradialectic coding sets up a series of conditions that both prescribes and describes the sign's "letters", this is the presences of the code. Antithetical to this are those absences which, through their absence, qualify the presences and enable them to exist. So a letter may be distinguished from a note, a card, a reminder, a memo, a telephone call—these become absent within the code and form the other point of the axis. This means that although they are absent they are of a particular order which is directly and necessarily connected to the presences of the code. Beyond these is an endless number of other absences which define the code in terms of both its presences and absences as such. These are *non-relevant* (as opposed to irrelevant, which would imply that they are not necessary) absences because they do not qualify the code within itself but rather for other codes/systems. These non-relevant absences are crucial in the interdialectic coding because they provide the infrastructure for the nodal points of connection. In interdialectic coding the formation of the new code system is based on the intradialectic coding of the two original code systems. It is the result of one system of presence and absence combining with a second (or more) system of presence and absence to produce gestures towards "synthesis" with a different set of presences and absences. In this sense the concept of synthesis necessarily operates as *Aufhebung*, with the reserve providing the paradigmatics of absences. We can speak of symphysis to include dialectical joins and the dynamics of growth.

Returning to the earlier example let us say that there is a code of letters dynamically functioning through the symphysis of intradialectic coding, which is then combined with another code, one of desire (which also operates with its own intradialectic coding). Through interdialectic coding these form the code of "love letters" which will in turn operate in terms of absences and presences (love letters of rejection as opposed to acceptance, letters which invite love, letters which invite passion—should letters of friendship be included?) and also can become part of another, distinct interdialectic coding system. The system is endless because its organising principle is the endless roll of absences. As codes combine in this manner so the various typologies of absences and presences must shift—a code of desire combined with a code of letters would suggest the need for a set of presences dealing with particular language structures. Issues such as truth and how it is determined, which may have been positioned as absent in both codes of letters and codes of desire, could become highly present in the interdialectic coding of love letters.

Dialectic subcoding tends to operate within the code itself and so is incorporated into the action of the code without dramatically altering it. Subcodes can form without requiring an extensive remodelling of the code itself, unlike both intradialectic and interdialectic coding where substantial alterations take place. However, what is often the case is that the subcode operates in terms of the larger order of absences and presences of the originary code(s) and also forms—synchronically and diachronically—particular rules within itself. Love letters can be a subcode of letters or desire or both, and it is when it is recognised as operating in this nodal sense of both that the other forms of dialectical coding—and the adhesive properties of symphysis—are critically useful. Once the subcode is established it emphasises absences and presences according to its own regulations, in fact it is precisely because of this particularity of absences and presences that subcodes are formed. Subcodes, like the order of codes (not originary but aetiological), can be defined precisely through their systems of absences and the operations of cohesion and assembly/production. A code of letters does not necessarily emphasise (make present) the amatory quality of some letters, so a subcode of love letters makes absent other possibilities of other types of letters. A subcode of love letters will absent those letters designed for hatred, unless, of course, the subcode is designed to include sadomasochistic relationships or the idea of meaning through opposition ("I say I hate you but really I love you", "you say you hate me but I read this as "I love you"", "I love your hatred for me", "I hate your love for me"). In cases such as this there is a transformation of the signified through a political rereading of the signifier for its opposite.

Syntagmatic and Paradigmatic; (Syn)tactical Readings

Syntagmatic and paradigmatic structures are obvious points of connection between the operation of codes and signs in terms of absence. A code formulates presence through the syntagmatic and provides the range of possibilities, that is absences, through the paradigmatic—the movement from possibility to actuality is an interplay between presence and absence. At this level we witness the code as a determinant of absence and presence through the selection and combination of signifiers and the organisation of other signifiers in a relational, "external" position. What this model suggests is a binarism, and the important aspect of things held in readiness tends to be at best de-emphasised and at worst totally ignored. The urgency of presence supports the figuring of the syntagmatic over the paradigmatic; however, other signifiers are just as essential to the construction of the sign(s).

The most self-evident operation of absence in terms of syntagmatic and paradigmatic is the choices made to construct the sign and the signifying chain. However just as there are paradigmatic absences above and below the signifier, there are also absences within the syntagmatic. This is the lacunae of the sign as it combines with other signs within a theory of codes. It is this same order of lacunae that becomes such an attractive idea for a phenomenological approach to the text. It is therefore not impossible to imagine that these syntagmatic absences also have paradigmatic relations. Of course, Ingarden argues that these syntagmatic lacunae are an essential part of the text and that they can never be totally "filled" by either the writer or the reader of the text, although his sense of textual spots of indeterminacy is different to the syntagmatic absences being dealt with here.

Absences of both syntagmatic and paradigmatic orders can be read as a type of syntax, devised in its own way through a grammatology and archaeology. Ways of reading these syntagmatic and paradigmatic absences require their recognition as well as an understanding of the operational systems within them and external to them. This is (syn)tactical reading—of *taxis* as an order (taxonomy) and also a strategy (tactic) for reading absences within the text. This concept of (syn)tactical readings extends to the system of absences determining codes and codes determining absences and this is part of the reason why a particular type of reading is required. The motivations and reasons behind the absences (from notions about the structure of the text to the ideological workings of censorship and repression) often mean that the actual state of absences are disguised. The sign and all its codes combine to suggest, sometimes compel, the idea of wholeness and completeness. (Syn)tactical reading is not a formula for the filling in of gaps however, although it is motivated by the same structure that engenders and requires such absences, the absences which constitute the split subject and the forces of desire as absence. Rather it is a methodological process that acknowledges the primary feature of splits, gaps, holes, blanks, and spaces—in short, the complex interplay of the heterology of absence.

Codes and Letters of Love

It was suggested earlier that there might be an interdialectic code of love letters arranged primarily around two aetiological codes of letters and of desire. Such an aetiology is constructed *after* the code production, which makes it a retrospective organising system. This is not a complete agenda of such a code (an impossibility in itself) but a consideration of the ways in which (syn)tactical readings might operate in the context of such a code system and its absences. It is necessary to consider some fundamental issues of the love letter code as it is determined here before examining some specific examples.

Letters share the fundamental aspect of transmission—they have a source (of writing) and a destination (of reading). Both Derrida and Lacan concur on this point: "The letter has a place of emission and of destination" (Derrida 1987: 437); "Thus we are confirmed in our detour by the very object which draws us into it; for we are quite simply dealing with a letter which has been diverted from its path" (Lacan 1975: 59), that is the *lettre en souffrance*—(the implication here is that for a letter to be diverted it must have an established sense of direction). The letter can be seen as representative of the simple communication model of sender/message/receiver, with the interplay of letters being made up of "letters" (graphic, but also other signifying systems) to construct the message. This model extends further when we note that the letter carries with it the need to be read and understood—there is an assumption made that the codes of reading competence are shared by both parties. The letter is perfectly positioned in terms of absence because it is written with one party absent and read with one party absent, and it spends time travelling absent from both parties; furthermore, it stands in for (acts as a presence) in both the writing and the reading processes. The letter also represents the signifier because there are constant attempts to possess the letter/signifier and there are continual dispossessions of it.

The second quality most obvious in the letter is that it conveys, or at least attempts to convey, information. This forms part of the reading competence, not that the competence assures a particular reading of the letter, but at the very least it suggests the capacity to recognise the materiality of the letter and its coded functions. Love letters occupy a particular position in terms of the information given as it forms part of the generic definition of the texts. All letters deal with information, but letters of love specify a type of information that bond the writer and reader together. Love letters do not always overtly (that is, in a denotative, monosemic manner) signify love (erotic, passionate, but other categories deal with different, related issues) nor do they express it in a uniform manner. It is largely because of this particular exchange and the polysemic potential that love letters are prone to misreading. Such aberrant decoding and encoding can result in a love letter not being recognised as such, or a letter of a different type being reread as a love letter. Both these permutations occur in Freud's case study of Dora—her love "letters" to another woman are not read as amatory and her dreams are read by Freud as love "letters" from her to himself. Reading competence is severely tested in the case of love letters because there must always be a contingency of the politics of desire.

A third aspect of this code is that the letter must engage in the complexities of desire. The most simple and straightforward case of this is when the letter is understood by both parties as being one of love. Misreadings, aberrant coding, misrecognitions all contribute to the very real possibility of the production of *méconnaissance*—particularly as emphasised in the Imaginary—so that the *glissement* of the bar slips the signified into another schema entirely. The extensive nature of the paradigmatic axis in this form, as well as the often excessive investment of the self (and the self's desires), contribute significantly to the operation of a failure to read, to acknowledge, to understand, or to recognise. This failure is based on the aphanisis of subjectivity invested in the interplay of absence and presence of desire in the letter and for the letter. Its possession determines the measure of fragmentation in the *Ichspaltung* through the coding of absences. This particular aspect is connected to the fourth quality that is not so readily apparent, which is the functional properties of absence to love letters.

Love letters are based on absence. Not only are there the usual aspects of absence—of writer and reader, of representation, of misunderstanding and *méconnaissance*—there are also the extensive structures of absence as part of the whole system of letters and love. These letters, motivated by desire and a desire to be present, necessarily engage in absence ("I am absent but this letter stands in my place", "love is absent from us", "in my absence this letter tells of my love"), and it is the absence which constructs and emphasises the desire for both reader and writer within the exchange, as well as the reader of the exchange and its texts. This is precisely what Derrida explores in the deconstructionalist love letters in *Carte Postale*.

The letter (its signifier and multiple signifieds) passes through these three qualifying codes of information, representation, and desire to construct the other code of absence and love letters. The letter passes through each one but is inflected on its way. The inflection occurs at the point of interception which is also the *point de capiton* but which is not, it should be noted, rigid, although it does fix certain meanings in the elastic and immeasurable systems of history and truth.

Ordering each of these codes is the system (and code) of absence—through its attributes of qualifying and enabling, this system unites the love letters. The code of information becomes hermeneutic as absences of meaning are devised and interpreted; the code of representation relates directly to the absences of subjectivity (of subject to subject, subject to self, egocentrism, masochism, narcissism, the self to others and the Other), included in this is the operation of the Imaginary in both a self-conscious (identificatory) process as well as considerations of representability to others, particularly the lover's other, as well as the interpretative; and the code of desire is necessarily constructed of absences—it exists and operates entirely on the sustained construction of absence. Desire splits in the attempts to portray it, and the fractured images are what become the signifiers, most notably of *jouissance* because it is here that the gaps become painful pleasures.

The *Lettre en souffrance* and the Investment of the Self

Part of the dispute which revolves around the Lacan/Derrida debate of *The Purloined Letter* and "Freud and the Scene of Writing" is the analytic frames that are set up and broken down. The debate becomes centred and decentred around open and closed readings, the capacity to attach meaning to anything, the dispute of transcendental signifiers—in short the history of meaning in all its political and ideological senses. For Derrida this is the positioning of *truth* as it arrives: "The remaining structure of the letter is that—contrary to what the Seminar says in its last words . . . —a letter can always not arrive at its destination. Its "materiality" and "typology" are due to its divisibility, its always possible partition" (Derrida 1987a: 443-444)—in which "truth" is employed to avoid the fragmentation of the letter. Yet Derrida fails to recognise this same interpretative sense of fragmentation—this same dissolution of the truth through absences (the failure to arrive)—in Lacan's seminar. Lacan does acknowledge this interpretation—it is the *la politique de l'autruiche*—even if Derrida denies the seminar this dimension. Meaning becomes connected to the subject and the presence and/or absence of meaning relates to the site of subjectivity. We can illustrate the significance of absence to this critical exchange between Lacan and Derrida and the Poe story by considering another French letter.

Eugenie Grandet has never experienced passion—*jouissance* in fact—until her cousin Charles visits her father's house from Paris. It is her father's house because the extreme miser Grandet owns and takes stock of every article, every splinter of wood, every aspect of being of his domain. Patriarchal and phallocentric Grandet represents the extreme of the Law of The-Name-of-the-Father because he controls everything—even emotion—within himself and his family. The law within this family is based on denial and repression, in fact absence—the powerful Phallic law becomes enmeshed in the French letter. This is the *lettre en souffrance* in its purest form for it denies spending, it constricts and it prevents the delivery of the message. The French letter acts as a form of (a signifier for) castration for both Grandet and Charles. Eugenie gives her gold (supposed gift from the Father) to the impoverished/castrated Charles (gold and masculinity are constantly aligned throughout the narrative) and in doing so usurps the traditional basis of power in the household—in fact the basis of capitalist economy. From this point on Eugenie moves to a more powerful and independent, and yet more hollow and infertile, position. It is noteworthy that masculine sexuality, and its demonstrations, is practically absent from the narrative. Grandet is impotent because he cannot spend anything—money, wealth, sperm are all held back—and Charles is castrated socially, mentally, physically (for a while) through his lack of wealth after the death of his father. The male cannot spend anything, and so he becomes the *lettre en souffrance* because nothing, especially passion, ever arrives at its destination. This is parallel to the wider issue of the formation of the subject and desire for Lacan in "Seminar on *The Purloined Letter*" : "the singularity of the letter, which as the title indicates, is the true subject of the tale: since it can be diverted, it must have a course which is proper to it: the trait by which its incidence as signifier is affirmed. . . . If what Freud discovered and rediscovers with a perpetually increasing sense of shock has a meaning, it is that the displacement of the signifier determines the subjects in their acts, in their destiny, in their refusals, in their blindness, in their end and in their fate" (Lacan 1975: 59; 60). This is the relationship of the subject to the signifier and the Other, the interplay between the *Ichspaltung*, its desires and absences, and the Symbolic.

Eugenie creeps into the bedroom where her beloved Charles fitfully sleeps. She sees a letter addressed to "My dear Annette" and is faced with a moral dilemma—whether or not to become the reader of that letter. This dilemma introduces a remarkable struggle—remarkable because Eugenie is a young woman and yet she has never encountered the difficulties of deciding between good and evil: "For the first time in her life there was a struggle between good and evil in her soul" (Balzac 1947: 116). She becomes the reader because of "love and curiosity" and in doing so transforms the letter into a love letter and also a *lettre en souffrance*. Her interception mirrors the reader of the narrative. Like Eugenie into Charles's bedroom, the reader creeps into the text and reads the letters, and in this sense *en souffrance* utilises its double meaning of suffering and to be in suspense/in abeyance rather than to miss its destination. Letters, and this is all letters, may have an intended destination, but this is not necessarily the only meaningful one. Charles's letter to Annette is absent from Annette (detoured) but finds a new destination with Eugenie. In one sense it misses its destination, but in another sense it arrives. Lacan makes this very point at the close of his seminar: "Thus it is that what the "purloined letter," nay, the *lettre en souffrance* means is that a letter always arrives at its destination" (Lacan 1975: 72). Derrida *seems* to be in opposition here when he writes: "The mishap of this perhaps, is that in order to be able not to arrive, there must be included in the idea a force and structure, a drift in the destination, such that it *must* also not arrive at all. Even by arriving . . . the letter carries the sense of not arriving. It arrives elsewhere, always, several times. You simply can't take hold of it. That is the structure of the letter" (Derrida 1987a: 135). At another point, however, there is a type of qualification to this: "a letter does not always arrive at its destination, and from the moment that this possibility belongs to its structure one can say that it never truly arrives, that when it does arrive its capacity not to arrive torments it with an internal drifting" (Derrida 1987a: 489).

Derrida's argument for the *restance* of the letter and its torment of internal drifting is at the very least comparable to *glissement*. To recoup essential arguments from these two ideas it is necessary to observe the centrality of absence. Both Lacan and Derrida are arguing in terms of absences and meaning. Lacan's arrival is *a* meaning, but not *the* meaning, just as Derrida refuses any meaning but in doing so acknowledges a point of meaningness, even if it is transitory. As we discover later in the narrative, Eugenie's reading of Charles's letter produces multiple meanings, that is, multiple points of arrival. In this sense it arrives but only for a moment before moving to another destination. This is the integration of temporality and absence in the interpretation of the signifier. This series of chains of significations, of a paradigmatics of *points de capiton*, is founded on the interplay of secondary absences and their counterparts of presences. However, more importantly, the action itself is a series of primary absences which come to determine the horizonality of signications, as well as the production of interpretative acts themselves.

Ultimately, what is in the letter is not important, and in effect it is absent from the central issues of the narrative. This sense of absence is mirrored in the narrative, for Eugenie sees two unsealed letters, but she only reads one and the other is never mentioned again—its absence confirms the other letter's immediate presence. This absence is a crucial aspect in a particular form of the love letter and this order of absence needs to be explicated further. In *The Purloined Letter* the point is that the letter is made absent (stolen) and only the analytic methodology of Dupin can recover it. The absence of the letter means that the reader never discovers what the letter contains; hence there is a further absence within the absence. This lacuna gives the reader certain interpretative rights, which both Lacan and Derrida take up to the point where the rights themselves come under question. Even outside of Lacan's reading, it is most tempting to see the Queen's letter as a love letter, but not directed towards the King. The story lends itself to this interpretation, but even if we were to resist this, dismiss it outright, the desire and passion for the letter by the Queen, the Minister, and Dupin make it a letter of passion—a desired letter. It is certainly a fetish in the absolute sense of the word. And as with fetishism the absence of the real object ensures its power and its position as a signifier of power through possession and its lack: "For it is clear that if the use of the letter, independent of its meaning, is obligatory for the Minister, its use for ends of power can only be potential, since it cannot become actual without vanishing in the process" (Lacan 1975: 63). This same sense of absence is evident in Eugenie's reading of the letter, for even though she, and the reader, "see" the letter, its interpretation is based on a sense of absence. What comes before and after the reading of the letter is more significant than what the letter actually says. Prior to its reading is the fundamental engagement with morality; during its reading is the insertion of action and demonstration of character ("Poor Charles, I did well to read this. I have money, and he shall have it"); and after reading it is the essential semiotic and hermeneutic question: "How was it possible that an inexperienced girl should discover the coldness and selfishness of this letter?" (Balzac 1947: 117).

This question, all the more extraordinary because it is imbued with meta-fictional qualities in a novel of Realist proportions, is not a rhetorical question—both the reader and Eugenie will be told the answer for the rest of the narrative. In effect it is a question that acknowledges a desire in the reader (both the reader of the novel and Eugenie as reader of the letter) to ask it, but is stated in the text to ensure that it is asked. Eugenie misreads the letter because of her desire to see one set of signifiers (Charles's love for her) while encountering the opposite. In her *méconnaissance*, her (syn)tactic reading, Eugenie transforms the cold, selfish letter into a love letter, and she is able to do this because of the syntagmatic and paradigmatic absences created by her and delivered into the letter. This action is motivated by desire, which in turn becomes the *glissement* which relocates the letter into the code of love letters.

This is the inflection at the *point de capiton* that is necessary to make the letter relevant to Eugenie and her passions.

This action of Eugenie's absenting of certain meanings and presenting of others is similar to a further issue in the "Seminar on *The Purloined Letter*" and *Carte Postale*; that of Lacan's aligning of the stolen letter with the signifier and by implication the subject. Charles's letter to Annette, which becomes Eugenie's letter, has this same infrastructure of lacunae that Lacan attributes to the purloined letter, at the levels of textuality, meaning, subjectivity, the Law and sexuality/desire. These gaps are represented in many ways throughout this passage. Typographically and through syntax and semantic open-endedness, there are spaces left to attract our gaze. Because of these we are as compelled as Eugenie to discover what is in the letter: "One of them began: "My dear Annette"----- She felt dazed, and could see nothing for a moment. Her heart beat fast, her feet seemed glued to the floor. "*His dear Annette*! He loves, he is beloved!---- "Then there is no more hope!---- What does he say to her?" (Balzac 1947: 116). Repetitions and returns abound ("My dear Annette" and its derivatives occur four times in less than a page) which formulate further gaps and multiple false starts and endings to the letter and its interpretation—Eugenie interrupts the letter three times in the course of reading it. The letter itself is incomplete, trailing off at the point where Charles addresses the issue of Eugenie herself, and sentences are left incomplete. Like Schreber's utterances, their endings are absent. The letter must end here; it becomes the critical point of the mirror phase, even in this divergent semiotic reading, when Eugenie sees herself in the encounter. The absences and readings become the site of subjectivity for Eugenie to the point where aphanisis takes over and desire and existence become inextricably linked in the encoding of the love letter. Such is her investment in the reading of the letter that she cannot allow its signifiers to mean anything else than a reiteration and confirmation of love.

The danger of such a (syn)tactical reading is that the sterility of the (French) letter, from Grandet to the dead Father, to Charles, is passed on to Eugenie herself. In her desire to possess the letter she loses control of meaning and the capacity to construct meaning. From this hermeneutic activity onwards Eugenie becomes constructed through an even more powerful Phallic Law—the movement from the fetish and castration to "phallicisation". Lacan expresses this point in terms of the Minister, but it is true also of the Queen and of Dupin (his reputation as analyst/detective rests on his success or failure to recover the letter): "The ascendancy which the Minister derives from the situation is thus not a function of the letter, but, whether he knows it or not, of the role it constitutes for him" (Lacan 1975: 63). Eugenie, her innocence undone through the seeming moral struggle of good and evil, becomes part of this paradigm, for she also attempts to gain from the knowledge within the letter. The difference between the Minister and Eugenie, however, is that the former attempts, through calculated actions, to manipulate whilst the latter becomes manipulated through her own actions of generosity. This is part of what Cixous sees as the distinction between the feminine and the masculine, the gift and the *propre*. Both Eugenie and the Minister become constructed by and through the letter/signifier and have their destinies tied to its fortunes. Gold and sexuality—being and desire—are paradigmatically and syntagmatically linked in these narratives: "Thus once more we meet the equation gold = penis" (Derrida 1987a: 448). Furthermore, Eugenie becomes masculinised and undergoes phallicisation whilst the Minister becomes feminised: "Not only has he [the Minister] become feminised through his possession of the letter, but the letter, whose relation to the unconscious I have told you of, even makes him forget the essential" (Lacan 1988b: 203). And all of this occurs because of their relationship to the letter and its textual, intertextual, and systemic absences. This is the form of narcissism, in terms of the signifier and the self, that becomes vital to the subject. As Kristeva puts it: " If narcissism is a defence against the emptiness of separation, then the whole contrivance of imagery, representations, identifications, and projections that accompany it on the way toward strengthening the Ego and the Subject is a means of exorcising that emptiness" (Kristeva 1987: 42).

Lacan makes the point that the deception of the purloined letter is that although it is made absent, it is never really hidden. Its apparentness as a letter becomes the thing that hides it from all but the keenest eye. But of course the eye that sees it is able to do so because it knows the letter of the law and the law of the letter. With both the Queen's purloined letter and Charles's letter to Annette, the defining and shared quality is that the content of the letter is not as significant as the property of *letterness* and absence. The sign of "letter", and in particular "love letter", becomes overdetermined because of its connections with subjectivity and desire. It fulfils that quality that led Bakhtin to formulate the idea of heteroglossia. This action of the absent letter (in various guises, literal or metaphoric) and the interplay of narcissistic self-investment, fetishisation of the object, desire, and power forms a central base for the code of absence and love letters.

10

Toward a Typology of the Absent Signifier

The sign is based on the idea of present signifiers and absent signifieds. To posit the concept of an absent signifier is not to reverse the semiotic model, nor is it to abide by some binarism of the sign itself. Rather, the absent signifier represents a typology—a logical type located in the larger class of signifiers (absent or present). It is this type which concerns us here.

A central difficulty in describing such a typology is allocating certain discriminatory features to a single rubric. This would appear to by an impossible task given the very nature of the signifier. This is not a complete agenda of the absent signifier, but an outline of a particular set of propositions which enable its operation within the text.

The Absent Signifier vs. the Repression of the Signifier

Part of the typology of the absent signifier is the system of intentionality in its design. The absent signifier as type is quite distinct from the repression of the signifier, which may appear similar but which has quite different textual and hermeneutic effects. This does not mean that the two cannot be linked; an absence of the signifier may be connected with its repression. The implication is that although there is an absent signifier (either through repression or as a type), the signified is present or more apparent.

The intentionality of the absent signifier defines it as a conscious structure—it operates in the text in a deliberate fashion. This means we can articulate its function as part of the text itself. However, the repression of the signifier must be an unconscious act; it exists as an extra-textual construct, to be brought to the text and determined. This is true of both the definition and nature of the repression. It must be acknowledged that distinguishing between intended absences and a repression of the signifier can be difficult, and in these cases there is something to be said for recognising absence as the central edict rather than examining why it presides in the text. Freud's account of his forgetting the name "Signorelli"—later analysed by Wilden (1984) as the repression of the signifier—is an example of how the signifier is traced back from the signified. The signifier is absent here, but the design of this absence is quite different from an absent signifier as type. Freud's account of the repression of Signorelli signals why we must view the repression of the signifier as distinct from its absence. He argued that this particular repression was linked with death and sexuality (giving him the groundwork for his later theories of neurosis), and so there are unconscious motivations behind its absence. The absent signifier, on the other hand, is consciously developed, and so is delivered as a textual device.

The absent signifier is distinct from the signifier which is absent because it has been repressed. It is also distinct from those signifiers which are absent because of the overall system of textual absences—that is, lacunae. Ingarden (1973) points out that spots of determinacy are a fundamental part of the artistic text. It is also noteworthy that Horst Ruthrof (1981) argues that this absence is an essential process of narrative development in a wider historical context. However, a system of absence such as lacunae does not guarantee the implementing of absent signifiers. All texts have a system of absence based on the reader's ability to encode the semiotic structures of absence and presence, but not all of these semiotic structures involve absent signifiers. Ingarden and Ruthrof detail the obligatory nature of such a system, locating it within the reader aesthetics of phenomenology. The absent signifier relies on this set of aesthetics, but also draws on the structure of the sign itself, positing that the reader's efforts allow meaning to be derived without the signifier being present.

The Absent Signifier in Metaphor and Metonymy - the Absent Signifier as *Ombrager*

Both metaphor and metonymy operate on a level of absence—the former as absence and replacement, the latter as absence and remainder. In either case the absent signifier is an *ombrager*—both shadow and shade. The *ombrager* signifier is not truly absent; rather, it is only partially visible—it is either a shadow of the present signifier (metaphor) or it is hidden by the other, present signifier (metonymy). We must avoid the error of confusing the signified with the *ombrager* signifier.

In the synecdochic utterance there are three processes of signification: the metonymic signifier (present); the *ombrager* signifier (obscured or absent); and the signified, with its potential semiosis. The metonymic signifier and its *ombrager* are not equivalent in the paradigmatic sense, as there are both textual and interpretative reasons for the presence of one and the absence of the other.

The contemporary lines of censorship or cultural fetishism are two possible forces of selection. This selection is also based on textual and interpretative levels of production and encoding.

The essence of the metonym is its partial representation of the whole, and as such relies on the absence of a part. It is this part which shades the *ombrager*, and so is obscured in the text. However, the metaphoric utterance is based on absence of the whole, so the *ombrager* signifier in this case acts more like a shadow. Once more there are three parts of the signification—the metaphoric signifier, *ombrager*, and signified—but the absence is construed in a different manner. The *ombrager* signifier in the metaphoric utterance is more likely to be eidetic in nature. In this way it resembles the Platonic *eidos* of substantial and accidental forms.

There are three syndetic actions at work in the relationship between the metaphor/metonym signifier, its *ombrager*, and the signified. The action between the metaphoric/metonymic signifier and its *ombrager* is less dynamic than the equivalent action between either of these signifier types and the signified, the reason being that the corpus of possibilities is limited by the structure of the absence itself. It is a paradigmatic sequence defined by the contextual locus. However, the syndetic relationships between the metaphor/metonym and the signified, and *ombrager* and the signified, are potentially diverse, and may in fact act in a dialectic. Such a dialectic operates in the syndetic action because of the encoding process. This is true of the general encoding activity and the more specific forms of extra-coding as proposed by Eco (1976).

The Absent Signifier as *Manque*

In Lacanian theory, the dependence of the subject on the signifier establishes the need for the subject to engage in the realm of the Other. Lacan offers the somewhat cold comfort that whenever we engage with the Other we must always commence from a new and uninitiated position of learning—a premise also founded on absence. Because the signifier is part of the Other, it is always exterior to the individual—it has the property of the Lack, or *manque*. The lack of the signifier fulfils Lacan's definition of desire, as it is something which cannot be attained. Furthermore, the signifier is positioned in the field of the Other, and so must possess qualities of the field.

The absent signifier acts as *manque* for two reasons: because, like lacunae, it establishes a gap in the text which the reader must fill; and because the absent signifier draws attention to itself at least at the textual level, and often at a critical one. In this sense its very absence makes it both specular and speculative. There is a desire to provide the absent signifier, to possess its Otherness by bringing it to the same plane as the present, established signifiers. However, this is the paradox of the absent signifier—it must always operate as a polymorph, a potential rather than an actual. Fixity of the absent signifier ultimately necessitates its presence in the signifying order. This is the curious thing regarding the absent signifier—it delivers up a series of possible signifiers, but will often yield only a single signified (or certainly a small number of them).

A further corollary of the absent signifier as *manque* is that the reader is committed to overdetermination to provide potential signifiers and signifieds. This relates to the syndetic action mentioned earlier, as the copula between present and absent signifiers, although partially established through the encoding process, is based on the exchange value of the sets of signifiers. The reader exchanges a series of potential signifiers to make sense of the textual utterances according to the interpretative frame currently operating. Overdetermination is required for this exchange to take place—meaning cannot simply be determined, because there is a lack or absence; consequently, there is a compulsion or desire to "complete" the text.

Discourse and the Absent Signifier

The absent signifier is analogic. Selections are not based on a process of either/or, but rely on context. The contextual interplay of the formation and reading of the absent signifier is more pronounced than those surrounding present signifiers, because the contextual provides *langue* for the absent signifier. Context as *langue* necessarily has more autonomy from a larger system, and rule-generating features may be derived from the textual source or borrowed from other, external systems (such as linguistics). This is not to argue that the absent signifier is beyond discourse or that it sets up a hermetic discourse within the text (although both are possible).

Discourse itself is problematic, resting somewhere between text and context, *langue* and *parole*. Foucault's "three great systems of exclusion which forge discourse—the forbidden speech, the division of madness and the will to truth" (Foucault 1981: 55) are rich caches of absent signifiers precisely because of this problematic. These systems of exclusion (or absence) both inform and articulate, and they do so outside the mainstream discourse of a sociocultural order. The position of absent signifiers in these systems will help to explain how they function overall and within the context of discourse. The forbidden speech—Foucault's term for the discourses of sexuality and politics—contains absent signifiers because the social (and by implication textual) regulations disallow their presence. Direct and manifest usage is forbidden, and (as was noted with the repression of the signifier) the absent signifier operates within the desire to articulate a political or sexual idea and the pervasive atmosphere of societal taboo that seeks to limit such articulations. Foucault argues that "discourse is not simply that which manifests (or hides) desire—it is the object of desire" (Foucault 1981: 55). Within this interplay of desire and the struggle for the power of discourse and discursive practices is the placement and use of absent signifiers. In this sense the absent signifier can be interpretative as well as subversive.

The discourse of madness is largely condemned as meaningless, and exists as an alternative to (and disjunctive of) the language of sanity. It functions in the same manner as schizophrenic utterances—merging the literal with the metaphoric—and relies heavily on absent signifiers as both type and convention. Foucault argues that the discourse of madness leads us to look for hidden meanings—and far from being meaningless, it compels us to find other interpretations of the world order. Part of this discourse is the convolution of the status of the utterance, and one way of doing this is by offsetting signifiers with absent ones, or establishing signifieds with no visible signifiers.

The third system of the will to truth encompasses both forbidden speech and the language of madness. Foucault indicates that it is the area to which both of these ultimately gravitate. Such a philosophical ethos is bound up with the idea of determination of meaning, and within this determination lies the processes of absence and presence. It is worth reiterating that this is not a binarism; just as Foucault does not argue for truth vs. falsity (in fact, he works towards the exact opposite of such a position), so there are no true or false solutions to absent signifiers and their signifieds. The will to truth proves to be not an issue of truth, but one of the determination of meaning—albeit a meaning established through interpretation!

If the absent signifier is indeed absent from the text, where then is it located? The point has already been made that, unlike the repressed signifier, the absent signifier is not extra-textual and does in fact occupy a position in the text. Similarly, a distinction has been made between the gap left by indeterminate spots and the absent signifier which exerts a deliberate space in the text. In one sense the absent signifier occupies a similar space to that of the *sémiotique*, the parargonal, and the Symbolic, because it calls on contributions from the reader to deliberate on a cave chipped from the text. It is the tangible that the absent signifier lacks, not the textual. Barthes's conditions of the textual pertain to the absent signifier—that it is mutable and gains any sense of fixation in the act of reading and interpretation.

Bibliography

Althusser, Louis (1971). *Lenin and Philosophy and Other Essays* (trans. Ben Brewster) New York and London: Monthly Review Press.

Bakhtin, Mikhail (1973). *Problems of Dostoyevsky's Poetics* (trans. W. W. Rotsel) Ann Arbor: Ardis.

--- (1981). *The Dialogic Imagination* (trans. Caryl Emerson and Michael Holquist; ed. Michael Holquist) Austin: University of Texas Press.

--- (1987). *Speech Genres and Other Late Essays* (trans. Vern W. McGee) Austin: University of Texas Press.

Balzac, Honoré de (1947). *Eugénie Grandet* (trans. George Saintsbury) New York: Charles C. Biglow & Co.

Barthes, Roland (1972). *Mythologies* (trans. Annette Lavers) Herts. Granada.

--- (1974). *S/Z: An Essay* (trans. Richard Miller) New York: Hill and Wang.

--- (1984). *Camera Lucida* (trans. Richard Howard) London: Fontana.

--- (1987a). *Image, Music, Text* (ed. and trans. Stephen Heath) London: Fontana.

--- (1987b). 'The Metaphor of the Eye' (trans. J. A. Underwood) in *The Story of the Eye* Middlesex: Penguin.

--- (1988). *The Pleasure of the Text* (trans. Richard Miller) New York: Noonday Press.

--- (1990). *A Lover's Discourse: Fragments* (trans. Richard Howard) Middlesex: Penguin.

Bataille, Georges (1970). *OEuvres complétes* Paris: Gallimard.

--- (1985). *Visions of Excess: Selected Writings 1927-1939* (trans. Allan Stockl, with C. R. Lovitt and D. M. Leslie) Minneapolis: University of Minnesota Press.

--- (1987). *The Story of the Eye* (trans. Joachim Neugroschal) Middlesex: Penguin.

Baudrillard, Jean (1988). *The Ecstacy of Communication* (trans. Bernard Schutze and Caroline Schutze; ed. Slyvere Lotringer) New York: Semiotext(e).

--- (1990). *Seduction* (trans. Brian Singer) London: MacMillan.

Baudry, Jean-Louis (1984). *Proust, Freud et l'Autre* Paris: Les Éditions de Minuit.

--- (1986). 'The Apparatus: Metapsychological Approaches to the Impression of Reality in Cinema' and 'Ideological Effects of the Basic Cinematographic Apparatus' in Philip Rosen (ed.) *Narrative, Apparatus, Ideology* New York:

Columbia University Press.

Cixous, Hélène (1976). 'The Laugh of the Medusa' (trans. Keith Cohen and Paula Cohen) in *Signs* Vol. 1, No. 4 (Summer).

--- (1981). 'Castration or Decapitation' in *Signs* Vol. 7, No. 1.

--- (1985). *Angst* (trans. Jo Levy) London: John Calder.

---, and Catherine Clément (1985). *The Newly Born Woman* (trans. B. Wing) Minneapolis: University of Minnesota Press.

Deleuze, Gilles (1983). *Nietzsche and Philosophy* (trans. Hugh Tomlinson) New York: Columbia University Press.

--- (1989). *Cinema 1: The Movement Image* (trans. Hugh Tomlinson and Robert Galeta) London: The Athlone Press.

--- (1989). *Cinema 2: The Time-Image* (trans. Hugh Tomlinson and Robert Galeta) London: The Athlone Press.

---, and Félix Guattari (1984) *Anti-Oedipus: Capitalism and Schizophrenia* (trans. Robert Hurley, Mark Seem, and Helen R. Lane) London: The Athlone Press.

Derrida, Jacques (1967). *De la grammatologie* Paris: Collection Critique.

--- (1972). *Marges de la Philosophie* Paris: Les Editions de Minuit.

--- (1973). *Speech and Phenomena and Other Essays on Husserl's Theory of Signs* (trans. David B. Allison) Evanston: Northwestern University Press.

--- (1976). *Of Grammatology* (trans. Gayatri Chakravorty Spivak) Baltimore and London: The Johns Hopkins University Press.

--- (1978a). 'Coming Into One's Own' in Geoffrey H. Hartman (ed.) *Psychoanalysis and the Question of the Text* Baltimore and London: The Johns Hopkins University Press.

--- (1978b). *Writing and Difference* (trans. Alan Bass) London: Routledge and Kegan Paul.

--- (1981). *Positions* (trans. Alan Bass) London: Athlone Press.

--- (1985). 'Nietzsche: Life as Metaphor' in David B. Allison (ed.) *The New Nietzsche* Cambridge, Mass.: The MIT Press.

--- (1986). *Margins of Philosophy* (trans. Alan Bass) Sussex: Harvester Press.

--- (1987a). *The Post Card: From Socrates to Freud and Beyond* (trans. Alan Bass) Chicago and London: University of Chicago Press.

--- (1987b). *The Truth in Painting* (trans. Geoff Bennington and Ian McLeod) Chicago and London: University of Chicago Press.

---, and Marie-Françoise Plissart (1989). 'Droit de regards' (trans. David Wills) in *Art and Text*, 32 (Autumn).

Descartes, René (1986). *Discourse on Method and the Meditations* (trans. F. E. Sutcliffe) Middlesex: Penguin.

Eco, Umberto (1976). *A Theory of Semiotics* Bloomington and London: Indiana University Press.

--- (1984). *Semiotics and the Philosophy of Language* London: MacMillan.

Foucault, Michel (1970). *The Order of Things: An Archaeology of the Human Sciences* London and New York: Tavistock.

--- (1972). *The Archaeology of Knowledge* (trans. A. M. Sheridan Smith) London and New York: Tavistock.

--- (1977). *Language, Counter-Memory, Practice* (trans. Donald Bouchard and Sherry Simon) Oxford: Blackwell.

--- (1981). 'The Order of Discourse' in Robert Young (ed.) *Untying the Text* Boston and London: Routledge and Kegan Paul.

--- (1983). *This is Not a Pipe* (trans. James Harkness) Berkeley: University of California Press.

--- (1984). *The History of Sexuality Volume One: An Introduction* (trans. Robert Hurley) Middlesex: Penguin.

--- (1986a). *The History of Sexuality Volume Two: The Use of Pleasure* (trans. Robert Hurley) New York: Vintage.

--- (1986b). *The Foucault Reader* (ed. Paul Rabinow) Middlesex: Penguin.

--- (1987a). *Discipline and Punish: The Birth of the Prison* (trans. Alan Sheridan) Middlesex: Penguin.

--- (1987b). *Madness and Civilization: A History of Insanity in the Age of Reason* (trans. Richard Howard) London: Tavistock.

Freud, Sigmund (1985a). *Case Studies I: 'Dora' and 'Little Hans'* (trans. James Strachey) Middlesex: Penguin.

--- (1985b). *Case Studies II: 'The Rat Man', Schreber, 'The Wolf Man', A Case of Female Homosexuality* (trans. James Strachey) Middlesex: Penguin.

--- (1986a). *The Interpretation of Dreams* (trans. James Strachey) Middlesex: Penguin.

--- (1986b). *Introductory Lectures on Psychoanalysis* (trans. James Strachey) Middlesex: Penguin.

--- (1986c). *Jokes and Their Relation to the Unconscious* (trans. James Strachey) Middlesex: Penguin.

--- (1987). *On Metapsychology: The Theory of Psychoanalysis* (trans. James Strachey) Middlesex: Penguin.

--- (1988). *The Psychopathology of Everyday Life* (trans. James Strachey) Middlesex: Penguin.

---, and Joseph Breuer (1980). *Studies on Hysteria* (trans. James Strachey and Alix Strachey) Middlesex: Penguin.

Gasché, Rodolphe (1986). *The Tain of the Mirror: Derrida and the Philosophy of Reflection* Cambridge, Mass.: Harvard

Hegel, G. W. F. (1971). *Philosophy of Mind* (trans. W. Wallace) New York: Oxford University Press.

--- (1975). *Aesthetics: Lectures on Fine Art* (3 volumes) (trans. T. M. Knox) New York: Oxford University Press.

--- (1978). *Philosophy of Subjective Spirit* (3 volumes) (trans. M. J. Petry)

Dordrecht, Holland: D. Reidel.

Heidegger, Martin (1971). *Poetry, Language Thought* New York: Harper and Row.

--- (1972). *On Time and Being* (trans. Joan Stambaugh) New York: Harper and Row.

--- (1973). *Being and Time* (trans. John MacQuarrie and Edward Robinson) Oxford: Basil Blackwell.

--- (1974). *The Question of Being* London: Vision Press.

--- (1982). *The Basic Problems of Phenomenology* (trans. Albert Hofstadter) Bloomington: Indiana University Press.

Hjelmslev, Louis (1969). *Prolegmena to a Theory of Language* (trans. Francis J. Whitfield) Madison: University of Wisconsin Press.

Husserl, Edmund (1960). *Cartesian Meditations* (trans. D. Cairns) The Hague: Martinus Nijhoff.

--- (1975). *The Paris Lectures* (trans. Peter Koestenbaum) The Hague: Martinus Nijhoff.

--- (1969). *Ideas: General Introduction to Pure Phenomenology* (trans. W. R. Boyce Gibson) London: Allen and Unwin.

--- (1982). *Ideas Pertaining to a Pure Phenomenology and to a Phenomenological Philosophy* (3 volumes) (trans. F. Kersten) The Hague: Martinus Nijhoff.

Hyppolite, J. (1956). 'Commentaire parlée sur la *Verneinung* de Freud' in *La Psychanalyse 1*. Reprinted and translated as an appendix in Jacques Lacan, *Freud's Papers on Technique* (trans. John Miller) Cambridge: Cambridge University Press, 1988a.

Ingarden, Roman (1973). *The Literary Work of Art* Evanston, Ill.: Northwestern University Press.

--- (1973). *Cognition of the Literary Work of Art* Evanston, Ill.: Northwest ern University Press.

Irigaray, Luce (1985a). *Speculum of the Other Woman* (trans. Gillian Gill) Ithaca: Cornell University Press.

--- (1985b). *This Sex Which Is Not One* (trans. Catherine Porter with Carolyn Burke) Ithaca: Cornell University Press.

Kant, Immanuel (1965). *Critique of Pure Reason* (trans. Norman Kemp Smith) New York: St. Martin's Press.

--- (1973). *Critique of Judgement* (trans. J. C. Meredith) New York: Oxford University Press.

Klein, Melanie (1932). *Psychoanalysis of Children* London: Hogarth.

--- (1988). *Love, Guilt and Reparation and Other Works 1921-1945* London: Virago.

Kojève, Alexandre (1969). *Introduction to the Reading of Hegel* (trans. J. H. Nichols; ed. A. Bloom) New York: Basic Books.

Kristeva, Julia (1973). 'The Semiotic Activity' (trans. Stephen Heath and

Christopher Prendergast) in *Screen* Vol. 14, No. 1/2.

\--- (1974). *La révolution du langage poétique* Paris: Seuil.

\--- (1982). *Powers of Horror: An Essay on Abjection* (trans. Leon S. Roudiez) New York: Columbia University Press.

\--- (1984a). '*Histoires d'Amour* - Love Stories' and 'Julia Kristeva in Conversation with Rosalind Coward' in Lisa Appignanesi (ed.) *Desire* London: Institute of Contemporary Arts.

\--- (1984b). *Desire in Language: A Semiotic Approach to Literature and Art* (trans. Thomas Gora, Alice Jardine, and Leon S. Roudiez; ed. Leon S. Roudiez) Oxford: Basil Blackwell.

\--- (1984c). *Revolution in Poetic Language* (trans. Margaret Waller) New York: Columbia University Press.

\--- (1985). 'The Speaking Subject' in M. Blonsky (ed.) *On Signs* Baltimore: The Johns Hopkins University Press.

\--- (1986). 'Ellipsis on Dread and the Specular Seduction' in Philip Rosen (ed.) *Narrative, Apparatus, Ideology* New York: Columbia University Press.

\--- (1987). *Tales of Love* (trans. Leon S. Roudiez) New York: Columbia University Press.

Lacan, Jacques (1966). *Écrits I* Paris: Seuil.

\--- (1971). *Écrits II* Paris: Seuil.

\--- (1973). *Livre XI: Les quatre concepts fondamentaux de la psychanalyse* Paris: Seuil.

\--- (1975). 'Seminar on *The Purloined Letter*' in *Yale French Studies* No. 52.

\--- (1980). 'Desire and the Interpretation of Desire in *Hamlet*' (trans. James Hulbert; ed. Jacques-Alain Miller) in Shoshana Felman (ed.) *Literature and Psychoanalysis-The Question of Reading: Otherwise* Baltimore: The Johns Hopkins University Press.

\--- (1982). 'God and the *Jouissance* of The Woman', 'Intervention on Transference' and 'A Love Letter' (trans. Jacqueline Rose) in Juliet Mitchell and Jacqueline Rose (eds.) *Feminine Sexuality: Jacques Lacan and the École freudienne* London: MacMillan.

\--- (1985). *Écrits: A Selection* (trans. Alan Sheridan) London: Tavistock.

\--- (1986). *The Four Fundamental Concepts of Psychoanalysis* (trans. Alan Sheridan) Middlesex: Penguin.

\--- (1987) 'Le ravissement de *Lol V. Stein*' in Marguerite Duras *Duras on Duras* (trans. Edith Cohen and Peter Connor) San Francisco: City Lights Books.

\--- (1988a). *Freud's Papers on Technique 1953-1954* (trans. John Forrester; ed. Jacques-Alain Miller) Cambridge: Cambridge University Press.

\--- (1988b). *The Ego in Freud's Theory and in the Technique of Psycho analysis 1954-1955* (trans. Sylvana Tomaselli; ed. Jacques-Alain Miller)

Cambridge: Cambridge University Press.

Laplanche, J., and J.-B. Pontalis (1980). *The Language of Psychoanalysis* (trans. Donald Nicholson-Smith) London: The Hogarth Press.

——— (1986). 'Fantasy and the Origins of Sexuality' in Victor Burgin, James Donald, and Cora Kaplin (eds.) *Formations of Fantasy* London and New York: Methuen.

Levinas, Emmanuel (1963). 'La trace de l'Autre' (trans. A. Lingis) in Mark C. Taylor (ed.) *Deconstruction in Context: Literature and Philosophy* Chicago: University of Chicago Press, 1986.

Miller, Jacques-Alain (1977-1978). 'Suture-Elements of the Logic of the Signifier' in *Screen* Vol. 18, No. 4.

Mitchell, Juliet, and Jacqueline Rose (eds. and trans.) (1987). *Feminine Sexuality: Jacques Lacan and the École freudienne* London: MacMillan.

Nietzsche, Friedrich (1957). *Thus Spoke Zarathustra* (trans. M. Cowan) Chicago: Henry Regnery.

——— (1966). *Beyond Good and Evil* (trans. W. Kaufmann) New York: Random House.

——— (1968). *The Will to Power* (trans. W. Kaufmann) New York: Random House.

Pascal, Blaise (1960). *Pensées: Bibliothèque de cluny* (eds. Zacharie Tourneur and Didier Anzieu) Paris: Libraire Armand Colin.

——— (1987). *Pensées* (trans. A. J. Krailsheimer) Middlesex: Penguin.

Ruthrof, Horst (1981). *The Reader's Construction of Narrative* Boston: Routledge and Kegan Paul.

——— (1992). *Pandora and Occam: On the Limits of Language and Literature* Bloomington: Indiana University Press.

Roudinesco, Elisabeth (1985). *Histoire de la psychanalyse en France* Paris: Seuil.

Sartre, Jean-Paul (1957). *Being and Nothingness* (trans. Hazel Barnes) London: Methuen.

——— (1963). *The Problem of Method* (trans. Hazel Barnes) London: Methuen.

——— (1973). 'The Transcendence of the Ego' in David Carr and Edward S. Casey (eds.) *Explorations in Phenomenology* The Hague: Martinus Nijhoff.

——— (1987). *Existentialism and Humanism* (trans. Philip Mairet) London: Methuen.

Scilicet Working Party (1987). 'The Phallic Phase and the Subjective Import of the Castration Complex' in Juliet Mitchell and Jacqueline Rose (eds. and trans.) *Feminine Sexuality: Jacques Lacan and the École freudienne* London: MacMillan.

Index